Vibe Mercha
The Sound Crea
Jamaican Popular Music

RAY HITCHINS
University of the West Indies, Jamaica

Routledge
Taylor & Francis Group
LONDON AND NEW YORK

First Published 2014 by Ashgate Publisher

Published 2016 by Routledge
2 Park Square, Milton Park, Abingdon, Oxon OX14 4RN
711 Third Avenue, New York, NY 10017, USA

Routledge is an imprint of the Taylor & Francis Group, an informa business

British Library Cataloguing in Publication Data
A catalogue record for this book is available from the British Library

The Library of Congress has cataloged the printed edition as follows:
Hitchins, Ray.
Vibe merchants : the sound creators of Jamaican popular music / by Ray Hitchins.

   pages cm. – (Ashgate popular and folk music series)
  Includes bibliographical references and index.
   ISBN 978-1-4724-2186-9 (hardcover : alk. paper) – ISBN 978-1-4724-2187-6 (ebook) – ISBN 978-1-4724-2188-3 (epub) 1. Popular music–Production and direction–Jamaica–History. 2. Sound recording executives and producers–Jamaica. I. Title.
  ML3486.J3H57 2014
  781.64097292–dc23

                                                                                        2014002733

ISBN 13: 978-1-472-42186-9 (hbk)
ISBN 13: 978-1-032-40425-7 (pbk)
ISBN 13: 978-1-315-54835-7 (ebk)

Bach musicological font developed by © Yo Tomita

VIBE MERCHANTS: THE SOUND CREATORS OF JAMAICAN POPULAR MUSIC

Contents

List of Figures

List of Music Examples

General Editors' Preface

Popular musicology embraces the field of musicological study that engages with popular forms of music, especially music associated with commerce, entertainment and leisure activities. The Ashgate Popular and Folk Music Series aims to present the best research in this field. Authors are concerned with criticism and analysis of the music itself, as well as locating musical practices, values and meanings in cultural context. The focus of the series is on popular music of the twentieth and twenty-first centuries, with a remit to encompass the entirety of the world's popular music.

Critical and analytical tools employed in the study of popular music are being continually developed and refined in the twenty-first century. Perspectives on the transcultural and intercultural uses of popular music have enriched understanding of social context, reception and subject position. Popular genres as distinct as reggae, township, bhangra, and flamenco are features of a shrinking, transnational world. The series recognizes and addresses the emergence of mixed genres and new global fusions, and utilizes a wide range of theoretical models drawn from anthropology, sociology, psychoanalysis, media studies, semiotics, postcolonial studies, feminism, gender studies and queer studies.

Stan Hawkins, Professor of Popular Musicology, University of Oslo and
Derek B. Scott, Professor of Critical Musicology, University of Leeds

Acknowledgements

The origins of this book lie in a Doctoral dissertation that was completed at Leeds University in 2011. First and foremost, I would like to thank Kevin Dawe, Rachel Cowgill (Leeds) and Anthony Clayton (University of the West Indies) who made up my advisory team. Their advice and support played a crucial role in the realization of these pages. A special thanks and 'respect' is extended to all those who were kind enough to offer their time and energy. I am much indebted to Graeme Goodall, Donald Hendry, Errol Brown, Gregory Morris, Glen Browne, Jeremy Harding and Cleveland Browne whose words and actions make up a considerable part of this study. Also Robbie Lyn, Jimmy Peart, Michael Fletcher, Glen Whitter and Noel Davy provided a critical range of information without which this study would have undoubtedly suffered. In addition, Mark Golding provided critical legal advice regarding content while Donna Hope at the Institute of Caribbean Studies (UWI) provided support during the final weeks of editing.

On a more personal level, Brigette Levy and Harry Abrikian provided critical shoulders for me to lean on during the early part of my research while my sister Alene was a stalwart pillar of support throughout the process, with cordon bleu cuisine thrown in. While my parents are no longer with us, their life story shaped the path that mine would follow and led me to Jamaica's shores in 1981. This book is in part a product of their love, support and encouragement. Last but by no means least, my wife Marie and daughters Rachel and Julianna have played a critical role in this book coming to fruition. They have been generous in their love and tolerant of my needs while encouraging my aspirations throughout the writing process.

Nuff respect due!

Introduction

Since the 1964 release of Millie Small's 'My Boy Lollipop', Jamaican popular music (JPM) has achieved a consistent presence in the very competitive and lucrative popular music markets of Europe, North America and Asia.[1] During the course of the last 50 years, JPM has evolved stylistically and is now represented by a range of popular music genres that include ska, rock steady, reggae and dancehall music. John McMillan writes: 'From Jamaica, reggae music has swept the world. You can hear reggae played in clubs from Senegal to Samoa' (2005, p. 1), while Kozul-Wright and Stanbury estimated that in 1996 'reggae generated approximately US$ 1.2 billion [worldwide sales]' (1998, p. 24). Jamaican recording artists have not only established a place for themselves among the world's most competitive and highly paid popular music entertainers, but their music has been adapted and exploited by a diverse range of international performers, from Harry Belafonte and The Beatles to David Bowie, demonstrating its marketability and influence on the world stage.[2]

This book explores the development of JPM, primarily through the experience of audio engineers and musicians as creative and technical innovators in their own right. While the academic orientation is centred on ethnomusicology, it is influenced by a range of thought, emerging from musicology, popular music studies and cultural studies as well as from historical perspectives on the development of the recording industry and recording technology.

Moreover, my research is directed and informed by my work as a professional musician who has lived in Jamaica since 1981. This long-term emersion in the field, working as a performer, programmer, audio engineer, writer and producer provides access to a musical world that is not easily penetrated by outsiders. The process of integration demands the balancing of formative and new value systems, in a commercial music environment where distinctions between professional and academic interests need to be maintained. As such, I am part of a group of ethnomusicologists who Gregory Barz and Timothy Cooley suggest are 'striving

---

[1] The *New Grove Dictionary* (2001, Vol. 21, p. 100) states 'Reggae: A term denoting the modern popular music of Jamaican and its diaspora.' This book uses the term 'Jamaican popular music' to denote the distinct styles of Jamaican boogie, ska, rock steady reggae and dancehall music but acknowledges the existence of other styles and what some authors term 'sub genres' (see Veal, 2007, p. 2).

[2] This list would include: Jackie Edwards, Desmond Decker and The Aces, Jimmy Cliff, Bob Marley, Bob Andy, Marcia Griffiths, Peter Tosh, Shabba Ranks, Super Cat, Boris Gardener, Chaka Demus and Pliers, Freddie McGreggor, Shaggy and Sean Paul.

to perceive and understand the liminal quality of musical meaning' (2008, p. 3); however, the boundaries and rationalization of insider/outsider perspectives are often difficult to decipher and evaluate.

My research has therefore been inspired by my experience of living and working in Jamaica, observing how the roles and responsibilities of recording participants differ from their counterparts in Europe and North America. Despite sharing the same fundamental technology, Roger Wallis and Krister Malm note that 'It is only in the sophisticated recording studios of Kingston that the reggae sound the world has learned to recognize is created' (1990, p.169). An investigation of what constitutes the 'reggae sound' lies at the heart of this study, where consideration is given to the creating, capturing and processing of sound in a Jamaican context.

A range of scholarly works has influenced my thinking in regard to the relationship between music and technology, which 'contain possibilities for many different ways of ordering human activity' (Winner, 1986, p. 5).[3] The process of music production in Jamaica, while influenced by technology, also probes and explores its function, looking for unique ways to interpret and manipulate its application. Paul Greene notes how 'the logic of a particular technology depends upon the logics of related technologies and preceding technologies that prefigure it' (2005, p. 5), highlighting the importance of understanding the way in which technologies develop, interconnect and assume relevance within a society and culture.

Lysloff and Gay's 'ontological, the pragmatic and the phenomenological' (2003, p. 6) methodologies for approaching the place of technology in society also offers a sound perspective for assessing the complex array of forces that influence music creation and capture. In addition to understanding the relationship between technology and the music creation, performance and capture process, it is also vital for the student of JPM to understand the influence of the sound system and forms of local media, reflecting meanings and associations, which are 'situational, fluid and polysemantic' (ibid., p. 15). My research has therefore led to the sounds of JPM being traced through the development and application of technology, which is adopted, adapted and reconfigured to meet local objectives, representing the cultural and creative pathways along which the logic of technology can evolve and transform sound.

My study of JPM, in the context of technology's influence, therefore resonates with Timothy Taylor's assertion that: 'Whatever music technology is, it is not one thing alone … In short music technology – any technology – is not simply an artefact or a collection of artefacts; it is, rather, always bound up in a social system, a "seamless web" as is often described' (2001, p. 7). While focused on JPM, this study offers examples of technology's application within the 'seamless web' that constitutes the JPM making experience.[4]

---

[3] See also: Louise Meintjes (2003), Timothy Warner (2003) and Deborah Wong (2003).
[4] See Lysloff and Gay (2003) and Hesmondhalgh (2002).

I therefore trace the development of Jamaican recording methodologies conscious of the debate that surrounds the relationship between technology, music and culture but also recognizing that the adaptation of technology has played a central role in the unprecedented global impact (on a per capita basis) that JPM has achieved. This study of JPM is made through analysis of the details of recording practice and the technology on which it depends. It is observed from an insider's perspective, which is sensitive to the local forces that direct music production. I agree with Timothy Warner who suggests that 'musical creativity in pop music is inextricably bound to developments in audio technology and the working practices which ensue' (2003, p. xi). In effect, this book responds to Curwen Best's criticism that 'The region does not yet have a substantial body of "formal" criticism which foregrounds a technology-sensitive reading of Caribbean culture' (2004, p. 3), therefore responding to a perceived gap in the literature.

My study of recording studio practice acknowledges that sound has the ability to migrate and influences diverse cultures through Wallis and Malm's concept of 'transculturation' (1990, p. 173). While considering the way in which sound can be exported and imported, there is also a need to make distinctions between the sounds of musical performance and the added sonic values that the recording process often introduces to sound recordings. From my perspective, these sounds are all too often assumed to be the product of the musician, in part because the details of recording practice are not readily evident and tangible to the listener. Much of my focus is therefore on what Mark Katz describes as 'phonograph effects ... the manifestations of sound recording's influence' (2004, p.3).[5] I therefore contend that it is vital in the study of post-war popular music for the listener to be able to differentiate between, what Virgil Moorefield describes as, 'the "illusion of reality" (mimetic space) to the "reality of illusion" (a virtual world in which every-thing is possible)'. (2010, p. 5). My thinking has therefore been influenced by a range of scholarship regarding the historical development of recorded sound and I agree with Steve Jones's observation that 'It's the technology of sound recording that organises our experience of popular music' (1992, p. 1).

In my investigation and analysis of JPM, sound is perceived as an element that can be traced and has the potential to provide critical information about the forces that direct music creation, performance and capture. I remain conscious of Michael Chanan's observation that 'recording, like news gathering is not a transparent process' (1995, p.69). I therefore conceptualize the process of creating, capturing, balancing, mixing and mastering musical sound as 'sonic rendering', not dissimilar to the process by which photographic images can be manipulated in layers of filtering and adjustment. The human agency that directs these processes has the potential to change the way not only in which we listen but also create and perform music. Moreover, the analysis of these mechanisms reveals much about the underlying values of music creators, performers and the forces that direct music production. The primary elements on which recorded sound depends are

---

[5] See also Evan Eisenberg (1987) and Steve Jones (1992).

represented by frequency, dynamics and the spatial characteristics of sound. These become the surface, light and texture that recording participants manipulate and sculpt sounds in an effort to stimulate the listener's emotions and sensibilities.

A wide array of music industry periodicals and enthusiast literature describe many of these processes in detail and represent a valuable resource for the student of popular music. In addition, there is a growing body of enthusiast literature with a focus on recording studios or the work of audio engineers and producers.[6] They document a variety of perspectives on the recording process and the actual merging of musical creativity and technology, and also provide detailed descriptions of how audio engineered dynamics, frequency response, balance and space are applied in the transformation of a musical performance into a musical product.

The commercial success and worldwide recognition of JPM has ensured a wide range of academic and enthusiast interest, much of which focuses on cultural, sociological and anthropological perspectives.[7] Notable musicological, ethnomusicological perspectives include works by Kenneth Bilby (1995), Peter Manuel and Wayne Marshall (2006), Michael Veal (2007) and others who grapple with the difficult task of understanding the complexities of JPM. As a subject of study, JPM is representative of a body of creative work, to which, as Théberge notes, 'Traditional musicology offers little assistance' (1997, p.6). In fact, post-1960s JPM is the product of a rhythmic and sonic sensibility, which is distinct from other forms of popular dance music and is often locally described in terms of 'vibe', 'groove' and 'feel'. While the music that these terms describe remains difficult to definitively notate, the analysis of sound in conjunction with detailed descriptions of recording practice can help to establish the shape, form and structure that underpins the amalgamation of music and sound in a Jamaican context. Although focused on recording process and technology, the ultimate objective of this study is to expand our understanding of the music that is locked into a dynamic system of creation, performance, capture and consumption.

The study of JPM is made more complex by the language and vocabulary that is often employed to describe the components of its construction. Despite my familiarity and understanding of JPM, and perhaps because of it, an early decision in my research was to establish an independent reference for music-specific terms. This decision was based on the fact that many terms can assume a wide range of meaning, typically defined by the context of their usage. Having functioned as a music creator and performer in rehearsals, stage shows and recording sessions, I was aware that the sonic nature of these events provide critical context, which is absent in interviews and discussions. I am conscious of the fact that it is possible

---

[6] See Mark Lewisohn (1988), Mark Cunningham (1996) and Geoff Emerick and Howard Massey (2006).

[7] See Dick Hebdige (1987a, 1987b), Carolyn Cooper (1993, 2004), Norman Stolzoff (2000), Lloyd Bradley (2000), Curwen Best (2004), David Katz (2003), Donna Hope (2006, 2010), Sonjah Stanley-Niaah (2006, 2010) and Brent Hagerman (2011).

for both informant and researcher to assume a common understanding where in fact none exists.

I have therefore tried to minimize the inevitable misunderstandings and misinterpretations that can arise by asking informants to respond to a questionnaire at the start of the interview (see the list of informants in Appendix B). During the course of the interview, the questionnaire provided a convenient reference point to confirm, amend and expand the meaning of terminology and proved to be an invaluable tool that has undoubtedly added rigor to the themes being discussed here. The questionnaire also provided a consensus of opinion in regard to terminology, which is provided in the form of a glossary as Appendix C. Although these definitions cannot be considered definitive, given the relatively small sample group, it is the first attempt, as far as I am aware, to establish a formal definition of common Jamaican music-related terms based on the descriptions of professional music practitioners.

I want to draw the attention of the reader to a key issue that informs my research concerning the perception of record production standards. Despite the success of JPM, it has had a number of detractors. According to Lloyd Bradley, these include Tony Blackburn who would 'denounce reggae as not being real music' (2000, p. 257), while de Koningh and Cane-Honeysett assert that accusations in the UK about JPM 'being boring and monotonous with incomprehensible lyrics' were 'reasons for its dismissal by the nation's hit-pickers' (2003, p. 35). Dick Hebdige assumes that these derogatory remarks were made in part because 'production standards in the Jamaican record industry were still not as high as in Europe and the States' (1987a, p. 93), a view, apparently supported by Simon Frith who discusses the creative use of the recording studio in commercial music, and refers to 'Jamaica's "hack" reggae engineers' (1981, p. 114). The issue of production standards is also commented on by Jason Toynbee, but in regard to the sound of British popular music of the early 1960s. He cites an example of The Beatles who 'began their recording careers by attempting to ape the sound of American rhythm and blues and pop. But had neither the technical means, nor the accumulated culture and expertise on which the big, transatlantic productions were premised' (2000, p. 89).[8]

I note the comments of these distinguished scholars at the outset of this study because they imply the existence of a pre-eminent music production standard, evident in recorded sound. This perception rests on several assumptions that this book will question. While Toynbee points to the significance of culture and technology in popular music, he fails to explain in what way British beat groups such as The Beatles had less accumulated culture and expertise than white American

---

[8] Toynbee does not define the term 'accumulated culture' but suggests the existence of common values that American pop and rhythm and blues artists shared. He also fails to define the term 'technical means' but suggests that this refers to the existence of superior American recording technology.

artists such as Elvis Presley or Bill Haley.[9] They also 'aped' the sound of American rhythm and blues, but did so with great effect. Toynbee also fails to explain how 'big transatlantic productions' often emerged from small and modestly equipped recording studios such as Sun, Stax, Chess, Atlantic, Motown, J&M and Sigma Sound. What 'technical means' were available in these recording studios that their British counterparts lacked?[10] I contend that, in the assessment of popular music, an understanding of recording process and methodology are critical in the analysis of 'production standards' and the role that culture and technology play.

While agreeing with Hebdige, Frith and Toynbee on the importance of recorded sound and the recording studio, I reject their notion of a pre-eminent production standard, as if it was the benchmark for every recording culture in the world.[11] The idea of a fixed recording standard does not appear to accord with actual experience, where we see the more complex parallel evolution and cross-fertilization of many different approaches in music production, where different music cultures employ different aesthetics and value systems (see Joli Jensen's discussion of the Nashville sound, 1998, pp. 118–35). In practice, therefore, we see a diverse range of production standards, each existing independently of the other and without hierarchy. In this sense, recording studios and the sounds they produce represent tools and products with an economic impetus. They are culturally driven and employ technology for the purpose of creating a specific product that responds, very often, to a local need.

Audio engineers as well as musicians are the primary users of these tools, and so the focus of this book is to better understand their work, but specifically within a Jamaican value system. My research is premised on the assumption that recorded sound can have a diverse range of legitimate interpretations, all worthy of study and without the need for placement in some form of hierarchy. I contend that it is by understanding the recording process and its relation to technical, economic and cultural forces that it is possible to understand the diversity of production standards and the worlds they serve.

Moreover, the above comments by Hebdige, Frith and Toynbee are worthy of note because they reflect a culture of recording and a value system, in terms of music production, that is associated with large corporations such as the British Broadcasting Corporation (BBC).[12] For these organizations the process of audio engineering was considered strictly as a technical skill that should follow

---

[9] See Chanan (1995, p. 102).

[10] See Cogan and Clark (2003) and their discussion of North American recording studios, compared to Martin and Hornsby (1979), Cunningham (1996) and Emerick and Massey (2006) who discuss recording studios in the UK.

[11] I employ the term 'recording culture' to suggest the existence of recording practices in different geographical locations, which are adapted, practised and relevant to local needs.

[12] I employ the term 'value system' to suggest the existence of an evaluation process that was used to judge the characteristics of electronically captured sound and promoted certain types of sonic characteristics while rejecting others.

predetermined recording procedures, intended to achieve a recorded product that could be consistently replicated and reproduced. In the production of popular music, this goal was considered outdated by the late 1950s and the focus of this book is on the production of music that, despite being technically derived, is fundamentally creative, musical and exploratory in its nature.[13] I contend that it is this attitude of creation and exploration within the field of music recording that not only marked the 'big transatlantic productions' of the 1950s and 1960s, but also much of the popular music that has dominated the European and North American popular music charts since that time.

This study therefore takes a pragmatic approach, grounded in interdisciplinary concepts involving theory, method and practice in ethnomusicology and popular music studies. Like Curwen Best I approach this study, which 'is not fixed to any one critical school or in its accompanying methodology or politics' (2004, p. 3) but draws widely to understand the relationship of music, culture and technology as demonstrated in the work of recording participants. I employ methodologies that include musical and comparative analysis, participation and observation, in-depth interviews with JPM practitioners and a graphic mixing analysis tool. This tool is designed by me to demonstrate the musical foundation of performance-mixing as a unique Jamaican music arranging process conducted by the audio engineer for the production of reusable riddims (reusable backing tracks). The combined results of this broad approach are designed to offer new insights into the work of recording participants, their influence on music production and ultimately provide new perspectives on how JPM developed.

The choice of themes presented herein are the product of a selection process that was initially driven by trying to identify and isolate the elements that make JPM different from other forms of popular music and to find ways of quantifying those differences. The chapters presented here are a product of that focus but presented in the context of the existing literature, which I build on, expand but at times also challenge. The perspective I bring to the study of JPM, at times, comes into conflict with established perceptions but in no way attempts to discredit or reduce the significance of existing scholarly research, often conducted in an environment that is unwelcoming and suspicious of outsiders. As a general guideline, I categorize the recorded popular music of Jamaica into the genres below. The associated dates are intended as a rough guide, representing the periods during which they might be considered the dominant form of locally recorded music:

Mento	1952–62
Jamaican Boogie	1955–60
Ska	1960–66
Rock Steady	1966–69

---

[13] See Emerick and Massey (2006) in which an institutional approach to recording methods by large corporations such as EMI and Decca is described.

Reggae   1969–82
Dancehall[14]   1982–present

Given the nature of my research and focus on the recording studio, audio engineer and musician, there was a need to establish an understanding of recording models as a framework from which JPM evolved . For the purpose of this book I define a 'recording model' as the template to which recording processes are tied, setting the creative and technical boundaries by which musical performance and sound can be captured and transformed into a commercial music product. Recording models represent the way in which the recording studio, as a complex tool, is designed and calibrated to function in the pursuit of a specific sonic objective. Recording models not only dictate how musical creations are captured, but this book will highlight the way in which the audio engineer's 'concentration of the "right" sounds for a given musical context can shift the musician's attention away from other, more familiar levels of musical form such as melody, rhythm and harmony' (Théberge, 1997, p. 186). Based on the testimony of my informants, the following descriptions highlight the primary recording models employed in Jamaica between the late 1940s and present day. A graphical display of each model is provided as Appendix A. These include:

1. **The single microphone/single-track recording model** (1948–58), where one microphone was used to capture the sound of instruments, musically balanced through their placement in the recording space.
2. **The multi-microphone/single-track recording model** (1958–63), where multiple microphones were placed on individual instruments allowing the position of the instrument in relation to the room, microphone in relation to the instrument and the electrical balance of microphone feeds to influence the recorded sound.
3. **The multi-microphone/multi-track recording model** (1963–82), where instrument and multiple microphone positioning, in addition to electrical balances, are employed, but also where additional recording tracks allow voices or instruments to be added (over-dubbed). The resulting collection of tracks can then be sonically treated and balanced through an independent post-recording process of mixing.
4. **The serial multi-track recording model** (1982–92), where electronic instruments no longer require the use of microphones, but where the introduction of sequencers and drum machines allows instrument parts to be captured serially one at a time and built into a collection of tracks that are then mixed.

---

[14] The term 'dancehall' refers to a genre of Jamaican music and should not be confused with the locations where dances are located, often referred to as a 'dance hall' or 'lawn'. These venues are typically situated in an outdoor, open-air space.

5. **The computer-based recording model** (1992–present), where musical elements are derived from samples, electronic instruments and microphones, but captured as digital sound files that can be manipulated using cut and paste editing. The mixing process becomes integrated into the process of capturing and arranging instruments.

This outline provides the broad umbrellas under which the recording process occurs but recognizes that they are also in a constant state of flux, as recording participants attempt to stretch their technical and creative boundaries. The concept of recording models are therefore used only as a guide to help us conceptualize how the process of recording responds to local values and the commercial forces that drive music production.

From my perspective there is great significance in the acquisition and use of equipment in the form of recording models, which I contend can provide a range of information about music and its creation. For example, Mark Lewisohn provides a range of data based on The Beatles' recording sessions conducted between 1962 and 1970. Lewisohn extracts information based on interviews with the recording participants as well as through analysis of the multi-track tapes, track sheets, recording notes and the administrative documentation required by the recording studio, Abbey Road.

Although Lewisohn makes no attempt to assess or categorize the recording processes employed by The Beatles, it becomes evident that they initially employed the multi-microphone, multi-track recording model as used in Jamaica during the 1960s. However, Lewisohn notes that on 3 November 1965, in the recording of the song 'Michelle', 'the Beatles [sic] concentrated on the rhythm track, using up all four tracks of the tape' (1988, p. 67). A process of 'tape reduction' was then employed, which entailed the rhythm track being mixed onto one track of a second four-track tape recorder, allowing additional over-dubs to be added to this new recording. This process was used on many of The Beatles' subsequent recording sessions and became the mechanism, in the form of a new recording model, for capturing the multiple instrument textures that mark a transition in the recorded sound of this group, culminating in *Sgt Pepper's Lonely Hearts Club Band* (Parlophone, 1967).

According to my informants, the above process was understood, available and tried in Jamaica, yet was rejected as a mechanism for producing JPM. This rejection raises a number of questions regarding the objectives of recording participants and the values that drive Jamaican music production. From my perspective, the understanding of the function and usage of recording equipment and instruments, in the recording process, is as important to the student of popular music as the rudiments of harmony are to the musicologist. They represent the form through which music and sound are merged to become a recorded musical product.

The focus of my research is therefore closely linked to the evolution of recording processes as mechanisms that reflect local values, in the form of sonic rendering applied to musical performance, sound creation and capture. As such, the discussion of specific music genres, or what might be considered important periods in the musical output of Jamaica, becomes secondary. This book investigates how recording participants and audio engineers in particular, influenced JPM through their manipulation and adaptation of technology. The themes contained in this study are often based on a correlation between changes in recording practice, which can be shown to have influenced the process of, or approach to, the act of creating music and sound. Although these themes are catalogued chronologically, I make no attempt to provide representation for each music genre, but rather reflect what, in my judgement, are the most pertinent examples that emerged from my research and could be accommodated within a limited number of pages.

Chapter 1 assesses the recording capabilities of Jamaica's first dedicated music recording studio and the role of Stanley Motta and Ken Khouri as pioneers of the Jamaican recording industry. The chapter considers the first recording model to be used in Motta's studio, the role of the audio engineer and musicians and the inclusion of a 'raw' sound aesthetic. The chapter also includes a comparison of local and foreign recordings, identifying ways in which the sound of local and foreign records of the period differed.

Chapter 2 considers the influence of the sound system on local recording and the first exclusive sound-system music products.[15] The sonic capability of studios available in Kingston during the 1950s are considered, in addition to the way in which access to recording studios was obtained, both formally and illicitly. The structure of Jamaica's fledgling recording industry is discussed and the role that class and race played in its early development. The chapter considers the way in which the process of music production emerged in Jamaica and the role of the music producer.

Chapter 3 assesses music listening trends in Kingston at the turn of the 1960s and how local audiences were exposed to a broad range of recorded music. The chapter discusses how local producers overcame the difficulty of gaining access to recording studios and achieving a sound that transcended mento music. The chapter details how the Radio Jamaica Rediffusion (RJR) studio was covertly transformed into a music production studio that produced Jamaica's first popular music recordings, which were able to directly compete with imported popular music. The chapter discusses the emergence of a new multi-microphone recording model in which the audio engineer assumed a role of ultimate authority and the way in which this provided the platform for a Jamaican sound to emerge.

Chapter 4 discusses the birth of the modern Jamaican recording industry with the opening of Federal Records and the impact that Federal had on local music-making and the consolidation of the multi-microphone, single track recording model. The chapter documents how a Federal recording session was conducted

---

[15] The term 'sound system', in a Jamaican context, refers to a large audio amplification system that includes a selection of popular and exclusive recordings, played primarily in Jamaica's dance halls, representing an entertainment system formulated around sound reproduction.

and considers the origins of emphasized bass as a sound-system aesthetic, which was transferred to the recording process. The role of Ken Khouri is assessed as well as his significance as an innovator who tailored music production and manufacturing to meet the demands of sound-system clients, helping to establish the earliest commercial distribution of sound-system music products.

Chapter 5 discusses the changes that occurred in Jamaican music production practice during the 1970s and 1980s. It assesses the existing commentary on dancehall music and the value system that is often employed to judge the creative and musical content of this music. The chapter challenges a common claim in the literature that a 'digital revolution' occurred after the release of the song entitled 'Under Mi Sleng Teng' (Jammys 1985). An evaluation of the actual introduction of instrument and recording technology to Jamaica is offered and an alternative explanation for the significant attention that the above song has attracted. This is based on interviews with the creator of the riddim over which the above song is performed but also a number of distinguished music industry participants.

Chapter 6 looks closely at the way in which synthesizers and drum machines influenced a transition in Jamaica's dominant recording model, employed to capture reggae and dancehall music. Consideration is given to how these new instruments changed the roles of musicians and audio engineers as well as how they fundamentally changed the way in which musicians interacted with sound, its creation, development and usage. In particular, attention is given to the way in which the drum machine allowed and encouraged the use of riddims and the development of performance-mixing as a music arranging tool that was performed by the audio engineer.

Chapter 7 provides an in-depth look at riddims with a categorization of type and function within local and foreign recording industry practice. It provides a performance-mixing analysis tool as a mechanism for extracting and documenting the musical elements that audio engineers are required to create. It describes the unique musical attributes and technical skills that Jamaican audio engineers have been required to develop in a unique production methodology in which 'vibe' and spontaneity play a critical role. Consideration is also given to the way in which the new technologies and production methodology encouraged recording participants to assume ownership of their creative works.

Chapter 8 considers the emergence of the multi-role producer in Jamaican popular music, representing a new kind of music practitioner who was often expected to perform all aspects of the music production process. The work of Jeremy Harding is considered along with his pioneering use of computer recording during the 1990s and the transition of Jamaican recording practice from analogue to digital technologies. The chapter discusses how Harding negotiated the challenge of gaining access to a recording industry using opportunities that the new technologies provided. It also accounts for how these technologies demanded a new perception of local and foreign sound aesthetics, and the way in which sound integrated with commercial exploitation.

Chapter 9 presents a recording studio ethnography conducted in 2008. The study provides a sense of how the historical development of JPM relates to actual recording practice in 2008. The study brings together the way in which humans interact with each other and with the technology they employ, and the way in which responsibility is assumed in a Jamaican recording context. Although providing only a small slice of recording practice in Jamaica, the study provides a real sense of how music and sound creation are captured and transformed into a commercial product.

The range of methodologies and approaches employed in this study are a product of planning that has been appropriately modified as data was gathered and assessed, and challenges emerged. During the course of assessing data, it became apparent that there was a need to question a number of established views, some of which are consistently repeated within the JPM literature but could not be reconciled with the historical record. While the content of this book has undoubtedly been influenced by the need to respond to some of these issues, it has remained focused on Jamaican recording studio culture and the recording practices that it represents. Although focused on JPM, it is hoped that themes that emerge from this study will find relevance in a wider context, where recording participants, irrespective of their location, are recognized as being directed and responding to a wide range of forces, the understanding of which can reveal much about music.

Chapter 1
Jamaica's First Recording Studio

The influence of recording studios, recording practices and their development are a central theme of this book. There is an underlying premise that the recording studio represents a complex tool, designed to perform a specific task, satisfy a range of local needs, and is often only one part of a larger commercial enterprise, driven by costs and profit. If we are able to understand how this tool is employed, we are likely to form a better understanding of the recorded musical product that it helps to create. My study of sound creation and capture in Jamaica therefore starts by addressing the dearth of information surrounding Jamaica's first recording studio and the recording models that emerged during the formative years of the Jamaican recording industry.

Throughout this book, the term 'recording studio' describes a physical structure that houses recording equipment, and has been acoustically prepared and treated, primarily to capture a musical performance. The early chapters focus on the testimony of Donald Hendry and Graeme Goodall, two audio engineers who worked in Jamaica's fledgling recording industry during the 1950s and who bring a level of authority to the discussion of this period, which remains largely overlooked in Jamaican popular music studies. Hendry, interviewed for the first time, is the only surviving audio engineer who was employed at Motta's Recording Studio (MRS) between 1953 and 1959. Graeme Goodall, a native Australian, was trained as a broadcast engineer, moved to London in 1951 and was contracted by RJR to work on the expansion of that company's Jamaican radio service in 1954.[1] Both informants provide critical information about the earliest Jamaican recording studios and the recording models they employed.

While Hendry provides the first account of a Motta recording session, Goodall is able to describe the transition in local recorded sound from the folk sounds of mento, a musical style that Bilby claims had 'Long been associated with a genre of topical songs reminiscent of other Caribbean styles such as calypso' (1995, p. 153), to the beat-dominated sound of the Jamaican boogie genre and out of which ska would emerge at the start of the 1960s. Goodall, as the only formally trained audio engineer working in Jamaica during the 1950s, would in fact play a critical role in not only introducing a recording model that allowed local recordings to compete with foreign imports, but also in assisting Ken Khouri in building the Records

---

[1] The term 'broadcast engineer' describes an individual whose duties not only include audio engineering and the capture of sound but also the transmission and distribution of sound via radio.

Limited studio in the mid 1950s and later Federal Records, which played a vital role in the early success of JPM.

Both Hendry and Goodall provide important accounts of how local recording practices evolved and how the audio engineer and musician assumed particular roles in response to the unique commercial and creative demands of Jamaica. Their testimony portrays an environment in which a complex array of forces influenced the development of Jamaica's fledgling music industry, which can be broken down under the headings of:

- **Economic**: Representing the amount of investment made in recording studios and the budgets available for recording projects, directly related to their perceived potential financial return.
- **Creative**: Representing the composition that was to be recorded, the genre, the musical structure and arrangement, and the recorded sounds that increasingly became a feature of recorded music in the 1950s.
- **Cultural**: Representing not just the local values associated with music and sound reproduction but the attitudes of musicians and audiences as well, and how they responded to the political and social changes taking place as Jamaica approached independence in 1962.

Recording Pioneers

Stanley Motta (1915–93) built Jamaica's first privately owned recording studio in 1951, for the purpose of recording local music. Although it is not clear when recording equipment was first introduced to the island, Kingston's sole radio station, ZQ1 had, according to Graeme Goodall, the capacity to make audio recordings during the 1940s, possibly using a wire recorder, used for radio broadcasting. Despite the importance of Motta as a founder of the Jamaican recording industry, there is limited information regarding the operation of his studio.

Stanley Motta's son, Brian, describes his father as a self-made businessman who was passionate about music and enjoyed acquiring and learning to use new technology and gadgets. Motta's business interests began as an electronic parts supplier prior to the Second World War, but his first involvement with commercial records started during the war years when he acquired a number of jukeboxes, which he rented and maintained. Brian Motta describes how his father acquired a disc recorder in 1950 and in 1951 opened the MRS studio, primarily intended to capture local music. Stanley Motta employed Jamaica's network of hotels to locate talent and contracted what he considered the best, to be recorded and commercially released on 78 rpm record, on the MRS label.[2]

---

[2] Also see Olive Lewin (2000), discussing the folk music of Jamaica and its connection to mento.

The details of these contracts are unknown and it is not clear if Motta ever pursued any commercial exploitation of these sound recordings outside the retail sale of records.[3] Brian Motta describes how musicians were commissioned on a work-for-hire, basis, meaning that a single payment was made for the exclusive rights contained in the sound recording.[4] According to Brian Motta, recordings were made on an acetate disc-cutting machine, were then sent to Decca in the UK for editing and mastering, and were manufactured into 78 rpm records.[5] The finished product was imported into Jamaica and sold in Motta's chain of retail stores, primarily aimed at the tourist market.

A contemporary of Motta, but more significant in the development of JPM, was Ken Khouri (1917–2003). I interviewed Khouri's son, Paul, in 2002, who claimed that his father purchased the first acetate-disc recorder to be brought into Jamaica in the late 1940s. Daniel Neely provides a perspective on Khouri's early work and challenges the above claim suggesting that 'there is much to critique in some of his [Ken Khouri's] claims of firstness' (2007, p.3). Given the introduction of the first Berliner recorders at the close of the nineteenth century, it would indeed be surprising if Khouri's disc recorder was the first to be introduced to the island (see Millard, 1995). Khouri does, however, represent the first of a new generation of recordists in Jamaica and he would do much to establish the modern Jamaican sound, which is discussed in Chapter 4. Ken Khouri is undoubtedly a seminal figure in the development of JPM, particularly through his creation of Federal Records at the close of the 1950s. I argue that his significance is not so much as a 'producer' who 'pre figured the "big three" of Dodd, Reid and King Edwards' as Neely suggests, but as the driving force behind the Jamaican recording industry, providing the 'big three' with a recording environment in which they could emerge as music producers.

At the end of the 1940s, Paul Khouri claims that his father began his career in the recording industry by capturing a variety of material including mento, performed on their home veranda in Vineyard Town, but also in other locations.[6] Ken Khouri, like Motta, was described as having a passion for music and although both men are pioneers of Jamaica's post-war recording industry, they are differentiated by their

---

[3] I have not been able to locate any evidence that Motta claimed ownership of the songs that his studio recorded, unlike Belafonte, Burgess and Attaway, who also recorded traditional Jamaican folk songs during the 1950s (see Wallis and Malm 1984, p. 191).

[4] I was not able to find any evidence that Motta or the groups he recorded tried to assert any rights associated with the respective creative works and possible publishing royalties.

[5] The term 'acetate' refers to a disc consisting of a glass or aluminium plate covered by a soft material in which grooves were cut to record music. The term 'lacquer', 'soft-wax' and 'dub-plate' are also used to describe the same item. Morton asserts that 'While a lacquer-based coating would eventually replace true acetate, the name "acetate" remained in use in the recording industry through the end of the disc era in the late twentieth century' (2004, p. 97). Here, I employ the term 'acetate' used by my informants but acknowledge that these discs might have been lacquer discs.

[6] See Daniel T. Neely (2007).

commercial focus. Khouri invested all his energy and financial resources into the development of that industry, whereas it represented only a small part of Motta's business interests.

According to Paul Khouri, his father consolidated his non-music business interests at the start of the 1950s to concentrate primarily on the manufacture, wholesale and distribution of records, which his recording of music supported. Graeme Goodall provides details of how Khouri's early manufacturing business operated, describing a trip that he made with Khouri to the Tower Isle hotel on the north coast of Jamaica. Goodall states that Khouri had secured a contract with Abe Issa, the hotel owner, to record the hotel's resident mento group. These recordings were made in the hotel and then taken back to Kingston where they were edited and sent to Miami to be mastered and have stampers manufactured.[7] Khouri was then able to locally press 78 rpm records, which were sold to Issa's hotel gift shop on an ongoing basis.

Khouri's eldest son Richard explained that, in 1954, his father expanded his record manufacturing business by successfully negotiating a licensing agreement with Mercury Records in the USA to manufacture and distribute their record catalogue in Jamaica. The significance of the Mercury contract is that it became the basis of a close symbiotic relationship between Ken Khouri and Coxsone Dodd, discussed in Chapter 2, but also suggests a significant growth in the local demand for records during the 1950s, although Lloyd Bradley suggests that 'there simply weren't enough phonographs on the island to warrant any kind of mass production' (2000, p. 23). While actual production figures are not available, the issuing and maintenance of a Mercury Records licence implies that a critical level of record consumption had been attained in Jamaica by 1954. Khouri was the first to recognize this potential and the introduction of record manufacturing to Jamaica represents an important step in the development of a local recording industry.

Local Recording Objectives

According to Graeme Goodall, Motta and Khouri's respective recording endeavours were initially responding to an international demand for what was commonly described and marketed as 'calypso music'. The origins and lineage of this music style is the subject of ongoing debate, but Goodall suggests that the term 'calypso' had international recognition as a generic 'Caribbean island music', whereas the term mento was relatively unknown outside of Jamaica. For this reason, many of the Jamaican mento recordings of the 1950s were marketed as calypso confirming the intended market for these products. Dedicated mento enthusiast sites, such as mentomusic.com, provide examples of albums recorded

---

[7] A 'stamper' is a negative copy of the master recording manufactured as a metal coated disc, used to stamp out positive copies of the actual vinyl record.

on the MRS label, entitled: *Authentic Jamaican Calypso*, *All Jamaican Calypsos* and *Calypso Date*.[8]

The choice of the term 'Authentic' in the above title provides a clue to how Motta positioned his recordings in the context of an international interest in Calypso music during the 1950s. It is interesting to compare Motta's mento recordings with contemporary foreign recordings of the mid-1950s that harness a Jamaican/Caribbean folk aesthetic. For example Harry Belafonte's 'Banna Boat Song' (RCA Victor, LPM-1248) recorded in the USA and Louise Bennett's (Miss Lou) 'Linstead Market' (Melodisc, MEL28 1139) recorded in the UK. The sophistication of Belafonte and Bennett's musical arrangement, performance and recording are in sharp contrast to an apparent rawness that is evident on many of the recordings captured in Motta's studio. There is a temptation to assume that this is the product of the basic equipment and recording method that Motta employed; however, this is not necessarily the case.

There was therefore a need to establish the basis on which Motta's recording studio operated and the creative goals it set out to achieve. According to Donald Hendry, Motta's studio was designed to capture small folk ensembles with what he describes as a 'country' mento sound, employing a single Reslo RV bi-directional microphone, which fed an acetate disc recorder. Hendry stated that the recording system selected by Motta was intentionally designed to be as simple as possible in order to minimize the harmonic distortion found in electronic equipment of the period. This claim would be consistent with Motta's experience as a supplier of jukeboxes and retailer of electronic components during the 1940s. According to Hendry, Motta reasoned that the simpler the system, the higher quality sound it would be able to capture and reproduce. It is also evident that during the course of the 1950s Motta saw no need to upgrade the studio and, according to Hendry, the equipment was considered adequate for the commercial and creative objectives that Motta set out to achieve.

As a successful and well-travelled businessman with an interest in electronics, Motta must have been aware of the multi-microphone recording technique, transition to tape and use of artificial reverb, which was increasingly heard on post-war recordings, including those by Belafonte and Bennett. According to Andre Millard the use of multiple microphones was 'commonplace in the larger studios' (1995, p. 287) by the close of the 1940s. Despite this, Motta designed his studio around a single microphone perhaps because, as Millard notes, multiple microphones demanded balancing by skilled audio engineers with a 'unique combination of creativity and technical know-how' (ibid., p. 288), which was unavailable in Jamaica. However, it is also possible that Motta's thinking on this issue was influenced by established recording theory of the period. As late as 1962, leading audio engineering manuals such as Alec Nisbett's *The Technique Of The Sound Studio: Radio & Recording* note how 'the balancers of "serious" music

---

[8] See photographs and documents relating to these and other mento albums at: http://www.mentomusic.com/1scans.htm#moremottainfo (accessed 19 May 2010).

generally prefer to use as few microphones as possible to create the "natural" sound' (Nisbett, 1962, p. 74). In addition, it is likely that the post-war transition to tape recording from disc, with the potential for editing was not seen by everyone as a positive attribute, not dissimilar to the way in which the merits of analogue and digital recording have been debated since the 1980s.

Hendry's testimony in conjunction with the known limitation of local technical resources, Motta's selection of recording equipment, the title of some MRS albums, and the sound of the resulting records suggest that Motta was not trying to replicate a foreign interpretation of recorded mento. It would appear that he set out to capture what he considered to be a 'true' representation of Jamaican mento, working within the limitations of his local setting but at the same time establishing a distinct sonic characteristic that was a reflection of live musical performances.

Recording Studio Practice

In order to try and understand the recording objectives of Motta I asked Hendry to describe the way in which recording sessions were approached and directed in an effort to reduce speculation. The objective was to establish whether a recording model existed and, if so, how it functioned. Hendry describes that during his tenure as audio engineer from 1953 to 1958 Motta was solely responsible for identifying the recording talent and he was notified when a recording was scheduled. Hendry describes the musicians that took part in recording sessions as being mostly well trained, consisting of professionals who worked in Jamaica's hotels and clubs performing a wide variety of music. When asked about musical discrepancies, such as changes in tempo and performance mistakes, evident in some sound recordings, Hendry suggested that this was part of an imitation process to achieve what he described as a 'country' sound, perhaps less confusingly referred to as being 'downhome' or 'rural' sounding, rather than the result of poor musicianship.[9]

Significantly, Hendry describes a recording process that was often spontaneous in nature, where audio engineer and musicians collaborated on the selection of material and crafting of a sound recording rather than it being directed by a producer and vetted through a process of material selection, musical arrangement, scoring, rehearsal and performance, which is certainly evident on the Belafonte and Bennett recordings. For example, Hendry claimed that the selection of material, which might have proved popular in a live performance setting, was often considered inappropriate for recording. Lyrical content could include sexual innuendo, which Motta discouraged, and Hendry confirms that the selection of material and musical arrangements were often impromptu, performed without scores and at times tried to capture what he described as a 'country sound', meaning rural Jamaica.

---

[9] In the context of mento I adopt Jeff Todd Titon's definition of 'downhome' as a term that 'refers not to a place but to a spirit, a *sense* of place evoked in singer and listener by a style of music' (1995, p. xv).

The scenario described by Hendry offers a new perspective on the way in which Jamaica's first recording studio was established. The selection of equipment and a recording methodology was tempered to meet the demands of mento music with consideration for the absence of trained audio engineers, while attempting to achieve a high sonic standard. The simplicity of the recording equipment was considered appropriate for the production of a music product, which Motta saw as representative of the 'authentic' sound of Jamaican mento, and uninfluenced by recording trends taking place in popular music outside of Jamaica. I make no attempt to evaluate these sound recordings on the basis of 'authenticity' but note that the concept has much in common with Joli Jensen's description of the 'Nashville Sound', in contrast to the 'downhome' interpretation of American country music. In Jensen's discussion she notes the fact that 'authenticity and commercialisation are vague and flexible concepts' (1998, p. 7), which, in the case of Jamaica's earliest commercial mento recordings, is an evaluation that I would agree with.

The important point I wish to make is that the sounds emerging from Motta's studio were the product of careful thought, design and planning. They reflect the rejection of the latest foreign recording trends, in terms of using tape and multiple microphones. Further, they reject a recording methodology where a producer oversees the selection of material, musical arrangements and use of the recording environment to create artificial musical balances and spatial characteristics, which mark the Belafonte and Bennett recordings. By contrast, Motta selected a single microphone/acetate disc recording model that harnessed spontaneity in pursuit of an 'authentic' mento sound, which is in sharp contrast to the North American and British recordings, representing distinct recording values.

Harnessing a 'Raw' Sound

Kenneth Bilby highlights the work-song origins of mento but makes a distinction between urban and rural mento.[10] 'Some looked down on it as "coming from country" [meaning rural Jamaica] and dismissed it as "unsophisticated"; others performed it with relish' (1995, p. 154). The recording techniques and musical performances in many of Motta's sound recordings provide evidence that elements of this 'unsophisticated' aesthetic were in fact embraced and accommodated by Motta. I contend that this is significant because it represents a local musical value that was recognized by Motta as being vibrant and was harnessed into the process of recording. This approach was contrary to mainstream foreign recording trends where the capture of music demanded the 'perfect performance', rejected by Motta and representing a raw sonic value that would transition into subsequent forms of JPM, despite changes in technology and music genres.

---

[10] See Olive Lewin's discussion of work songs and other types of Jamaican folk music (2000).

In O'Brien-Chang and Chen's *Reggae Routes*, Winston Wright, a prominent keyboard session player who emerged in the 1960s, discusses the need for Jamaican musicians during the ska era to be able to play both sophisticated and raw (1998, p. 33). Wright suggests that professional musicians were not only required to be competent technical performers but also able to incorporate this 'raw' style into their playing, which was often considered necessary for some musical interpretations.

I draw on my own experience of working with Wright in a recording session in the early 1990s at Couch Recording Studio for Toots Hibbert, where we were employed to record keyboard and guitar overdubs. During the session, Wright was playing an organ rhythmic pattern, referred to as an 'organ bubble'. The part consisted of a rhythmic figure based on the last three semi-quavers of each crotchet beat in the bar, with a rest on the first semi-quaver. As Wright began to perform the part over a two-chord progression from G major to A minor, Hibbert stopped the recording and instructed Wright to perform the bubble in the 'old time way'. The performance adjustment required by Hibbert was for Wright to play the same rhythmic figure but on the lower register of the keyboard, as if playing a congo drum, with no attempt to follow the harmonic changes of the song. Although the organ part created a distinct element of discordance, which initially seemed out of place to my musical sensibilities, it was unanimously accepted by the other recording participants. By the end of the session, with the organ part balanced in the mix, the discordance provided by the organ created a musical tension that undoubtedly helped to provide a distinct and characteristic to the sound recording. This is not dissimilar to the irregularities found in some sound recordings made at Motta's studio and the description by Hendry of a recording aesthetic that allowed some musical discrepancies if the overall musical effect was considered pleasing.

In 2002 I discussed this approach to recording and the integration of 'raw' or 'discordant' sounds into the production of Jamaican popular music with Paul Khouri. He made the point that, locally, the recording goal was not to create a technically or musically perfect recording: 'When it felt good and sounded good it was on the right path', suggesting an approach that is driven by intuitiveness and spontaneity rather than by concepts of perfection in regard to performance or sound. While the origins of this approach are difficult to determine, the testimony of Hendry suggests that spontaneity and the acceptance of 'imperfect performances' were first formalized into a recording methodology at Motta's studio and represents an important thread of continuity that has permeated every subsequent genre of JPM.

The Making of an Audio Engineer

I was interested in discovering how this recording aesthetic evolved because it represented a radical rejection of recording practices and trends found in North America and the UK. I asked Hendry about his training, the recording methods he employed and his awareness of developments taking place in popular music outside Jamaica. Hendry explained that he was employed by Motta in 1953, initially to work with the company's public-address systems that were rented for private functions. He was quickly transferred to work in the recording studio as a trainee audio engineer under the guidance of Frank Jeffery. Hendry claimed that neither Motta, who acted as the studio's first audio engineer, nor Jeffery, who succeeded him, had any formal training in audio engineering. Likewise, Hendry did not receive any formal training and, during my initial interview, he described the scope of his duties as follows:

> Actually recording took up very little of my time. Maybe 10 per cent or 15 per cent at the most. There were long periods when not much was done. I was in charge of the public address equipment dept. responsible for repairs to cables, amplifiers, etc., etc. And also taking rental systems out and installing them for public meetings or political meetings. Two huge ones were the visit of [Louis] Armstrong and Marion Anderson. Another task included making sure the [Off-Course] Betting sound requirements were met on race days. Installation of permanent systems for background music in hotels like Tower Isle hotel and the Arawak hotel.

Hendry claimed that, in terms of Motta's business interests, 'The recording thing was not a big thing ever, I don't know how many records we made but if we made 50 [78 rpm discs] we made a lot.'[11] Hendry implies that the recording studio and retail record business it served was like a hobby for Stanley Motta. Hendry states that the recording studio set-up was very simple, employing the Reslo ribbon microphone and a Presto desktop disc recorder. He recalls this being a model N6 and that it looked very similar to the unit shown in a photograph that he provided (see Figure 1.2). Hendry describes the features and working conditions of the recording studio as follows:

> The recording studio was a very basic affair. It was a room of about 12 feet by 12 at the most. It had an upright piano and a table for the 78 rpm recorder. It had a small window air conditioner which was turned off just prior to recording. The walls and door were panelled [sic] with that soft ¾ inch sugar cane bagass [sic] with multiple sheets of it to damp down noise from without. It was on the

---

[11] I have not been able to establish an estimate of the size of the Stanley Motta group of companies in the late 1950s. Motta's business interests included import, distribution and retail of electronic and photographic equipment. The company also manufactured household furniture items, installed commercial sound equipment, rented sound equipment, and repaired electronic equipment and photographic equipment. By all accounts the company was one of the largest locally owned companies in Jamaica and by the 1950s had become a household name.

ground floor. We all chain-smoked profusely and the air was very thick and blue. We all sweated copiously and were usually very happy to quit the sessions.

Hendry also stated that a typical session would last from 10 am until 3 pm in which time it was possible to complete the recording of three discs, but he emphasizes that the studio conditions were uncomfortable and 'as hot as hell'. This recording schedule, conducted during the hottest time of the day, perhaps reflects the 9-to-5 nature of Hendry's employment but also suggests that some musicians would not have been able to work during cooler times of the day because of evening performance commitments.

When discussing the method used to balance instruments, in preparation for recording, Hendry claimed that 'the musicians were very skilled at their trade'. He describes how maracas were particularly difficult to record at a desired level because of the loudness of the instrument and how the performer had to 'step back to reduce it (referring to the volume level). On some occasions the performer was required to play the maracas behind his back to help reduce the level. Hendry describes a recording practice where the physical size of Motta's recording space limited the size of the ensemble to five or six musicians but it also restricted the way in which individual instruments could be balanced through their physical position in relation to the single microphone. In addition, because the disc recorder was located in the same room as the performers, it would have been impossible to monitor the actual balance of instruments, as they were being recorded onto disc (see Figure 1.1).

Figure 1.1.   Donald Hendry pictured in the mid 1950s, at his desk in Motta's parts department. From Hendry's private archive, reproduced with his permission

According to Hendry, the recorded balance of instruments was established through trial and error, relying on the audio engineer's intuition, experience and judgment. There simply was no way of accurately adjusting the balance of instruments in response to the monitored feed from the microphone, as in an isolated studio control-room. Hendry claimed that this recording model had been established by Stanley Motta who saw no need to change or modify it for the production of mento and was content with the sound that the studio achieved.

It would be accurate to describe the recording model employed at Motta's studio as a tried and tested method established by Motta in 1951. The method was taught to Hendry who in turn passed it onto his successor, Jim Taylor, in 1958. Taylor, who was still in contact with Hendy at the time of my interviews, confirmed in an email that although Motta upgraded the studio to a tape recorder at the start of the 1960s the recording methodology remained consistent until the studio closed in the first years of that decade. Hendry claimed that during his tenure as audio engineer, if a disc was discarded, it was generally due to a mechanical problem during the cutting process and his primary duty during the recording was 'trying to keep the damn swarf out of the way' of the cutting head.[12] The musicians were able to ask for a new disc to be cut if they felt it was necessary, typically due to a serious error in the musical performance, but Hendry confirmed that this did not happen often.

It would be fair to describe the recording model being practised at Motta's as outdated when compared to North America or British recording practices of the 1950s.[13] One of the most significant advances that the transition from mechanical to electronic recording had facilitated in the 1920s had been the ability to isolate the studio control room from the performing space.[14] This allowed audio engineers to accurately monitor the signal form the microphone(s) and adjust the relative position of instruments accordingly. However, the practice also allowed and encouraged the intervention and reinterpretation of the natural musical balance of an ensemble. Andre Millard notes how 'The great maestro Stokowski was one of the first conductors to record his orchestra with the Western Electric System [using multiple microphones]. When he was told of the function of the mixer he replied: "you're paying the wrong man. He's the conductor and I'm not"' (1995, p. 288). See also Figure 1.2.

By locating recording and performance activities in the same room and employing a single microphone, Motta removed the need for a mixing console and minimized the ability of the audio engineer to alter the balance, tone, timbre or character of the recorded instruments. However, the rationale for this seemingly outdated recording methodology may have been based on the fact that Motta's primary focus was on one genre of music that he felt could be standardized and formulated into a set recording method. Despite criticism of Motta's studio, the sound recordings that it produced are accurate representations of live mento performances, where the maracas or shaker tend to overpower instruments with less natural amplitude such as the acoustic guitar or rhumba box. By comparison, in the interpretation of 'Lindstead Market' by Louise Bennett, cited above, the shaker is subdued in the recording, whereas in Harry Belafonte's recording of

---

[12] The 'swarf' is the waste material removed from the acetate disc by the cutting head. Hendry had to ensure that this was removed from the disc and did not get caught in the path of the cutting head, creating an audible noise that would cause the disc to be discarded.

[13] See Millard's discussion on developments in the American recording industry (1995).

[14] See Millard's discussion on electrical recording (ibid., pp. 139–47).

Figure 1.2   BBC type C disc-cutter. Courtesy of Neil Wilson and the Washford Radio Museum[15]

'Day Oh' the conga slide is clearly amplified and pushed to the forefront of the instrument balance, both creating pleasing recorded musical sounds but not what one could fairly describe as 'natural'. In this sense, the sound recordings made in Motta's recording studio might be considered representative of music where the intervention and influence of technology was limited, despite the fact that this practice was increasingly considered out of sync with contemporary North American and British recording practices of the 1950s.

A Comparison of Two Popular Sound Recordings of the 1950s

I asked Hendry whether any attempt was made by him to alter or modify the sound characteristic of individual or collective groups of instruments, in terms of their

---

[15] Hendry directed me to this picture and claims that this unit is very similar to the unit employed in the MRS facility.

frequency and dynamic range, and, in particular, emphasizing low frequencies. Hendry stated that his role was to try and capture the musical performance and reproduce it as a facsimile. He claimed that the natural low frequency content of mento music, produced by the rumba box, was relatively small, and said that 'In our case [meaning MRS] we never emphasized the bass, we couldn't, we just cut the damn disc on the RIAA curve', implying that the process of emphasizing low frequencies or interpreting the sonic characteristics of the music was not considered.[16] This is a significant point because it confirms a recording rationale that aimed to produce sound recordings that were representative of a live musical performance, whereas the popular music sound recordings emerging from North America and elsewhere increasingly used multiple microphones and their strategic placement as a means of altering the sound, frequency emphasis and natural musical balance of instruments.

While entrepreneurs such as Motta and Khouri were exploring the potential of record manufacturing and retailing during the 1950s, the sound systems had grown into a significant local entertainment industry. They reproduced mostly foreign music on large outdoor reproduction systems with extended frequency and dynamic ranges, which became a major form of entertainment for Jamaica's lower socioeconomic groups. Although Motta and Khouri's mento recordings were largely targeted at the tourist market there is evidence to suggest that some of these mento sound recordings made their way onto the play lists of sound systems.[17]

Winston Blake claims that 'When you weren't dancing to American music, mento was the dance music. When you put on mento the place went wild. It was our music' (Salewicz and Boot, 2001, p. 23). Blake implies that locally recorded mento records earned a place in the early sound-system's programming as good dancing music, but, more significantly, because local audiences responded enthusiastically to recordings of local music performed by local talent. It is reasonable to assume that part of this enthusiasm was based on a growing sense of identity and nationalism as Jamaica approached independence in 1962.[18]

In order to try and understand the extent of the difference between the American and Jamaican recorded sound of this period, and how it might have been perceived in the dance halls of Kingston, I conducted a comparative analysis of two recordings, both of which are known to have been locally popular in the early 1950s:

---

[16] RIAA curve refers to a specification established by the Recording Industry Association of America to standardize the specification for the manufacture of records and recording devices. This specification reduced the low frequency content of source material during recording and then emphasized it during playback, allowing the maximum amount of level to be fed to the recording device with, what was considered, an optimum signal-to-noise ratio.

[17] The term 'sound-system operator' describes the owner of a sound system.

[18] See Philip Sherlock and Hazel Bennett's discussion of Jamaica's move toward independence in *The Story of the Jamaican People* (1998).

- Harold Land's composition entitled 'San Diego Bounce', recorded in 1949 in Los Angeles, taken from a compilation, double compact disc album entitled *Jump 'n' Jive* (Union Square Music Ltd, metrocd540, 2004).
- Lord Composer and The Silver Seas Orchestra's interpretation of a traditional mento composition entitled 'Hill and Gully Ride/Mandeville Road', recorded during the early 1950s at MRS. (The recording was made by Hendry but he could not verify the date.) The recording is taken from the compilation compact disc entitled *Mento Madness* (V2 Records, Universal CD6733431, 2004).

In Norman Stolzoff's interview with Winston Blake (2000, p. 53), Blake claims that the Harold Land sound recording was regularly featured on Coxsone Dodd's sound system. This therefore provides an example of a foreign sound recording that is known to have been popular during the mid-1950s.[19] For comparison, I have selected the Lord Composer and Silver Seas Orchestra performance of 'Hill and Gully Ride', which Hendry recorded and confirmed was one of the more popular mento recordings of the same period.

The comparison of these two examples and the recording standards they represent cannot be considered definitive because they have each undergone a re-mastering process during their transfer to a digital medium. Compact disc was the only medium through which I could access the recordings, and I acknowledge that the digitizing process would have altered their original sonic characteristics. However, the digitization and re-mastering process would not have significantly influenced the balance of instruments or spatial characteristics of the original recordings.

In 2007 I interviewed Paul Coote, who was a co-producer for the compact disc collection from which 'Hill and Gully Ride' was selected. Coote claimed that 'Hill and Gully Ride' was copied from his personal collection of 78 rpm MRS discs. According to Coote, the original production masters, in the form of acetate discs, were no longer available. Coote, who was present at the re-mastering session, claimed that, to the best of his knowledge, very little additive processing was performed on the recordings but he was unable to provide specific details regarding re-mastering and the subdued levels of surface noise on the compact disc suggest that some audio restoration occurred. Even less information was available for the Harold Land recording; however, it would be reasonable to assume that it was made on acetate disc or the first generation of commercial tape recorders.[20] Either way, a tape or disc recording medium would have suffered some level of physical, chemical or magnetic deterioration after at least 30 years of storage. It therefore

---

[19] According to Norman Stolzoff, in an interview with Winston Blake, Coxsone Dodd originally acquired this particular record. Dodd kept the identity of the song and artist hidden from the public. The song became known locally as 'The Down Beat Shuffle' (2000, p. 53).

[20] See Morton's discussion on the introduction of the commercial tape recorder in 1948 (2004, p. 117).

seems likely that both recordings were exposed to some form of digital audio restoration, even though, according to Coote, the difference between the original 78 rpm mento record and the re-mastered compact disc version is not substantial.

The evaluation of the recordings is limited by these facts, but, in addition, it is difficult to assess how the original records would have been perceived when played on a sound system during the 1950s. Sound systems of this period employed custom-built vacuum-tube amplifiers that, according to a number of local informants, sounded very different from the transistor amplifiers that eventually replaced them. In addition, sound systems were played outdoors at very high volume levels with extended frequency ranges and did not suffer the boundary effects of an enclosed space.[21] The closest approximation I could achieve was to play the recordings at high volume levels on a studio monitoring system, which provided only a sense of their original sonic impact.

The most obvious difference between the two recordings is in the performance and style of the music. Land's composition is an instrumental based on a 12-bar blues (I, IV, V chord progression) in the key of F major, with a $\frac{4}{4}$ signature at a brisk 152 bpm. Instrumentation includes drums, double bass, piano, tenor saxophone, horn section and hand claps.[22] The musical performance is well executed, typical of professional musicians working with a scored arrangement who provide a steady driving rhythm that is consistent in timing and pitch.

By contrast, 'Hill and Gully Ride/Mandeville Road' is a traditional call-and-response vocal composition, but is also based on a I, IV, V chord progression. Instrumentation includes maracas, acoustic guitar, banjo, bamboo flute, rumba box backing and lead voices.[23] The song is in the key of C major but the pitching of the instruments are 40 cents below concert pitch. Although Hendry could not recall the details of how this particular song was recorded, he claimed that instruments like the rumba box and flute were typically home-made and built from local materials, implying that a reliable source of concert pitch might not have been available during their manufacture.[24]

---

[21] Robert Teape, Glen Whitter and a number of other informants spoke about the superior sound of vacuum-tube amplifiers. There was a consensus that these amplifiers produced a particular type of full bass, which the terms 'warm' and 'big' were often used to describe.

[22] The make-up of Land's horn section sounds consistent with that used in popular music, comprising trombone, trumpet and tenor or alto saxophone, but one or more of these instruments might have been duplicated. No information was provided in the recording notes provided with the compact disc.

[23] The name 'rumba box' is given to a local instrument that falls into the Sachs Hornbostel classification system (1914) as a plucked idiophone with a comb form (112). The instruments are often home made and measure approximately $36 \times 24 \times 10$ inches with five or six tuned, metal keys, plucked by the performer who sits on the instrument.

[24] The variation in pitch could also have been caused by inaccuracies in one of the mechanical devices on which the recording was made, by the original mastering equipment or by the re-mastering process.

The mento composition is in $\frac{2}{4}$ and starts out at 100 bpm, which by the end of the recording has increased to 108 bpm.[25] The performance of the song is less refined than its American counterpart. For example, there is an obvious mistake by the guitarist during the first flute solo, where an incorrect chord appears to have been initially played but is quickly corrected. However, as discussed above, it should not be assumed that these performance errors, in addition to the tempo increase, are the product of poor musicianship as opposed to the creation of what was considered an 'authentic' mento performance.

In the analysis of the above recordings there is a significant difference, not only in their performance and instrumentation, but also in the characteristic of the recorded sound. This is a crucial point because although musicians with the appropriate instrumentation were performing American music styles at live music venues in Kingston, local recording studios, audio engineering processes and expertise were unable to capture them and replicate the sound of American sound recordings.

The Harold Land recording sounds sophisticated and smooth, in part, because of the way that the instruments have been balanced and sit together in the recording. The notes of the double bass are particularly well articulated and it is given prominence in the instrument balance, providing a sense that the bass player is closer to the listener than the other instrumentalists as he performs a driving walking-bass line. By contrast, instruments in the MRS recording are less well defined and not as evenly balanced. For example, the clave and maracas dominate the sound, at times competing in volume with the lead voice. In addition, the backing voices are dominated by one strong voice that stands out rather than being evenly blended with the other voices, and fails to effectively synchronize. The rumba box on the Jamaican recording provides the bass part for the song, but the notes are indistinct and masked by what appear to be over-tones, with an uneven dynamic. The recorded level of the lead-voice varies during the performance and is reduced significantly toward the end of the song. This is indicative of a recording method where the only means of changing the balance of instruments is to have the performer move physically closer to, or further away from, the single microphone.

Overall, the Jamaican recording provides the impression of a performance that is spontaneous in nature, and Hendry confirmed that the choice of songs and arrangements were generally made in an impromptu manner at the start of the recording session. Hendry felt that this approach was representative of the way

---

[25] Both recordings were analysed using wave-form analysis in the music-editing program Sound Forge. An average bpm rate was obtained by measuring the length of the recording in minutes and dividing that number into the number of total beats for an average bpm rate. Each song was then divided into eight-bar segments representing 32 beats and the time for each segment was measured in seconds. The measured time of each eight-bar segment was then divided into 60 seconds and the resulting figure was used to multiply 32 (beats) representing the average bpm rate for the eight-bar segment. Comparison could then be made between each segment as a means to analyse the steadiness of the performance.

in which many mento groups worked, which he tried to facilitate and encourage during recording. He explained that at the start of each recording, the song arrangement and interpretation would have to be altered to fit the time limitations of the acetate disc. Changes were then made to the musical arrangement but without using scores or taking notes.

Although both of the above recordings were made with one-track recording devices, the separation and definition of instrument sounds suggests that the American sound recording was made in a large acoustically treated room employing multiple microphones that were balanced and mixed during recording. The volume levels of individual instruments, or groups of instruments, change in a controlled fashion and reverb is added to the alto sax solo, representing progressive recording and mixing techniques that are absent in the mento recording. Despite these significant differences in the recorded sound, the Jamaican recording maintains a strong appeal, if very different to that of the American sound recording, and this, in part, undoubtedly comes from the energy that is captured in the musical interpretation and performance.

Hendry's account of the recording practices employed in Motta's studio explains many of the differences between the sound of 'Hill and Gully Ride/ Mandeville Road' and 'San Diego Bounce'. In addition to the limitations of using one room to perform and record, the size of Motta's recording room was also an important factor that negatively influenced the sound of the resulting recordings. Alton Everest states: 'The experience of the British Broadcasting Corporation (BBC) with their many talk studios is that volumes from 1,500 to 4,000 cubic feet (43 to 113 cubic meters) are generally satisfactory' (1991, p. 53), implying that the BBC considered 1,500 cubic feet as a minimum size requirement for a recording room. According to Hendry, Motta's studio measured approximately $12 \times 12 \times 8$ feet, and so had a volume of only 1,152 cubic feet, falling well below those standards set by the BBC. As a means of establishing a perspective for studio sizes in the 1950s, 'United Recording Corporation in Hollywood comprised three studios of 65,000, 27,000 and 3,000 cubic feet, respectively' (Millard, 1995, p. 297). Even smaller independent studios, such as Atlantic, had a recording room of 20×15 feet, and Sun had one of 30×18 feet.[26] Assuming even a minimum ceiling height, the cubic volume of these recording rooms exceeded the BBC's minimum requirement.

The small size, shape and similarity in two of the room's three dimensions of Motta's studio would have caused an increase in unwanted modal frequencies with a negative impact on the sonic characteristic of the resulting recordings.[27]

---

[26] See Cogan and Clark (2003) and Millard (1995) regarding the size and layout of American recording studios.

[27] Although the accurate dimensions of the room are not known the estimate of two dimensions being 12 feet would have resulted in an approximate reinforcement of the 94 Hz frequency. Calculated by dividing the speed of sound estimated at 1130 feet/second by the length of the room.

The duplication of any single room dimension had the effect of reinforcing the resulting resonant frequency. Everest states that 'A cubical room is the worst possible selection' (1991, p. 53), because with every room dimension being the same, one frequency would be heavily emphasized. Perhaps most significantly, the limited size of the room would have made the recording of a modern popular music ensemble using drums, bass, guitar, piano and horns difficult if not impossible. It is not just the physical layout of the performers and size of the instruments but the significant increase in decibel (volume) level that a rhythm section would have produced.

It seems evident that Motta's studio suffered from significant·design flaws, proof of which is found in the balance and timbre of the instruments in the above recording. The limited size of the recording space made it difficult to place a loud instrument far enough away from the single microphone to effectively reduce its level, in relation to other instruments. In addition, disc recording was being replaced by tape during the 1950s and the new medium allowed and encouraged a new range of recording techniques that MRS was unable to provide. One of the most significant changes was that the new tape medium encouraged the crafting of a recording, which could now be stopped if a mistake was made and restarted without having to discard the recording medium.[28] In addition, the best parts of several performances could now be physically edited into a composite version. Despite these advances, Motta's studio continued to use a disc recorder throughout the 1950s and the sonic characteristic of its recordings remained static. Other local recording facilities such as Ken Khouri's Records Limited and RJR had adopted tape and a limited use of multiple microphones, which only contributed to the perception that MRS was inadequate and outdated. As the 1950s progressed, Motta's studio became increasingly disconnected from post-war recording trends taking place in North America and, to a lesser extent, the UK. Independent recording studios such as Sun, Chess and Atlantic were driven by a new generation of progressive audio-engineering techniques employing tape and multiple microphones, pioneered and promoted by audio engineers such as Sam Philips and Tom Dowd who helped to reshape the sound of popular music.

George Martin, while discussing the changing practice of using multiple microphones during the late 1950s, said that, traditionally, 'The way to make good records was to use as few mikes as possible' ('mike' is the spelling used by Martin and Hornsby), but he goes on to explain why there was a reluctance by some of the older audio engineers to change this practice, saying: 'There was great skill in the relative placing of mikes, because that, and the placing of the instruments, was

---

[28] I use the term 'crafting' in relation to the work of the audio engineer and to suggest that many of the tasks he or she performs are technical and repetitive by their nature but require a creative application. The introduction of tape and its potential for being repeatedly recorded on seems to have encouraged this approach.

much more critical than it is today' (1979, p. 108).[29] Martin notes the changes in microphone usage by acknowledging that the successful recording of groups such as The Beatles depended on the use of multiple microphones and also on the skills of audio engineers such as Norman Smith and Geoff Emerick.

The Limitations of Motta's Studio

When considering the legacy of Motta's studio, it is evident that Hendry did not engage in any of the new recording practices that were evident in popular music emerging from North American and the UK. This was certainly due, in part, to the physical and technical limitations of the studio, but was also the product of Hendry's lack of exposure and limited training.[30] The net effect was that Motta's studio, although considered adequate for recording mento, was simply not suitable for recording the new styles of popular music emerging from North America such as rhythm and blues. The studio was not intended to capture groups that included a contemporary rhythm section and was simply unable to create the sounds that North American popular music had begun to embody during the 1950s.

Hendry was very candid about his own technical ability and described himself as an audio enthusiast, keenly interested in technology and classical music. He was trained to create competent recordings in the setting of Motta's studio but acknowledged that he did not listen to a lot of popular music and never attended a dance where a sound system played records. Hendry did not give much consideration to the sonic developments taking place in the wider recording industry. In addition, the equipment at his disposal did not encourage or allow for much experimentation and Hendry's training was limited to that environment. He offered an example of the difficulty he experienced as an audio engineer when Stanley Motta made arrangements to record the Jamaican Military Band. The band was too large to fit in Motta's studio and so Motta arranged to conduct the recording at the RJR recording studio, a much larger room of approximately 27,000 cubic feet. Hendry's attempt to record multiple instrumentalists in the large RJR studio using one microphone produced unsatisfactory results. Hendry states that he 'messed it up' and, as a result, Graeme Goodall (at that time employed by RJR)

---

[29] Martin seems to be referring to the fact that many older microphone designs were not directional and using multiple microphones could therefore introduce unwanted sound aberrations due to phase cancellation. See Ballou (1991, p. 393). As the popularity of using multiple microphones increased, microphone manufacturers designed specialist microphones that were very directional, intended specifically for this type of usage.

[30] Hendry did confirm that he had access to a mixing console and additional microphones from Motta's public address systems but did not see the need to modify the recording model based on his perception of the demands of Mento.

was asked to complete the session. [31] Goodall, in a July 2006 interview, confirmed that he 'salvaged the session' and used a variety of audio-engineering techniques, including the use of multiple microphones that were positioned and then balanced through an audio mixer in an isolated control room; representing audio-recording techniques that were simply beyond Hendry's ability and experience at that time. Goodall sums up the potential of MRS in writing: 'Nothing could EVER be as primitive as Motta's' (email extract from Goodall, 30 July 2008) however it is important to qualify this statement by noting that Goodall is using production values associated with North American popular music to judge Motta's recording facility. He confirms (in the same email) that it would have been impossible for Motta's studio to replicate anything close to Harold Land's 'San Diego Bounce' given the nature of the equipment and recording methodology.

Despite these limitations, the 50 or so albums that were created in Motta's studio are not insignificant and that number suggests the possibility that many local musicians experienced their first recording session in this studio. They would have therefore been exposed to the recording model established by Motta, where audio engineer and musicians collaborated during the recording process without a formal producer and often without an arranger or written scores, representing a rejection of a music production system that was common in North America and Europe. The Motta recording model recognized the importance of spontaneity, intuitiveness and the fact that a 'raw' sound could provide vibrancy and energize a sound recording. I contend that these values became embedded in the local recording process even though the recording model of single microphone and disc recorder was widely rejected in Jamaica by the close of the 1950s.

It therefore seems fair to say that the recording practices of Motta's studio, although technically outdated, established, consolidated and came to embody a sound that represented local values and an assertion that they were equal to values being practised elsewhere. They included a rejection of the producer in favour of the audio engineer and musicians who assumed creative direction of a sound recording, and embraced spontaneity as a creative process that could include a 'raw' sound as a positive attribute. These practices would play an influential role in the development of JPM, despite changes in technology and the growing availability of audio engineering expertise, which the following chapters continue to explore.

---

[31] Goodall confirmed that he was asked to 'salvage the session', that multiple microphones were used, and that they were balanced through a mixing console being fed to a one-track tape machine.

Chapter 2
The Demand for New Styles of Recorded Music

In order to understand how Jamaica's post-1960s popular recorded music emerged from the folk sounds of Motta's studio, it is necessary to bring together a range of information regarding the growing influence of the sound system as a sponsor of locally recorded music. This chapter discusses the earliest exclusive sound-system recordings, how they differed from mass-produced records and how this related to the nature of the sound system as a mechanism for reproducing music.[1] In addition, there is a need to consider how independent producers gained access to recording studios and how the roles of recording participants evolved.

Sound-system Sponsored Music: Restricted Acetate Discs

It is not known when the first locally recorded music was produced specifically for the sound system but there is consensus that sound-system operators during the 1950s began to purchase or commission local non-mento recordings to be played solely on their respective sound system. This practice was consistent with the sound-system policy of attracting patrons by offering a range of music that their competitors did not have access to. One of the distinct advantages of commissioning or purchasing locally recorded music was that it guaranteed exclusivity and, as a sound-system product, was the antithesis of the commercially mass-produced record on which Motta and Khouri's respective operations, depended.[2]

Unlike Khouri or Motta, who funded their recording of music through the manufacture, distribution and sale of records, sound-system operators depended on the generation of entrance fees, liquor and food sales to cover the cost of music production. It should also be noted that very few local restrictions stood in the way of music production, in regard to copyright laws and weak or non-existent music

---

[1] I employ the term 'exclusive' to describe the general practice of locating records from a variety of sources that competing sound systems did not have access to. These could include commercial records as well as commissioned or purchased recordings for which the sound system maintained exclusive rights. The exclusive nature of these recordings could, however, change through their discovery by a competitor or through the decision to release the recording commercially.

[2] See Bradley (2000); Stolzoff (2000) and Katz (2003).

industry unions, which in effect encouraged the creation of innovative but often-exploitative music production systems.

To date, I have not been able to locate any surviving examples of these earliest sound-system commissioned recordings, which were made only on acetate disc and I refer to as 'restricted recordings'. I use this term to describe these earliest forms of exclusive recording, which were neither mastered nor mass-produced as records. This type of recording should not be confused with other types of exclusive recordings that included foreign commercial records, from which the label was removed to hide their identity, and pre-releases of locally produced records. As such, restricted recordings are characterized by the fact that they were solely created for the purpose of promoting a sound-system brand prior to the sound system's involvement with the distribution and retailing of records.[3]

The acetate disc, commonly referred to as a dub plate or soft wax in Jamaica, is made from a thin aluminium disc, covered on each side by a soft acetate material on which sound can be recorded. Unlike 78 rpm or 45 rpm vinyl records, which acquired their grooves from a process of stamping a metal impression of a record onto heated vinyl, the grooves of the acetate disc were cut by a recording head on a device that looks similar to a record player (see Figure 1.2). The soft nature of the acetate material meant that discs had a relatively short life span, deteriorating progressively each time the disc was played. However, the cost of copying new discs from the master tape was significantly cheaper than having vinyl records locally pressed, requiring the master tape to be sent to Miami for mastering and stamper manufacture.

The benefits of using acetate discs was their relatively low cost of production for short-term usage compared to vinyl records and that they could be taken directly from the recording studio to the sound-system venue and played – an important consideration if the subject of a lyric was topical. Even after sound-system owners began to record music for commercial sale, the acetate disc continued to play a vital role in testing a sound recording's commercial potential and acting as a pre-release. In the case of a restricted recording not intended for mass production, the fragile nature of the acetate disc meant that a popular sound recording would need to have additional copies made as existing copies became worn, and this represented a recurring cost for the sound-system owner. Restricted recordings therefore represent the very earliest examples of the sound-system operators' venture into the world of music production; however, I have not been able to locate any examples of these recordings.

When I met with Coxsone Dodd in early 2002 to discuss aspects of his recording operation, I took the opportunity to ask if he still possessed any of the restricted recordings associated with by his Down Beat sound system, commissioned during the 1950s or early 1960s. Dodd confirmed that none of these discs had survived because they not only wore out quickly but also deteriorated with

---

[3] I use the term 'brand' because the larger sound systems such as Trojan or Down Beat had multiple systems that worked concurrently.

long-term exposure to the extreme heat and humidity of the tropical Caribbean. The significance of this fact is that surviving examples of a Jamaican sound recordings from the 1950s and early 1960s appear to be the products of vinyl mass-produced records, which, by definition, cannot be considered representative of restricted recordings made only on acetate disc, specifically for the sound system.

This piece of information is critical because it highlights a much-needed definition between two new music products that were emerging from Jamaican recording studios at the close of the 1950s, which were sonically and creatively distinct. One was recorded on acetate disc and was intended for the exclusive use of the sound system and the other was intended for commercial sale in the form of mass-produced vinyl records. Because only the latter of these two products have survived, there is a risk of assuming that these commercial mass produced records reflect the technical and creative parameters of the restricted recordings used by the sound system, but this is not the case.

The sonic characteristics of an acetate disc would have been significantly different from that of a vinyl record. An acetate disc represented a first-generation copy of a master recording whereas a vinyl record is a third-, and possibly fifth-generation copy, with a resulting loss of sonic detail. Moreover, the mastering process, which is necessary for the manufacture of a vinyl record, altered the frequency and dynamic range of the sound recording to conform to the RIAA curve mentioned in Chapter 1. This process was aimed at conforming the wide dynamics and frequency range of the studio recording to the sonic limitations of domestic music reproduction equipment. In addition to these differences, the acetate disc was not required to conform to broadcasting standards that restricted lyrical and thematic content of commercial records. Furthermore, it is important to remember that acetate discs were played exclusively on sound systems that could often sonically out-perform the recording studio in terms of volume, dynamics and frequency range.

It is important to understand that listening to music on a sound system represents an experience that is not quickly forgotten. They are typically designed to reproduce extended low frequencies that despite being inaudible are physically experienced by the listener. The use of first-generation unmastered recordings, in the form of acetate discs, simply added to the sonic detail of the listening experience, which contributed to the unique characteristics of this Jamaican entertainment system. Dick Hebdige quotes 'Junior Lincoln, a Jamaican record producer', who explains: "'A sound system is just like what you call a disco'" (1987a, p. 63); however, Lincoln is no doubt referring to the fact that the disco and sound system were both intended to reproduce commercially recorded music for the purpose of dancing. He significantly understates the performance capability of the sound systems of which the physical, aural and entertainment experience are notably different.

Our understanding of the impact of restricted recordings therefore needs to be made not only in the context of how they differed from sound recordings that were intended for mass production but also how the sound system was capable of reproducing a range of sonic detail and at levels that, to the best of my knowledge, were unique to Jamaica during the period being discussed. In the absence of actual examples of these earliest restricted acetate disc recordings, we are forced to assess their characteristics based on descriptive accounts of their production, creative content and what we can deduce from our understanding of the available recording technology.

The Growing Demand for a New Locally Recorded Music

The sound-system phenomenon has been widely discussed in the JPM literature and is correctly cited as the driving force behind the popular music that emerged in Jamaica during the 1960s. Lloyd Bradley claims that: 'Everything that is Jamaican music today can be traced back to those first sound-system operations' (2000, p. 11), while Michael Veal states: 'Ultimately the most relevant and organic context in which to ground any discussion of an electronic aesthetic within Jamaican music (besides the recording studio) is the local institution known as the sound system, which has been asserted by many observers as the site of most that is unique to Jamaican music' (2007, p. 42). While recognizing the dominant nature of the sound system's influence, I contend that other influences played a critical role in the early development of JPM that this and the following chapters will explore. The above comments reflect a widely accepted narrative that describes JPM emerging from the sound system, but closer analysis reveals a complex web of forces and influences that ultimately led to the emergence of ska at the start of the 1960s.

This narrative provides a rationale for the first attempts to locally produce popular music, which Kevin O'Brien Chang and Wayne Chen describe, stating: 'American music started to change from rhythm and blues to rock and roll but Jamaicans didn't like rock and roll much' (1998, p. 21).[4] Norman Stolzoff adds that 'Faced with this shortage of new tunes in the late 1950s, Coxsone Dodd started producing and recording rhythm and blues music with Jamaican singers and musicians in the local studios' (Stolzoff, 2000, p. 58).[5]

While O' Brien Chang, Chen and Stolzoff's claim appears to be widely accepted, it raises questions regarding the divergence in North American and Jamaican musical tastes at the close of the 1950s. It also raises pertinent questions

---

[4] In the popular music literature the term R&B is used to describe a wide variety of black American music styles. When some of my informants were asked to name artists that they defined as R&B, there were occasions when what are commonly considered pop or country and western artists were named, for example Jim Reeves and Patsy Cline. I have intentionally avoided using the term 'R&B' because of this ambiguity. My preference is to describe the music as 'American popular music'.

[5] Coxsone Dodd's legal name is Clement Dodd but he is widely referred to as Coxsone or Downbeat. The alias Downbeat is taken from the name of his sound system.

regarding the function of Jamaican recording studios and how they transitioned from tools designed to record folk instruments or for radio broadcasting into commercial recording studios with the capacity to replicate the multi-microphone sound of American popular sound recordings. Moreover, Stolzoff's comment begs the question: How and where did a sound-system operator such as Dodd, learn to produce 'rhythm and blues music'?

Lloyd Bradley offers a description of how an early sound-system-inspired restricted recording was produced, citing the recording of Derrick Harriot's song 'Lollipop Girl', made at Motta's studio between 1956 and 1957. Harriot claims 'We went to Stanley Motta's to cut a disc of our original R&B song "Lollipop Girl". This was sometime in 1956' (Bradley, 2000, p. 40). Bradley goes on to describe 'Lollipop Girl' as a rhythm and blues style song that Harriot composed, which achieved considerable local success with one of Kingston's smaller sound systems, despite consisting of only voice, piano and handclaps. Bradley's account provides an invaluable perspective on the instrumentation and performance of a restricted recording that was sold to a sound system in the form of an acetate disc. While it is difficult to accurately assess the sonic characteristics of this particular sound recording, the technical limitations of Motta's studio provide a sense of how it might have sounded. The single microphone, disc recorder and inability to monitor the balance of the voice, piano and handclaps, suggest that the resulting sound might be described as unsophisticated.

During my 2007 interview with Harriot, he confirmed that a sound system purchased the acetate disc on which the song was recorded, and to the best of his knowledge, there were no surviving copies of this first rendition of the song. Harriot reiterated Bradley's account saying: 'We recorded a demo of 'Lollipop Girl' at Motta's in 1957.'[6] However, Harriot's account raises questions regarding the extent to which the song was 'produced'. The title producer, in a European and North American context of the 1950s, represented a role that was assigned to an individual, who selected material to be recorded, oversaw the writing of musical arrangements, selecting musicians, recording studio and audio engineer. The production continued with the editing and mastering of the sound recording as it moved through a process of testing before being approved for release as a vinyl record that could compete in a commercial market with similar products.

Harriot's recording of 'Lollipop Girl' does not reflect this particular production process and is perhaps best described as a 'novelty recording' that achieved

---

[6] Note that the two references to Harriot's song in Katz (2003, p. 26), and Bradley (2000, p. 40), provide different dates for the recording, and in my own discussion with Harriot he provided a third date. Harriot's use of the term 'demo' was for the purpose of differentiating between the original version recorded at Motta's studio with piano accompaniment and hand clap and a later version recorded for Duke Reid at Federal Recording Studios with a full rhythm section. Harriot confirmed that although he describes the Motta recording as a demo, it was originally recorded as a complete work, considered adequate for use by a sound system.

interest not by competing directly with North American sound recordings but as a unique example of a local talent emulating foreign popular music. Stolzoff characterizes this practice by saying: 'Foreign music was held up as an example of sophistication that Jamaicans could only strive to attain through emulation' (2000, p. 36). It is therefore appropriate to consider in what way Harriot's recording of 'Lollipop Girl' was limited by breaking down the 'foreign sophistication' of North American sound popular records into three distinct elements:

- Instrumentation: The types of musical instruments being employed.
- Musical performance: The ability of musicians to perform 'authentic' representations of rhythm and blues, jive or other popular American music styles.
- Recording aesthetic: The recorded representation of instrument and vocal sounds, their balance, spatial setting, frequency range, sound dynamic, definition and clarity.

For those who wished to emulate the sound of North American records, achieving these three elements was critical. Through analysis of Harriot's description of 'Lollipop Girl', it is possible to surmise that while the performance and instrumentation was inadequate, the capability of the recording studio undoubtedly represented the weakest element. Stolzoff suggests that instrumentation and performers were locally available during this period because, 'approximately twenty to twenty-five big bands and small combos actively played clubs and holiday dates ... The big bands, which modelled themselves after their American counterparts both in terms of style and repertoire, played swing music in night clubs and dancehalls all over Kingston' (2000, p. 35).

Stolzoff therefore confirms that there was a vibrant community of musicians available in Kingston who constituted these 'bands and small combos' during the 1950s. The modelling of these groups 'after their American counterparts' suggests a local availability of performers able to provide the appropriate musical performance, using appropriate instruments; however, recording studios such as Motta's would not have been able to accommodate these groups and lacked the multi-microphone capability that Harriot's instrumentation of piano, voice and handclaps reflect. It would therefore be fair to say that, without a recording studio and audio engineer that could offer the multi-microphone recording model on which the sound of foreign popular music depended, Jamaican music production was limited to mento or a rudimentary emulation of foreign popular music.

Kingston Recording Facilities at the Close of the 1950s

In trying to better understand how the process of music production evolved in Kingston's recording studios it is necessary to consider how the recording of American inspired performances with appropriate instrumentation was achieved.

I asked Graeme Goodall to provide an assessment of the available recording facilities in Kingston between 1955 and 1960. Goodall claimed that the RJR studio was by far the best recording facility on the island during the 1950s in terms of studio design, size of the recording room, available equipment and trained personnel. However, RJR functioned as a broadcast facility, and so if live music was performed, it was intended for radio broadcast and not record production. Goodall went on to make the point that unlike the UK, where the Musicians' Union successfully negotiated for limited 'needle time' that demanded the daily inclusion of live music in radio programming, this was not the case in Jamaica. Therefore the capture of live music was not a daily event at RJR, despite the fact that RJR's broadcast engineers had been trained by Goodall to use multiple microphones. In addition, Goodall makes the point that although governed by the same fundamental audio-engineering principles, capturing music for broadcast and record production demanded a different recording technique, attitude and approach.

Goodall provides an appraisal of the available recording studios in Kingston in the mid 1950s citing Motta's and Ken Khouri's relatively new Records Limited studio as the principal facilities.[7] In 1955, Khouri built the Records Limited studio and upgraded his recording equipment from disc to tape with the purchase of a Magnachorda one-track tape machine. He also purchased a three-channel mixer, which offered multi-microphone capability and the new studio had separate control and recording rooms. This represented a substantial improvement over Motta's studio as a recording facility but as Goodall explains, the studio's limited selection of microphones, number of mixing console inputs, lack of a reverb chamber and limited recording space meant that Khouri's studio was still unable to achieve the recorded sounds associated with North American popular music.

Based on Goodall's assessment, as the only formally trained audio engineer working in Jamaica during the 1950s, it is evident that the available recording facilities were not capable of producing the sounds associated with North American popular music. The restricted recordings made by or for the sound system during the 1950s would therefore have been characterized by these technical limitations, although as acetate discs, restricted recordings, including Harriot's 'Lollipop Girl', would have provided the listener with a range of sonic details not found on commercial vinyl records.

---

[7] David Katz mentions Dada Tawari whom he describes as 'Another early entrepreneur cutting local product using basic equipment' (2003, p. 14) and Dan Neely mentions how Ivan Chin purchased Khouri's disc recorded in 1955 (2007, p. 2). While little is known about the details of Tawari's and Chin's respective recording operations, it is likely that they employed similar technology and recording approaches to those associated with Motta and Khouri.

Gaining Access to Kingston's Studios

During the course of my discussions with Hendry and Goodall, the issue of recording studio access was raised and both informants contradicted a widely held perception that Kingston recording studios were available to the public and independent producers during the 1950s. In Daniel Neely's research on the early development of commercial recording in Jamaica, he notes that in 1947 and 1950 Khouri and Motta respectively placed advertisements in the *Daily Gleaner* offering recording services to the general public.[8] However, it is not known where or for how long these services were offered or the response that Khouri and Motta received, but between 1953 and 1958, Hendry claims that Motta's recording studio was not offered to the public for rental although the studio did occasionally provide location-recording services.

Khouri's Records Limited Studio was not functional until 1955 and, according to Goodall, although a recording financier could approach Khouri and request studio time, Khouri felt no obligation to provide that service. The access to both studios, at the rear of an industrial woodwork department in the case of Motta, and behind Khouri's record presses, suggests that they were established without consideration for public access. In addition, the close proximity of industrial machinery suggests that recordings were conducted during periods when the machinery was not in use or had low levels of usage. Goodall claimed that the first recording studio in Kingston that could be routinely rented by the public was Ken Khouri's Federal Records, which opened in 1959.

In light of this information, I asked Donald Hendry to account for Derrick Harriot's claim that 'Lollipop Girl' was recorded at Motta's studio. Hendry could not account for this recording and was adamant that, as Motta's audio engineer, he would have been aware of this recording session or informed if such a recording session had taken place in his absence. Hendry reiterated that during his tenure as audio engineer with responsibility for the studio between 1953 and 1958, the only recordings made in Motta's studio were those intended for commercial release on Motta's record label.

In my interview with Derrick Harriot I asked who had acted as the audio engineer on the 'Lollipop Girl' recording session, which initially he could not recall. After informing Harriot of Hendry's claim that, 'We never rented out the recording studio to individuals or groups', Harriot recalled: 'It was Stanley Motta who cut the dub plate for us.' In a subsequent email exchange with Hendry, I asked him about the possibility of Stanley Motta assuming the role of audio engineer for the Harriot session without notifying him. Hendry replied: 'Would be unusual in the extreme. I cannot picture Stanley operating the recorder, which was fairly involved especially if a session was required, as he would not have had the time.' Hendry is referring to the fact that Motta owned and managed a number of large

---

[8] See Neely (2007). *The Daily Gleaner* is one of the daily newspapers available in Jamaica with a large readership.

prominent businesses by the 1950s. Motta had not been involved in recording since approximately 1952 and Hendry suggests that he would have not had the time or interest to personally conduct a recording session.

Hendry explained that, on the rare occasions when the studio recording equipment was rented for location recording, the booking process was administered through the company's main office, which then notified him.[9] While not doubting Harriot's claim, it remains unclear how this recording session was arranged and Harriot could not recall many of the details surrounding the session, such as who paid for the studio time, how much was paid, who received the payment and the mechanism through which the session was arranged.

Graeme Goodall offered an independent assessment of Motta and his recording operation. He describes Stanley Motta as a well-established businessman who ran a large corporation of which his record company and studio was a minor part. Motta did not appear to be interested in developing his studio beyond the role for which it was initially established in 1951, to record mento. By the late 1950s, Motta's studio was considered old fashioned and out of date. Goodall was unaware of Motta's studio being rented to the public or, for that matter, any Kingston studio of the period. By the early 1960s, Motta had closed his recording operation and Hendry had moved on to a successful career in electronics servicing.

Claims regarding the availability of Kingston recording studios during the 1950s are not limited to Bradley and Katz or Motta's facility, but include the two radio stations, RJR and Jamaican Broadcasting Corporating (JBC), each of which, according to Norman Stolzoff, 'Had a recording studio that was available to independent producers' (2000, p. 61). This claim is however refuted by Goodall who states that RJR and JBC, as broadcast facilities, did not offer their respective studios for rental – a standard policy for radio stations that continues in 2013.[10] However, Goodall went on to say that there were occasions when the station's recording studios might be made available to a politician or patron, such as an advertising agency, to record a public message or a radio commercial. If live music was recorded, it was usually confined to that usage and intended for radio broadcast, which was the function that the studio served. Goodall states that exceptions to this rule, such as Stanley Motta's recording of the Jamaican Military Band mentioned in Chapter 1, happened only occasionally and by special arrangement with the management of the station.

To this extent, Stolzoff's claim might be considered accurate, but in the context of his discussion on JPM it is misleading. He implies that independent

---

[9] Hendry states that 'When customers wanted recordings of weddings etc. these were booked by the workshop manager at Hanover St or by the record dept at the main store on Harbour St.' Hendry was then informed of the date, location and nature of the event, and would transport the equipment to that location to conduct the recording.

[10] In an interview I conducted with Melvis Cummings, the current head of RJR engineering, he claimed that the studio-rental market would be too disruptive for their core business of radio broadcasting.

music producers, intending to produce restricted recordings for the sound system or to manufacture records for mass distribution, had legitimate access to these studios, but that was not the case. More importantly, the claim risks concealing an underlying dynamic that existed between recording financiers and audio engineers during this important transitional period of JPM at the close of the 1950s. According to Goodall, audio engineers employed by RJR and JBC, which had the best recording facilities on the island, were increasingly being approached by recording financiers to provide studio time illicitly.[11] It would be reasonable to assume that the working relationships that evolved from these illicit recordings would be different from those of a formal recording session, where the rented studio typically included the services of an audio engineer, as practised in the UK and North America.

It therefore seems evident that the mechanism used by independent financiers to commission the recording of a piece of music was not a straightforward process. They were required to first establish a relationship with an audio engineer or studio owner and develop a sense of trust that would result in a recording studio being made available and in some cases illicitly, typically in return for some form of payment. This is an important consideration when trying to understand Jamaica's early studio culture, the process of music production and the significance of the audio engineer. It appears that the audio engineer was not only a technical and creative participant but was a provider of studio time with the ability to dictate the duration of the recording session and from this position of authority influence the material being captured.

As an employee of RJR at the end of the 1950s, Goodall was in a unique position to comment on this illicit solicitation for studio time with some authority. He was very candid about his own experiences and confirms that several of his early popular-music recordings were made at the RJR studio in this way. In an August 2009 email, Goodall writes:

> I suppose, in theory, that RJR & JBC studios could be rented but to the best of my knowledge most of the sessions [meaning music production sessions for independent producers] were moonlighting. Chris [Chris Blackwell] tried JBC studios a couple of times because of his inability to deal with Papa Koo, [Ken Khouri] but was unhappy with the results. He tried to smuggle me in to handle the sessions but 'it' hit the fan. ... from the guys @ JBC because they wanted the extra 'bread'.[12]

Goodall describes the existence of a complex environment where personal relationships, social and professional status as well as financial means played an

---

[11] The first audio engineers to be employed at JBC were RJR employees and had been trained by Goodall.

[12] Goodall claimed that the JBC audio engineers, Donald Wellington and Mervyn Carby were both trained by him while previously employed to RJR.

important role in the acquisition of studio time. The above statement also suggests that Blackwell was either unable to gain access to Khouri's Records Limited studio or was unhappy with the authority that Khouri was able to exert over the recording process. Goodall explains that he became involved with Chris Blackwell after meeting him at a social event where Blackwell asked him if he would be interested in helping him make some 'great sounding records'. Goodall agreed to do this and clarified his position in a July 2008 email, saying:

> Yes I was still working for Radio Jamaica but can't recall if I was ever paid by Chris ... Yes I 'moon lighted' ... [*sic*] (a Bechstein Grand Piano no less) after hours and after The Caribs had finished their regular gig. But you've got to remember this was all fun. And, to this day, I don't believe those records would sound as good if they had been done in daylight ... .think about it! [sic]

Goodall refers to the fact that the RJR recording facilities included a Bechstein grand piano, and also highlights the enjoyment he experienced in trying to make contemporary sounding records. This and other testimony of Goodall and Hendry demands a reassessment of the way in which the new transitional JPM of the late 1950s is considered. Studios such as MRS, Records Limited, RJR and JBC lacked the means to routinely offer their facilities for rental, lacking the appropriate location, infrastructure, advertising, booking, billing, collections and security necessary to operate a studio rental service.[13] The significant point to be made here is that Jamaica's transition from recording mento to the North American influenced sound of Jamaican boogie is a complex process in which the sound system initially represented only one influence. Surviving sound recordings such as 'Boogie In My Bones' (1958), financed by Blackwell and recorded illicitly at RJR by Goodall, were intended for the commercial record market and not to be used as a restricted recording for the sound system. As such, the record had to compete directly with foreign imports on the strengths of its instrumentation and performance, but most importantly, its recorded sound.

Details of this recording session will be discussed in Chapter 3, where it becomes evident that this recording process represents a significant investment of time, energy and resources. Although Blackwell was unavailable for comment, it would be reasonable to assume that this relatively high cost of production could be justified by a growing local and international record market, and therefore potential revenues. By contrast, sound-system operators in 1959 were producing restricted recordings that had to be financed from entrance fees, liquor and food sales.

---

[13] The revenue-earning strategy of Records Limited is more complex than the other Kingston studios, because Khouri's recording set-up was originally intended to be used as a portable facility, recording novelty discs for paying customers. Khouri was the owner and audio engineer for the studio and recognized a growing demand for a studio rental facility and the development of the Federal Records Studio was, in part, a response to that growing demand.

I contend that the significance of commercial records such as 'Boogie In My Bones' was that they demonstrated in unequivocal terms that the 'American sound' could be produced locally and therefore local record production could move beyond being a novelty product and compete directly with North American records for the public's attention. However, it is also significant that the illicit nature of the 'Boogie In My Bones' recording further established the authority of the audio engineer in the recording studio and strengthened the audio engineer/ musician production model first seen in Motta's studio. The following chapters will discuss how Jamaican music production built on the recording practices first established at Motta's studio, where the audio engineer and musicians assumed the creative and sonic responsibilities for the recording session while the financier contracted the various participants, paid for their services and exploited the resulting music product.[14]

Why information regarding the availability of recording studios does not surface more readily in the literature is not known, but it can perhaps be explained by an understandable reluctance on the part of prominent Jamaican artists or music financiers to admit publicly to researchers that they used illicit means to acquire studio time. It is also possible that they felt that this kind of disclosure would betray a trust placed in them by the audio engineers, studio managers, or those who made these recording sessions possible. With this in mind, the discrepancy between Hendry and Harriot's claim, regarding the availability of Motta's studio, acquires a new possible explanation. Although Hendry felt that the illicit use of Motta's studio was unlikely, he agreed that it was possible.

I do not wish to suggest that every independent recording session in Kingston at the end of the 1950s was illicit, because clearly that was not the case. Motta's recording of the Jamaican Military Band (mentioned in Chapter 1) at the RJR studio and recordings made at Ken Khouri's Records Limited provide examples. However, the fact remains that prior to the establishing of Federal Records, there simply was no recording facility available to the general public in Kingston, where studio time could be routinely booked. The music production process included the nurturing and maintenance of a relationship with an audio engineer, whether in the form of Ken Khouri at Records Limited or Graeme Goodall at RJR, yet this vitally important piece of information is absent in the literature.

On the basis of this new information, it is interesting to reconsider the accounts found in the literature regarding other early Jamaican recording sessions. For example, Lloyd Bradley discusses the production of the seminal song 'Oh Carolina' (1960), produced by Prince Buster, recorded at the newly opened, government-

---

[14] I have avoided using the term 'producer' in this discussion simply because it is not apparent what creative role individuals such as Blackwell and Coxsone Dodd performed, outside of financing these early, pre-1960 recording sessions. Coxsone would later build his own recording studio and learnt the skills associated with record production, including the ability to function as audio engineer. However, this does not mean that every recording financed by Coxsone was also produced by him.

owned, JBC studio (2000, pp. 59–61), but makes no mention of the mechanism by which the session was arranged. The recording is notable for a number of reasons, including the performance by a group of Rastafarian drummers led by Count Ossie. However, Laurie Gunst reminds us that in pre-independent Jamaica (1962), with a recent history of 'War between the Rastas and society ... when the locksmen ventured out of the dungle [sic] they were hounded through the streets and beaten by the police, who took special pleasure in shearing their dreads' (1995, p. 76).[15] Is it therefore likely or feasible that the management of this government-owned studio would welcome an independent recording session featuring Rastafarians? If so, there is an inconsistency with JBC's subsequent reaction to the song's commercial release, as documented by David Katz, who states: 'Demand for the song was so intense that both radio stations [RJR and JBC] were forced to give it regular airing, despite initial bans' (2003, p. 34).

Issues of Class and Race

Information regarding how access to recording studios was acquired by independent producers is clearly an important issue that needs further investigation in light of the above discussion. The general assumption that the existence of a recording studio or a recording session indicates legitimate public access is erroneous. However, this assumption has not only been widely accepted in the JPM literature but on occasion has become the basis for interpretations that are clearly in need of reassessment. For example, Lloyd Bradley not only makes the assumption that Motta's studio was available for public rental but goes on to assert that Motta's rental policy was based on criteria other than the studio's availability, because:

> Men like them [Motta and Khouri] were never going to be part of the shifting cultural development of an indigenous black Jamaican music. Simply because, unlike the sound-system barons, they were uptown men and it wouldn't have made sense. Motta even operated a door policy to restrict usage of his studios. (2000, p. 25)

Bradley implies that Motta, in particular, was not interested in the development of 'indigenous black Jamaican music' despite his well-documented and pioneering work with recording mento, what many might consider to be the 'most indigenous' of Jamaican popular music genres. In addition, Bradley's assertion that the objective of the 'sound-system barons' was to develop an 'indigenous black Jamaican music' is misleading given that early restricted recordings, such

---

[15] The 'dungle' refers to one of Kingston's most impoverished 'shanty town' communities. Some years later, Edward Seaga (then the Member of Parliament for Western Kingston) was to undertake a slum-clearing exercise that removed the 'dungle' and replaced it with a community now known as Tivoli Gardens.

as 'Lollipop Girl', were firmly grounded in the mimicking of North American popular music, and by the early 1960s, the fledgling Jamaican recording industry had attracted musicians from a wide range of ethnic backgrounds, both of foreign and local extraction.[16]

It is also worth noting that Stanley Motta was a member of Jamaica's Jewish community, while Ken Khouri was of Lebanese descent, representing two minority groups in Jamaica's complex Eurocentric society, of which racism and class prejudice were prominent features.[17] Bradley's stereotype perspective, implying that Motta was an, uptown oppressor, employing a 'door policy' to restrict selected individuals from gaining access to recording, while the 'sound-system barons' represent the black, downtown sufferers, trying to promote 'indigenous black Jamaican music', is not only inaccurate but risks hiding important underlying information. Although this narrative might be considered consistent with some political rhetoric associated with the 1970s, it fails to reflect Jamaican music production of the late 1950s and the complex relationship between music, economics, and race, which remains largely unexplored.

Although it is difficult to establish the exact nature of Stanley Motta's views on class and race, based on Hendry's testimony, the only 'door policy' employed by Motta was one that restricted the general public and independent producers from using his studio. According to Hendry, during his tenure as audio engineer, the studio was simply not set up or intended to function as a rental facility, and did not have the equipment or technical skills to record music that went beyond the folk sound of mento. Hendry's testimony not only offers new information on the culture of recording at Motta's studio but demands a reassessment of the part that class and colour played in the early development of JPM, and to what extent Jamaica's first recorded music financiers set out to create an indigenous music.

Hendry and Goodall not only contradict the assertions made by Bradley and other writers regarding the availability of recording studios, but suggest that the early development of JPM was much less concerned with race, cultural development, door policies or the establishing of an indigenous black Jamaican music than it was with economics and creating profit from the production of music. In this sense, the difference between Motta, Khouri, Reid, Dodd and even Harriot was perhaps less than their differences in ethnicity, religion or uptown, downtown status would imply.

---

[16] It is not clear how Bradley defines 'indigenous black Jamaican music', but the group known as The Caribs consisted of three white Australian members, including Dennis Sindrey and Lyle Morris, who during the late 1950s and early 1960s worked on many of Coxsone Dodd's recording sessions. In addition, stalwarts of the early Jamaican recording industry included Tommy Mc Cook, Rudolph Alphonso, Rico Rodriquez and Laurel Aitken, some of whom are racially mixed and all are of Cuban, or part-Cuban extraction.

[17] Information regarding the ethnic background of Stanley Motta and Ken Khouri was obtained during interviews with their respective children, Brian Motta and Paul Khouri.

How was the New Music Produced?

Although Hendry's testimony challenges the legitimacy of Bradley's claim, Bradley does raise a number of valid questions because if 'Crowds embraced records made by local artists with added vigour' (2000, p. 25), which Harriot's account of the success of 'Lollipop Girl' substantiates, why did Motta fail to recognize and profit from, what appears to have been, an increasing demand for locally recorded, non-mento popular music? Why did a well-known entrepreneur like Motta fail to capitalize on this new emerging recording market by either providing a studio rental service or by becoming a producer of this new music?

I asked Hendry to comment on this and what appears to have been a growing demand for recording services by independent producers, including sound-system operators, during the late 1950s. Hendry explained that there were logistical problems with the location of MRS, situated behind Motta's woodworking factory with no easy public access, but he also noted that:

> The fact was that other influences, including some Jazz, and rhythm and blues were on the way in. I don't recall when SM Ltd closed down their recording business. One of the reasons for closure would have been that there were better-trained sound technicians around and they were aware of the trends.

Hendry suggests that Motta's studio simply did not have the technical expertise that was required to produce the sounds associated with North American popular music. Based on his description of a mento recording session in Chapter 1, it is also evident that MRS would not have been equipped to accommodate a contemporary popular music ensemble with drums, bass, piano, guitar and horns. It is also significant that Hendry admitted to not attending local dances where sound systems played nor did he have any particular interest in popular music. Hendry stated that his personal preference was for classical music and therefore he was not fully aware of the latest musical trends and sounds that were influencing local audiences.

I was interested in discovering to what extent Ken Khouri's Records Limited studio was involved with the making of restricted recordings and how sound-system operators might have gained access to his studio. Lloyd Bradley notes that Khouri 'actively courted the sound-system men, going to find them at the lawns, cutting affordable deals with them' (2000, p. 46). Although Ken Khouri's son Richard was unable to substantiate Bradley's claim, he was able to describe the basis on which his father's relationship with Coxsone Dodd was established. Richard Khouri explained that he spent much of his childhood in and around the Records Limited office on King Street, and witnessed the development of his father's record manufacturing plant, and later the building of the Records Limited studio, on the same premises (see Figure 2.1).

Richard Khouri stated that, in 1954, his father obtained a licensing agreement with Mercury Records in the USA to manufacture selections of their record

Figure 2.1   129 King Street as it stood in 2009. The location of Records Ltd. From the author's archive

catalogue in Jamaica. Khouri recalls that the first foreign record to be manufactured locally was entitled 'Little Shoe Maker', performed by the Gaylords (Mercury Records, Number 70403, 1954). According to Khouri, the nature of the Mercury contract was that they would send samples of their latest North American releases to his father on a regular basis. Ken Khouri would then select the records best suited to the Jamaican market and Mercury would provide the appropriate stampers and artwork for those records to be pressed and printed under licence and distributed in Jamaica by Khouri.

Richard Khouri provides an important insight into the mechanism that his father employed for selecting records to be locally pressed. He explains that Coxsone Dodd was a regular visitor to his father's King Street office, and that his father gave Dodd many of the Mercury record samples to play on his sound system. Although Richard Khouri was not privy to the details of the business arrangement between Dodd and his father, he understood there to be a mutual exchange where Khouri received information from Dodd regarding records that were well received by his patrons and were therefore likely to sell locally, and in return Dodd received a regular supply of the latest Mercury releases prior to them becoming commercially available in Jamaica.

Richard Khouri seems to suggest that a business relationship and then friendship evolved between his father and Dodd from their mutual exploitation of the Mercury

Records licensing contract. Both men mutually profited from this relationship but more significantly the relationship provided a basis on which studio time at the Records Limited recording facility could have been offered to or requested by Dodd.[18] This information also substantiates Goodall's claim that recording sessions were the product of a complex network of associations, friendships and business interests, from which potential recording financiers would obtain studio time. In addition, the above information is significant because it suggests that both Khouri and Dodd would have gained insights into the functioning of the other's respective business, which would prove critical during the early 1960s. For Khouri, understanding how the sound system employed recorded music would become the foundation on which the Federal Recording studio achieved local and international success and Dodd would have undoubtedly noticed the growing demand for records and the potential economic reward from their mass distribution, which would later become the primary focus of his business interests.

Richard Khouri's testimony is therefore significant because it explains how a sound-system owner such as Dodd, established a working relationship with a studio owner/audio engineer such as Ken Khouri, and the possible avenue through which Dodd would have gained access to a recording studio and created his first restricted recordings. Richard Khouri's testimony also contradicts Lloyd Bradley's characterization of studio owners, such as Ken Khouri, claiming that: 'Although Kingston's vibrant dancehall scene was virtually on their doorsteps in the mid-1950s, it's no surprise there were no dealings between the studio owners and sound system operators'. (2000, p. 24). Once again Bradley appears to assume a stereotype perspective based on race and class, which in the case of Ken Khouri certainly needs to be reassessed.

Richard Khouri's testimony provides vital information regarding the existence of a complex network of relationships and economic opportunities that contributed to the formation of the Jamaican music industry, but also a culture of recording. With this in mind, the 'producing and recording', which Stolzoff refers to earlier in this chapter, represents a wide array of activities that are rarely defined, quantified or traced in regard to their development. They undoubtedly assumed a Jamaican characteristic during this transformational period that is distinct from music production practices developed elsewhere. The assessment of the capabilities of Jamaican recording studios, their available recording models and the practice of selecting and processing music products allows a more reasoned and detailed appraisal of what 'producing and recording' might have entailed during the late 1950s.

Despite being influenced by 'foreign sophistication', elements of spontaneity and rawness, first formalized at Motta's studio, appear to permeate later recording approaches and evolve as a sound aesthetic that becomes distinctly Jamaican. While these core values are in much need of study, they were recognized and formulated by a production model that depended on the collaboration of the audio engineer

---

[18] This would provide an explanation for where and how early Dodd sound recordings, such as Theophilus Beckford's 'Easy Snappin', were recorded.

and musician, representing a practice that continues to dominate JPM. While we see two distinct music products emerging from Jamaica at the close of the 1950s in the form of commercial mass produced vinyl records and restricted recordings on acetate discs, music production is in fact largely directed by audio engineers and musicians with 'producers' functioning primarily as financiers and marketers of the resulting music products.

The next chapter will consider how local values were integrated with 'foreign sophistication' established through a multi-microphone recording model and how issues regarding studio access and technical facilities were ultimately overcome. However, it is also appropriate to consider how Jamaican audiences were evolving, to what extent they were exposed to recorded music and how this influenced the work of recording participants.

Chapter 3
Establishing an Internationally Competitive Recording Model

Although I have not been able to locate any examples of restricted recordings from the late 1950s, the testimony of Derrick Harriot in conjunction with the availability and technical capability of local studios suggest that these recordings are best described as novelty music products. Despite the fact that Motta and Khouri's studios were not equipped to replicate the sound of North American records, they could provide recordings of home grown talent mimicking the latest trends in North American music. These sound recordings also had the potential of addressing topical subjects, presented with a range of sonic details on acetate disc, which commercial vinyl records lacked. The success of these early sound-system recordings suggests that they offered music consumers a range of attributes despite lacking 'foreign sophistication'. This might in part be explained by widespread growing nationalism, as Jamaica approached independence in 1962.

However, in 1958 we see the local release of a mass produced vinyl record, performed by Laurel Aitken entitled 'Boogie In My Bones', which somehow achieves much of the 'foreign sophistication' that Motta and Khouri's respective studios were unable to create. This chapter therefore considers the circumstances surrounding the creation of this pivotal recording and the recording model that it introduced; however, it is first necessary to look closer at how recorded music was consumed by local audiences and to what extent they were able to critically evaluate recorded music production standards.

Music Listening Trends in Kingston

While assessing the capability of local recording facilities and tracing the way in which music was captured, it is also appropriate to consider how the financiers of local recorded products were influenced by trends in music consumption. A widely accepted theme is that local music tastes were influenced by the reception of US-based radio stations, '[p]articularly by small r&b stations situated in and around Miami. On a clear day these broadcasts could be picked up fairly easily even on a battered transistor' (Hebdige, 1987a, p. 62). While this claim is repeated in the literature, there is no attempt to reconcile the existence of these 'r&b radio stations' with the change in American taste 'from rhythm and blues to rock and roll' as noted in the previous chapter.

The apparent inconsistency, of on the one hand, suggesting that American tastes had transitioned to rock and roll, which Jamaicans disliked, but on the other, suggesting that American 'r&b stations' continued to exist and presumably, obtain new rhythm and blues music from somewhere, is in need of investigation. I was interested in establishing to what extent ordinary Jamaicans had access to these American radio transmissions during the 1950s and early 1960s. I interviewed Walter Mathews, an English broadcasting engineer in 2006. Mathews was recruited by Rediffusion in the UK to help establish Jamaica's fledging radio service in 1948, and he became head of engineering at RJR, a position he maintained for over 25 years. Mathews suggested that the claims made by Hebdige are misleading.[1] He asserts that although it was possible to pick up American radio stations in Jamaica, it would depend on the listener having access to a supply of electricity, a relatively expensive tube radio receiver with a good antenna and/or the correct atmospheric conditions, prior to the early 1960s.

During the 1950s this type of equipment was relatively expensive and was not generally owned by the majority of Jamaicans but, in addition, many homes in Kingston's poor communities did not have an electrical supply. Moreover, Mathews stated that radio sets of the period were vacuum tube designs, intended to run on a 110 volt, 60 cycle supply however, during the 1950s, Kingston's electrical supply was 110-volt, 40-cycle. The difference in cycles is critical for tube equipment, which depends on step-up transformers that multiply the voltage on which the vacuum tubes operate and fewer cycles reduced the rate of multiplication resulting in lower voltages and equipment running inefficiently, overheating or unable to function. Electrical repair businesses such as Galbraith's and Wonard's could manufacture mechanical parts to compensate for the speed of record turntables or rewind electrical motors and transformers to operate on a 40-cycle supply but this only added to the high cost of audio equipment . By the 1960s companies such as Stanley Motta were commercially retailing locally assembled audio equipment, manufactured to this local specification but presumably at a premium cost.

During my interview with Donald Hendry, he commented on the commercial introduction of affordable battery-powered transistor radios to Jamaica, stating that this did not take place until the early 1960s. According to Hendry, Stanley Motta Ltd was the distributor for the first hand-held transistor radios to be imported into Jamaica (manufactured by Sony), and he confirms that their receivers were not strong enough to pick up American radio transmissions.[2] The local reception of US-based radio stations, according to Walter Mathews, was haphazard at best and often only possible with customized antennas or short-wave receivers during the 1950s and 1960s; even then, the quality of the reception was relatively poor.

---

[1] See O'Brien-Chang and Chen (1998); Stolzoff (2000); Bradley (2000); and Katz (2003), who all repeat this claim.

[2] Kingston to Miami is a distance of 935 kilometres, the same distance as London to Berlin.

While some Jamaicans undoubtedly obtained access to American music via long-distance radio transmissions, according to Mathews, the most likely source for the majority of Kingstonians to hear popular American music during the 1950s was through either the sound system or increasingly through a cable radio service provided by RJR. According to Mathews, the RJR service was significant, although its influence is sparingly mentioned in the literature.[3] Mathews played a major role in setting up, and running this service at the start of the 1950s and claims that 'it became very popular, especially in the poorer communities'. The service provided subscribers with a loudspeaker and volume control that was self-powered and hard-wired to RJR's broadcast facilities.[4] The equipment was rented for a small weekly fee and according to Mathews, the absence of the need for an electrical supply made the system universally popular.

I contend that this RJR service represented a significant development for many Jamaicans, especially those in the lower socioeconomic groups, who for the first time could obtain affordable access to foreign-recorded music on a regular and consistent basis. Mathews explained that the Rediffusion equipment was offered to the public in a variety of sizes and finishes, and priced accordingly. According to Graeme Goodall, the cheapest option included a good quality, Grampian eight-inch loudspeaker in a locally manufactured, solid wooden cabinet that sounded very good. Goodall claimed that the units had a reasonable frequency response and the volume level was superior to many domestic radio sets of the period and without the issues associated with poor radio-signal reception or atmospheric interference.[5]

Mathews stated that at its peak, in the early 1960s, the RJR service had over 20,000 paying subscribers in the Kingston area alone. Mathews went on to explain that the system eventually became unprofitable in the mid 1960s, because the cable network was suffering from a significant number of illegal connections that made the service increasingly expensive to maintain and difficult to expand. Mathews explained that in many of Kingston's poorer communities, illegal connections would be added to a single legitimate connection, with the additional users providing their own loudspeaker. Given the fact that each loudspeaker potentially provided a family residence or business place with radio service, and that illegal connections were common, it would be reasonable to assume that the actual number of Kingstonians who enjoyed this service was considerably higher than the 20,000 subscribers.

---

[3] Rediffusion was a UK-based company started in 1928. They 'set up their wired networks in many UK towns and cities during the 1940's and 1950's'. See http://www.rediffusion.info/ (accessed April 2010). This wired service was offered to Jamaica through a partnership with Radio Jamaica.

[4] Mathews, now retired, still lives in Jamaica and at the time of the interview was 92 years of age. This was his first interview and he proved to be a lucid and articulate informant.

[5] Goodall also confirmed that even the cheapest speaker box produced respectable volume levels, which were more than adequate for a domestic setting. The Grampian loudspeaker, according to Goodall, was a good quality unit, manufactured in the UK.

Based on this new evidence, I contend that the RJR service provided Kingstonians of all classes with their first widely accessible and reliable form of recorded music, with a consistent sound quality, on a daily basis. Donald Hendry provides a sense of the impact that the service had, describing it as a 'bloody nuisance', because the perception was that 'everybody had it, and never turned the speaker off'. According to Hendry, everywhere you went in Kingston the RJR service could be heard playing somewhere in the background.

It is not know why the literature tends to ignore the existence of the RJR service, which undoubtedly represents the primary source of recorded music to a large number of Kingstonians between the 1950s and 1960s. Lloyd Bradley dismisses the influence of the RJR service on the basis that it represented music programming that 'Played it safe leaning toward the insipid' (Bradley, 2000, p. 9), with a 'BBC Radio 2-style schedule of American and British popular hits and easily digestible classics' (ibid., p. 88).[6] However, Frith comments that: 'Most record companies agree ... that the most effective form of promotion is airplay' (1981, p. 117). I therefore contend that the significance of the service was not located in the 'insipid' selection of the RJR programmers but that it offered the only reliable, affordable and regularly accessible form of recorded music consumption that, despite its conservative programming, was popular with all classes of Jamaican society. The RJR service was therefore directly responsible for exposing many Jamaicans to a wide range of recorded music and music production standards considered 'good' by North Americans and Europeans. Although programming would have certainly been dictated by RJR policy, the actual selection of recorded music was predominantly made by Jamaicans for Jamaicans.[7]

This information demands a reassessment of the claim that ordinary Jamaicans enjoyed a musical diet of predominantly American rhythm and blues, via a long distance radio services as suggested by Hebdige and other scholars. Furthermore, it suggests an avenue through which Jamaicans seemed to have developed a taste for North American country music evidenced by the local popularity of recording artists such as Patsy Klien and Jim Reeves during the late 1950s and early 1960s.[8] In addition, the fact that the RJR service was paid for by an inclusive rental fee meant that users tended to leave their loudspeaker turned on, as testified by

---

[6] I was unable to obtain a programme schedule for the RJR service that included examples of selected materials that were presented to the Jamaican public.

[7] It should be noted that both Duke Reid and Coxsone Dodd bought half-hour radio slots from RJR that featured a selection of music. It is assumed that these programmes represented an advertising mechanism for their respective sound system, presenting largely American popular music, but I have not been able to locate any recordings of these programmes or lists of music that they featured.

[8] John Holt and Alton Ellis are two of Jamaica's most popular singers from the rock steady and reggae periods. While touring with them in the 1990s I was surprised that both singers cited the influence of North American country music along with rhythm and blues and other forms of North American popular music.

Hendry. This information suggests that the Kingston soundscape of the 1950s and early 1960s changed dramatically as a direct result of this radio service. Although it is difficult to estimate the influence that this had on the listening tastes of Kingstonians, it seems evident that the average sound-system patron was becoming a more widely exposed and discerning listener by the end of the 1950s, even if the sound system or foreign radio stations, when available, provided their preferred choice of music.[9]

Local radio broadcasting services were also expanded in Jamaica in 1958, with the opening of the government-owned JBC. This station was given a mandate to 'Promote the indigenous arts and to reflect local tastes accurately' (Bradley, 2000, p. 88). In addition, during the mid-1950s, the local capacity for manufacturing records was expanded with the opening of Edward Seaga's West Indies Records, initially a manufacturing facility for foreign records made under licence. This apparent increase in levels of access, affordability and consumption of popular recorded music can be explained in-part by 'A 10 per cent year-on-year Gross National Product growth up to 57' (ibid. p. 12), representing an unusual period of economic prosperity and optimism as Jamaica approached independence.

It therefore seems evident that the musical landscape of Kingston changed dramatically during the 1950s, with the first studio recordings of local music in the form of mento, and a growing demand for the more sophisticated sounds of American contemporary popular music styles in the form of restricted recordings as well as locally produced popular music records. Further, the sound systems were offering Jamaicans a unique mechanism for music consumption at a time when exposure to a wide array of recorded music and production standards was becoming routinely available. This was experienced primarily through the RJR cable service, but would have also been through the growth in locally owned record decks and distribution of American popular music; however, jukeboxes and long-distance radio receivers would have also undoubtedly played a role in the dissemination of recorded music. This information is cause for a reassessment of the way in which local and foreign music tastes diverged at the end of the 1950s and the forces that were driving the tastes of Jamaican music consumers. I contend that these issues represent a complex array of factors that are not easy to quantify or measure and are in much need of further research.

The testimony of Goodall, Hendry and Mathews provides a new sense of the Kingston soundscape at the turn of the 1960s, but, more significantly, they imply the emergence of a sonically well-educated music consumer who was exposed to a wide range of recorded music at a high standard of reproduction through the sound

---

[9] On a personal note I recall a comment by my father in the early 1960s after returning to the UK from a trip to Jamaica to visit his mother. He commented on a number of occasions in subsequent years that one of the most memorable things about Kingston was that 'music was everywhere' and this represented a marked difference from when he had left the island in 1942. In addition, the souvenirs he brought back to the UK were records by Jamaican artists.

system and domestically through the Rediffusion service. I contend that this is a significant point because it suggests that local music production was responding to a critical audience, which is an important consideration as we look at how the Jamaican recording industry transitioned from the recording models established by Motta and Khouri to a new multi-microphone model that was able to compete directly with the sound of foreign records.

Illicit Recording Sessions

As stated above, the song entitled 'Boogie In My Bones' (1958) represents one of the first local recordings of which the sound can be considered comparable, in terms of instruments, musicianship and recorded sound, to a North American recording. This chapter provides a detailed analysis of the recording session for the above song, conducted by Graeme Goodall at the RJR studio. The song is notably not the product of the sound-system operators but was financed by Chris Blackwell as an independent producer and was intended for commercial mass production. I contend that this recording session and the recording model it introduced acted as a catalyst for seismic change in the Jamaican recording industry. It was one of the first local sound recordings to overcome the challenge of achieving the 'foreign sophistication', which up to that time had seemed unobtainable. Its significance includes the fact that it confirmed the potential for a local recording industry, which was on par with North America and Europe and this was noted by sound-system operators, studio owners, would-be producers and musicians alike.

Goodall confirmed that the recording of 'Boogie In My Bones' was the first illicit recording that he made using the RJR studio and that the recording set out to satisfy two requirements for Blackwell. Goodall explained that Blackwell operated a jukebox rental business and the recording was intended to reduce his recurring cost of restocking jukeboxes with new foreign records while also providing his entrance into the growing local commercial record market. Goodall explained that for Blackwell, matching the sound of American popular records, in regard to their instrumentation, performance and recorded sound was essential. However, Blackwell had no previous experience as a record producer and was dependent on Goodall's technical and creative ability to bring these various elements together in a sound recording. Unlike the restricted recordings of the sound system, which were hyped by the sound system's 'selector' and 'chatter', Blackwell would have to depend on the sound of his record being able to compete directly with foreign imports on the basis of its creative and sonic values.[10] As one of many records on

---

[10] A 'selector' and 'chatter' are part of a team who operate the sound system and their primary role is to read the mood of the audience and then select appropriate discs, which they are able to promote and heighten its appeal.

a jukebox, Blackwell's recording had to appeal directly to local audiences on the basis of its inherent sound.[11]

The recordings conducted illicitly by Goodall at RJR are significant because, in 1958, the radio station's studio represented the only recording facility in Jamaica that owned all the technical resources required to meet Blackwell's objective. However, the contribution of Goodall is critical because he was the only audio engineer working in Jamaica at that time who understood how to employ these resources and break down the sound of American recordings into specific production techniques, an area that will be explored in the next chapter. Blackwell's decision to underwrite the relatively high cost of this recording, in the hope of making back his investment from jukebox revenues and the sale of records, is also significant. It is unlikely that this exploratory and relatively expensive recording approach would have been considered by sound-system operators, whose potential earnings-to-cost ratio for a restricted recording would have been significantly less. The sound-system recording strategy depended on minimum music production costs and a regular turnover of new music that would continue to attract patrons and ensure large gate receipts and high volumes of merchandise sales. I make the assumption that the production cost of music was directly linked to these revenues.

Goodall's consolidation of RJR's technical resources, employing them in a seven-hour recording session to record just two songs for Blackwell, was unprecedented in Jamaica in 1958. However, the results of this and similar illicit recording sessions that followed were nothing less than transformational for the fledgling Jamaican music industry. For the first time, a local recording was able to compete with foreign records in terms of their instrumentation, performance and sound. As a result, 'Boogie In My Bones' was not only successful on Blackwell's jukeboxes, but became a local hit through the radio and the sound-system network.

Goodall spoke at length, during his interview, about the recording of the song and the fact that it was arranged and performed by three Australian and two Jamaican musicians. This song is a prime example of the Jamaican boogie genre and evidence of its enthusiastic acceptance can be found in the fact that it 'Entered the JBC chart in October 1959 and stayed at number one for thirteen weeks' (Katz, 2003, p. 20). The song can therefore be fairly described as one of a small group of seminal recordings that mark the transition of local recorded sound from the mento recording models of MRS and Records Limited to the new multi-microphone recording model, which Khouri's Federal Records would soon adapt and emulate with great success.

The success of 'Boogie In My Bones' therefore suggests that the early development of the Jamaican recording industry is more complex than previously suggested, with independent music financiers such as Blackwell playing a critical role. By underwriting the relatively high cost of what must be considered an

---

[11] Blackwell's personal assistant was contacted to try and arrange an interview concerning these issues. Blackwell insisted that I submit a list of questions, which he would then answer, but no responses materialized.

exploratory recording session, Blackwell demonstrated that local recordings could compete directly with foreign records in regard to their core values of performance, instrumentation and now produced sound. However, this achievement would not have been possible without an audio engineer such as Goodall who was able to translate the sound of North American records into recording techniques based on the tools that were locally available. By assembling the best RJR resources, Goodall was able to apply his knowledge and understanding of recorded sound to establish the first Jamaican recordings, which could compete directly with North American and European popular music.

A New Music Production Model

Given the critical role played by Goodall in the transition of Jamaican recorded music from the raw sound of 'Hill and Gully Ride' (see Chapter 1) to the relatively sophisticated sound of 'Boogie In My Bones', I was interested in learning where and how Goodall, as a broadcast engineer, learnt the art and craft of record production. Specifically, I was interested in discovering:

- How did Goodall acquire the knowledge of recording techniques associated with foreign record production?
- To what extent was he given instruction by the producer of the 'Boogie In My Bones' recording session?
- What impact did the release of this song have locally?

Goodall explained that as a member of the RJR staff during the 1950s, he was involved with the capture, reproduction and transmission of sound for the purpose of radio broadcast, but describes himself as being passionately interested in the new sounds that were evident on many American popular-music recordings, especially after travelling across the United States in 1957. In a 2008 email Goodall writes:

> Returned, on 'Home leave' to Australia leaving JA November 57. Greyhound across the U.S. to LA. In Burbank, still the quintessential broadcaster, made an absolute pest of myself going to EVERY TV studio that I could talk myself into … saw every 'live' show that I could … very important later on in my life as you can imagine. Also went to Capital Records Studios.

Goodall returned to Jamaica in April 1958, inspired by the developments taking place in the North American recording industry, but with very few opportunities to use this knowledge and experience during the course of his everyday work with RJR. Therefore, when Chris Blackwell approached Goodall to make a record, which was sonically comparable to contemporary North American recordings, it represented an attractive challenge.[12]

It was important to discover the specific recording techniques that Goodall introduced during this session and I asked him to provide details of his recording approach. What mechanisms did he employ to shape the sound and the sonic characteristics of this particular record? I also surveyed the RJR recording studio in 2008 (see Figure 3.1), which has not changed structurally since 1958 and is still in use as RJR's principal recording studio. The main recording room is acoustically treated, measuring approximately 50 × 30 × 16 feet (24,000 cubic feet), with a small isolated control room to which microphone signals can be fed and balanced electronically through a mixing console. The room represented the largest professionally designed recording space available in Jamaica at that time, and allowed instruments to be effectively isolated, with independent microphone feeds. In addition, the complete isolation of the recording and control room was an important improvement over MRS, allowing the audio engineer to hear accurately

Figure 3.1   RJR main studio pictured in 2008. From the author's archive

---

[12] The term 'contemporary' is being used here to describe the popular music recordings coming predominantly from North America at the end of the 1950s.

what the microphones were picking up. This was critical for the process of adjusting and balancing instrument sounds, an essential element in the recording of contemporary popular music.[13]

Goodall explained that as a commercial broadcasting facility, RJR had a wide range of equipment available in several studios, including an outside-broadcast vehicle. After the station closed for the evening, he was able to commandeer a selection of the best equipment that could be used for the recording session. He collected the best microphones, which were used to capture individual instruments during recording; however, to provide enough microphone inputs, Goodall temporarily installed the station's outside-broadcast mixing console in the main studio control room, alongside the resident Gates console. Goodall states that he used an RCA 44BX ribbon microphone exclusively for the upright bass and placed an Electrovoice 666 microphone on the 'kick drum' that was then balanced with the bass to provide the driving rhythmic sound that contemporary American popular music employed.[14]

Goodall explained that the quality and selection of the microphones at the RJR studio, although the best available in Jamaica, were still limited, especially for instruments such as the kick drum. Up to that point, drums and bass were often subdued in the balance of instruments on popular music records, treated as a rhythmic unit and captured with a minimal number of microphones. However, Goodall reasoned that this recording approach was unable to reproduce the new sounds being heard on some American recordings and particularly music intended for dance. He explained that by micing the kick drum and bass independently, he hoped to achieve this American sound but there were problems to overcome.

The kick drum in particular represented a challenge because it generated too much energy for a sensitive ribbon microphone and dynamic microphones such as the Electrovoice 666 did not have an effective low-frequency response. The extent to which this was considered an issue is demonstrated by the fact that Goodall experimented with converting a car radio loudspeaker into a makeshift microphone that proved to be very effective for picking up the low frequency content of the kick-drum and was employed on subsequent recordings.

Goodall explains that the sound he achieved on his recordings was largely due to the way in which he employed the microphones and worked around their various limitations. For example, the RCA 44BX microphone, used on the upright bass, needed to be positioned carefully because its pickup pattern was restricted to a figure eight pattern, meaning that it was equally sensitive to sound in front and behind but less sensitive to sounds coming from each side. A degree of skill was

---

[13] Although Khouri's Records Limited studio was built with a separate control and recording rooms, the recording space was approximately 12 × 12 feet. The microphone selection was also very limited and only three mixing channels were available.

[14] The term 'kick drum' or bass drum refers to the largest drum in a modern drum set (sometimes referred to as a trap set) and produces the lowest frequency. It is played with a foot-operated pedal, hence the term 'kick'.

therefore needed to position the performers, their instruments and microphones in relation to the room boundaries and each other, so that well-defined instrument separation was achieved and maintained.

The fact that Goodall was using what he considered his 'best microphone' on the upright bass and placing a separate microphone on the kick drum is significant and indicates a sonic focus that was very different from any previous music recording made in Jamaica. Goodall also experimented with different recording techniques and devised a way of recording the electric guitar by using a high to low impedance transformer, typically found on the input of a tape recorder. This allowed Goodall to record the electric guitar without using a microphone, further improving instrument separation and his ability to balance and control the sound of the instruments from the mixing console.[15]

Goodall appears to be the first audio engineer to record with reverb in Jamaica and he achieved this by running a loudspeaker and microphone to the men's bathroom, in the adjoining corridor to the studio. He was then able to establish a rudimentary send-and-return channel, so that the vocal performance could be fed to the bathroom speaker and by adjusting the distance of the microphone from the speaker, mix the reverberant sound of the bathroom to the vocal.[16] The isolation of RJR's studio control room allowed sound to be accurately balanced, and Goodall was able to identify any sonic discrepancies evident in the quality of individual instrument sounds. This could include the squeak of a kick-drum pedal that needed mechanical adjustment or any unwanted sounds unwittingly made by the performers. These were painstakingly corrected and adjusted before recording began.

Goodall explained that using a tape recorder was a significant improvement over disc recorders because they allowed repeated takes to be made of a performance with a cost-effective recording medium. This encouraged the crafting of both musical performance and sound in a way not facilitated by disc recording. In addition, tape offered an improved frequency response and dynamic range and, when used by a skilled operator, natural occurring tape compression could be employed as a useful and creative recording tool.[17] The phenomenon of tape compression was experienced when recording levels approached the saturation point of the magnetic tape, but before audible distortion became audible. In effect, this phenomenon could be creatively used to compress the dynamic level of the

---

[15] This recording technique is now commonly referred to as 'direct inject' or DI. The technique, although common now, would have been considered pioneering at the end of the 1950s.

[16] 'Send-and-return' refers to a facility that is now commonly available on mixing consoles, whereby a feed from each mixing channel can be sent to a sound-altering device and then returned to the mixing console to be mixed with the original signal. The RJR mixer did not offer this facility and so Goodall had to configure the equipment specially to allow reverb to be added to the voice.

[17] See Balllou (1991), Chapter 25, 'Disc Recording and Playback'.

Figure 3.2   The RJR main studio control room in 2008. From the author's archive

recorded material and Goodall describes how this helped to create the sense of a driving sound, especially in rhythmic music. The use of tape also made it feasible to record several performances and choose the best one, or physically edit those performances into a single composite master (see Figure 3.2).

The significance of the recording techniques described by Goodall is not that they were new, because by 1958 many North American recording studios were routinely using multiple microphone feeds and reverb chambers. However, they were considered groundbreaking for Jamaica, and a revolutionary departure from the single microphone approach that had been practised at Motta's studio and the three microphones that Khouri's Records Limited employed. Despite the fact that these RJR recordings were illicit and makeshift in nature, they represent the first local attempt to sonically alter the instrumental characteristics of a musical performance and successfully achieve the 'foreign sophistication' that up to that point had been associated with foreign records. However, while the sound of 'Boogie In My Bones' became aligned with the sound of North America, the mechanisms of producing the sound was distinct. The commercial success of this sound recording, evident in the unprecedented 13 weeks at the number one position in the local charts, attracted the attention of the public, music and sound-system fraternity alike. The sound recording must not only have caused many to re-evaluate what could be achieved in a local recording studio but also established a foothold for what would become a uniquely Jamaican music production model.

A Jamaican Approach to Producing Music

A feature of JPM is that it represents an industry that, from its inception, was dominated by independent financiers, of which few, if any, had received formal training in music production. As a result, individuals given the title 'producer' were often performing an executive function. Information provided by my informants and the literature, as well as my own experience, suggests that the actual technical and creative decisions made during recording sessions are often delegated to the audio engineer and/or musicians.[18] This practice is first noted in Motta's studio and while it might not represent a conscious rejection of foreign recording practice it emerged as a method that was locally embraced and became established as part of a recording approach that helps to define and distinguish the sound and character of JPM. This audio engineer-/musician-driven production model had a significant influence on the way in which local recording-studio culture evolved.

The practice is also indicative of a recording industry influenced by the absence of corporate record companies directing music production through a chain of hierarchies and music production specialists . Their absence nurtured and encouraged a recording process that was spontaneous and informal compared to recording practice of North America or the UK. Andre Millard comments on the North American record industry saying: 'Although the record business in the 1960s appeared to be a profusion of many independent companies, this was only an illusion. Behind the mass of labels and exotic company names were a small number of integrated entertainment corporations' (1995, p. 333). From the boardrooms of these corporations creative and commercial goals were largely dictated, but that was not the case in Jamaica.

The large 'entertainment corporations' referred to by Millard incorporated employment structures based on stratified technical and creative roles, often unionized and supported by appropriate training and apprenticeship programmes. For example, the music producer George Martin qualified for employment with Electric and Musical Industries Limited (EMI), as an assistant to Oscar Preuss (head of Parlophone Records), through his formal training at the Guildhall School of Music.[19] Martin's additional training at EMI prepared him to take creative responsibility for the production of records in terms of the choice of artist, material, studio, arranger and musicians, all representing aspects of recording that were considered the responsibility of the producer.

According to Geoff Emerick, in this corporate world, the role of the audio engineer was seen as purely technical and divided into specialized tasks: 'The EMI "way" was to move inexorably upward from assistant to playback lacquer to mastering to balance engineer whether that's what you wanted to do or not'

---

[18] See Bradley (2000, p. 41), Veal (2007, p. 48).
[19] See Martin And Hornsby (1979, p. 37).

(Emerick and Massey, 2006, p. 105).[20] In this environment technicians 'Followed the unspoken rule, which was that the balance engineer – and, of course, the assistant – keep his mouth shut unless spoken to. Any unsolicited opinions were perceived as undermining the role of the producer' (ibid., p. 58).

By contrast, the emerging studio culture and production methodology described by Goodall in Jamaica was one where the audio engineer took responsibility for all aspects of the sound recording while the musicians took responsibility for the writing, arrangement and performance of the music. However, this did not mean that the financier for 'Boogie In My Bones' was not involved in the creative and technical direction of the recording.

The dominance of the audio engineer/musician in regard to production decisions is independently confirmed by Dennis Sindrey, who not only played guitar on the 'Boogie In My Bones' recording session but on a significant number of recording sessions during the 1960s in Jamaica.[21] The important point to make here is that the audio engineer, in this newly emerging multi-microphone recording model, assumed responsibilities that included the recorded balance and mix of instruments and voice, a task that in the UK and North America was typically supervised by the producer.

I asked Goodall: To what extent did Chris Blackwell, as the 'producer', assume responsibility for directing the 'Boogie In My Bones' session? Did he provide reference recordings for the type of sound he wanted, discuss or comment on the modification or treatment of sound or the balance of instruments? Goodall explained that control over the recording methods and how sound was interpreted and balanced were left up to him as the audio engineer. There were no specific references from Blackwell and the recorded sound was simply left up to his experience and judgment.

Chris Blackwell was unavailable for comment on these issues but in an attempt to explore the nature of these early recording sessions and the relationship and perception of participants, I interviewed Edward Seaga in February 2008, a contemporary of Blackwell who was also active in record production during this transitional stage of JPM's development.[22] I asked Seaga specifically about the recording of the song 'Oh Manny Oh' (1960), performed by Higgs and Wilson. Seaga explained: 'The song was already popular through *Vere John's Opportunity*

---

[20]   Emerick goes on to describe the influence of unions and how this affected creative aspects of audio engineering. Terms such as 'playback lacquer' describe a particular set of audio-engineering specified tasks established by the EMI management and structured into a hierarchy of positions. The authors do not provide specific details of what these tasks included.

[21]   Sindrey is an Australian guitarist who was interviewed in 2006. He came to Jamaica in 1956 and worked with the group known as the Caribs. He also worked as a freelance session player and on a substantial number of the early recording sessions of this period.

[22]   See note 13 in Chapter 2 regarding my request for an interview with Blackwell.

Hour and I offered the artists the opportunity of recording the song.'[23] The resulting record achieved significant commercial success for Seaga and I asked for his opinion on who was responsible for the creation of the recorded sound? He responded: 'The creative direction and music arrangements were made by the singers and musicians', implying that they were responsible for the sonic characteristics and success of the record. Seaga went on to say that: 'The musicians were chosen by the singers and Graeme Goodall was the best engineer available at that time and so the recording was made at RJR where he worked.'[24] Based on Seaga's recollection, only he, Goodall and a trainee engineer were present in the control room during the recording of 'Oh Manny Oh'. According to Seaga, the singers and musicians were not invited into the control room at any time to listen to or comment on the sounds that represented their respective instruments and group performance. It was he and Goodall who decided when the recording was complete.

I then asked Seaga if he gave the audio engineer any instructions in regard to the balancing of instruments and how they were interpreted through the mixing console. Seaga responded: 'No, but there was little Goodall could do because the recording was made in mono, this was long before the introduction of multi-track recorders.' I then pointed out to Seaga that a mono recording did not limit the number of microphones being used during the recording. As such, the song would have been balanced and mixed by the audio engineer live during the capture of the performance to tape. Seaga explained that he had not been aware of this and reminded me that in 1960 he was new to the recording industry and inexperienced in regard to how recordings were made.[25]

The description of this recording session by Seaga is significant because, as the 'producer', he confirms that the audio engineer took unilateral responsibility for how instruments were represented, balanced and mixed, yet, as the producer, Seaga was unaware that these sonic modifications were possible and the extent to which they were influencing the sound of the recording. I contend that Seaga makes a common assumption that the sonic characteristic, balance of instruments and dynamics evident on 'Oh Manny Oh' were the product of the musicians and singer. However, this sound recording, like 'Boogie In My Bones', achieved the

---

[23] *Vere John's Opportunity Hour* was a weekly talent show at the end of the 1950s through which many of Jamaica's early singers first came to prominence.

[24] Seaga, who is a Harvard trained anthropologist, explained that his move into politics at the start of the 1960s ended his interest in the Jamaican recording industry. As an elder statesman of Jamaica, including prime minister from 1980 to 1989, I felt it inappropriate to ask Seaga if the RJR session was conducted illicitly. At the end of the 1950s, Seaga was well enough connected to formally obtain permission to use the RJR studio.

[25] Seaga was very candid about his limited experience as a producer, which lasted for only a short period of time before his entrance into politics. Goodall commented that this lack of understanding was typical of Jamaican producers from that period, who had very little knowledge or experience of the recording process.

'foreign sophistication' because sound and its modification played as important a role as the musical performances. The musicians' absence from the studio control room confirms that they played no part in the alteration of sound through microphone choice, placement and balance, which ultimately played a critical role in the record's commercial success. Seaga's testimony highlights how the creative contribution of the audio engineer becomes masked by the technical nature of the tools and mechanisms that he employs in the capture and reproduction of music. Goodall's contribution to this and other recordings is located in the sonic rendering that is applied to the musical performance, but to measure and quantify that rendering is difficult and is all too often attributed to the performance of the musicians.

Lloyd Bradley aptly sums up the role of many Jamaican producers, claiming he was the man who 'sponsored the recording rather than the man who twiddled the knobs' (2000, p. 40), but I contend that in many cases the producer did not even understand the significance of 'twiddling the knobs'. This claim is not intended to discredit or devalue the role of Seaga or Blackwell and other Jamaican financiers of local recordings, but to highlight the fact that a producer in a Jamaican context generally played a different role from his foreign counterpart. Based on the testimony of Goodall, Seaga and Sindrey, it would be accurate to describe the role of the producer in the examples cited here as someone who established the objective of a recording, financed the production and manufacture of the record, located ways to earn a profit from the record but had little direct input on how the creative and technical production of the record was achieved. I contend that this is distinct from music production models practised elsewhere.

Goodall describes a scenario where he was required to assert himself as a decision maker in the recording studio, primarily because he was the only person on these early recording sessions that fully understood the recording process and how it influenced sound. His role as the audio engineer, responsible for the capture of sound, was seen in Jamaica as a position of authority, allowing him a level of creative and technical freedom that many of his British or North American peers did not share. Goodall also implied an underlying significance that the audio engineer had on these transitional recordings: because he was often responsible for illicitly providing access to the recording studio and could not be treated as just a hired technician. It is also important to note that although the new multi-microphone recording model established by Goodall, at RJR, differed in many technical aspects to those practised at MRS and Records Limited, the collaboration of musician and audio engineer, as the primary recording practitioners remained consistent.

A New Type of Audio Engineer

In my assessment of early Jamaican recording practices, the objective is to discover specific methods and/or approaches in which local music production diverged from that practised elsewhere. After identifying these differences it is possible to trace the causes for divergence and in so doing focus on unique aspects of music-making and production in Jamaica. It is therefore appropriate to consider the descriptions provided by Hendry and Goodall in an effort to position Jamaica's fledgling recording industry in a wider context. During my discussions with Goodall, he described the working environment that he experienced in London at the beginning of the 1950s before moving to Jamaica. He describes a scenario where younger engineers such as he were starting to question the traditional methods of recording music, placing him in direct conflict with the recording establishment. Mark Cunningham notes this conflict in audio engineering attitudes a decade later commenting: 'By 1967, it was apparent that Decca's die-hard engineers of the older generation had become too old and detached from the progressive pop world to have anything in common with the new breed of engineers' (1996, p. 100). Goodall added that traditional recording methods, especially in larger electronic media organizations, followed set practices, leaving very little room for creativity or the personal interpretation of sound through the selection and placement of microphones and instruments.

Goodall claimed that his earliest training in Australia, had included the use of multi-microphone techniques, which were a necessary part of capturing live radio broadcasts. In these situations the audio engineer had to contend with excluding unwanted sounds from microphone feeds, in part facilitated through using close micing techniques and exploiting the pickup-pattern characteristic of different microphones. The demanding nature of this work required a thorough understanding of the sound characteristics of microphones and what their real-world limitations were, as opposed to the recommended usage stated in their operation manual or the prescribed recording techniques of media organizations, largely designed to create a controlled and consistent studio environment.

When Goodall moved to London and started working with the International Broadcasting Corporation (IBC) at the start of the 1950s, he claims that they represented one of the few independent production companies in the UK, otherwise dominated by multi-national corporations such as EMI, Decca, RCA, Phillips and Pye. According to Goodall, IBC had a reputation for being very progressive in its attitudes towards recording and the company encouraged its audio engineers to maximize the potential of recording equipment, experimenting if necessary but with a focus on providing its recording clients with the best production sounds that they were able to achieve. The recording environment described by Goodall is in contrast to conservative organizations such as the BBC or EMI, whose audio engineers were required to follow strict company guidelines and practices, formally prescribed in company recording manuals.

In 2007, I conducted a search of the BBC Written Archives Centre, Caversham and found evidence supporting Goodall's claim in a *Programme Operating Handbook* dating from 1956, compiled by J.N. Borwick. This BBC handbook provided audio engineers with explicit instructions on where to place the microphone in relation to different sound sources, and states: 'It is very important to avoid working too close, with the resultant exaggeration of bass frequencies.

A minimum of 2 feet should be observed' (Borwick, 1956, p. 171).[26] It is evident that the increased low frequency, resulting from close micing, was considered undesirable by the BBC. However, in the 1950s that view was already at odds with the increasing use of close micing techniques being heard on American recordings, and was embraced by Goodall in Jamaica.[27]

Steve Jones comments on the issue that close micing represented, quoting J.P. Maxfield, who in 1933 suggested that it 'Accentuates the trend in popular taste toward acceptance of the unreal' (1992, p. 67), while Mark Katz offers an example of the impact of close micing and says, 'The sensitivity of the microphone also provided the means for new sounds and performance practices. Consider "Crooning"' (2004, p. 40).[28] These authors are referring to the 'unreal' effect that close micing could achieve, such as the intimate sound of a vocal, captured as if being performed next to the listener's ear, yet remaining balanced with a music ensemble, perceived in a much deeper sound field.

Goodall's comments reflect an ongoing contest of recording philosophy that existed in British recording studios but was most evident in the sound of the new popular music being produced in North America, during the 1950s. As a young audio engineer and firm believer in the use of close micing and the licence for audio engineers to craft the sonic characteristics of music, Goodall introduced to Jamaica a recording attitude that might be considered 'cutting edge' for the time period. With the absence of an established audio engineering community in Jamaica, the introduction of Goodall's recording practices were accepted without question and were unchallenged. When I interviewed Goodall in 2006, he emphasized the transition in the attitude of audio engineers, evident in both North America and Europe, as an important consideration when looking at the changes that took place in popular music during the 1950s and 1960s. He makes an important distinction between the older generations of audio engineer, whom he refers to as 'The White Coats'. They followed prescribed recording and production practices, but by the early 1960s, these established approaches were simply inadequate for recording the sounds that were becoming a part of the new popular music.[29]

---

[26] Using microphones close to their sound source generally causes a phenomenon known as the 'proximity effect', where closer positioning to the sound source increases the low-frequency content.

[27] Close microphone techniques were used to produce the rich vocal sounds of Bing Crosby but were also used to enhance the separation of instruments. See Chanan (1995, p. 67) and Millard (1995, p. 177).

[28] 'Crooning' Is the term applied to the singing style used by Bing Crosby and others where the voice was projected at low volume levels by the singer and this allowed the microphone to be placed in close proximity to the singer's mouth. This accentuated the low-frequency content of the voice.

[29] See: Nat King Cole's recordings of 'Mona Lisa' (Capital Records T-357, 1953), 'Unforgettable' (Capital Records T-357, 1953). The 'crooning' vocal style is evident resulting from a closely miced voice. Also, Little Richard's 'Tutti Frutti' (Speciality

A significant but overlooked influence that Goodall had on the developing recording industry in Jamaica, was his rejection of what he considered old-fashioned, formulated recording methodologies and the technical hierarchy employed by British studios such as Abbey Road. Their system of employing a balance engineer, a tape operator, mastering engineer and technicians who set up microphones, while others were responsible for moving equipment, represented, to him, a restrictive creative environment, limited to a formulated recording process. The net effect in this system was that a balance engineer was unable to choose which microphone to use or how it would be placed on an instrument representing a system enforced by strict trade-union codes.[30]

Each position represented a specialized post and a division of recording tasks into a company hierarchy where a team of technicians were collectively responsible for recording a piece of music. In an interview with Geoff Emerick, Mark Cunningham discusses the microphone placement practices in use when Emerick worked with The Beatles at EMI's Abbey Road studios during the 1960s. Emerick states that: 'There was a rule here that you couldn't place the mic closer than eighteen inches from the bass drum ... so I had to get a letter from the management which gave me permission to go in closer with the mics' (1996, p. 144). The technique of close microphone placement could accentuate the low frequency of the sound source but it also, in effect, reduced the level of other ambient sounds and therefore allowed the audio engineer to achieve greater definition between instruments. Ultimately, this allowed the audio engineer greater control over the electronic balance, mix and sonic characteristic of the instruments.

Goodall, perhaps out of necessity in the Jamaican environment, practised and taught a system of recording where the audio engineer was responsible for every aspect of music production. However, with that responsibility came a creative licence and opportunity to influence sound that was absent in many European and North American recording studios. This process centred on the audio engineer using his ears to decide what equipment could, and could not do, as opposed to trusting what the equipment manual recommended. In this sense, the recording practices introduced by Goodall to Jamaica in 1958, might be considered progressive and more in line with some independent North American recording studios such as Sun Records and Atlantic Records. In these studios Sam Philips and Tom Dowd also performed all aspects of the recording process, recording some of the most influential popular records of the 1950s. They and others pioneered a creative approach to audio engineering and music production where sound was crafted and shaped, with the intention of adding form and character to a musical performance, through the medium of recording.[31] It is also worth noting

---

Records, SP-100, 1957), where the kick drum is clearly heard and the drums have a prominent position in the mix compared, for example, to the piano.

[30] See Emerick and Massey (2006) and Martin and Hornsby (1979).

[31] The audio-engineering practices mentioned here refer to the recording process and do not include mastering. I exclude Motta's studio and its engineering practices: they cannot

that Goodall developed a personal and professional relationship with Dowd, who nominated Goodall's entrance to the Audio Engineering Society (AES) of North America. André Millard, notes the increasing influence of the audio engineer and technology that 'Blurred the line between technician and performer. Technology did not completely replace the artistic act of creation, it changed it' (1995, p. 302).

The recording of 'Boogie in My Bones' represents the establishing of a new recording model in Jamaica where the audio engineer not only assumed command of the recording session from a technical standpoint, but employed that technology to alter and change the sound of instruments and their musical balance. In 1958, Goodall was the only audio engineer working in Jamaica able to create the new sounds that 'Boogie in My Bones' came to represent. Goodall describes his attitude towards audio engineering as creating a picture that employs sound as colour, hue and texture. I therefore contend that Goodall represented a critical element in the development of the Jamaican recording industry, not only pioneering the use of new technologies but introducing an attitude towards the recording process where the audio engineer assumed responsibility for all aspects of sound creation and capture as a creative rather than technical endeavour.

Ken Khouri, himself an audio engineer, recognized the importance of Goodall's achievement and hired him in 1961 to reconfigure the newly built Federal Recording Studio. With the assistance of Goodall, Khouri revolutionized the production of music in Jamaica by enabling Federal to routinely produce the sounds associated with 'Boogie In My Bones', and offered this new recording facility to the general public for rental.

The success and dominance of Federal at the start of the 1960s not only indicated a general acceptance and embrace of Goodall's recording model and the audio engineer's authoritative role, but also ensured that it was passed on and disseminated by the first generation of Jamaican audio engineers who worked and trained under Goodall at RJR and then Federal. Goodall therefore helped to establish a recording culture in Jamaica where the audio engineer became responsible for the creation of sound and asserted that position with very little interference from financiers (producers) or musicians. This positioning was undoubtedly assisted by the practice of audio engineers and musicians assuming responsibility for the creative direction of the recording process and the authority of the audio engineer as a provider of studio time.

Goodall states that the net effect of these unique circumstances was that the audio engineer was seen as the final figure of authority in regard to the sound of a recording at the start of the 1960s. When asked for an example to support this claim, Goodall describes how some financiers of recording sessions might dislike the creative direction of a particular song or musical treatment but did not feel comfortable, as a musical layman, challenging the musicians directly. Goodall

---

be considered contemporary, as discussed in the previous chapter, and the construction of the studio limited the ability of the audio engineer to predictably influence or interpret the musical performance through the act of recording.

described a session at Federal for Coxsone Dodd during the early 1960s and claims that when Dodd was displeased with the direction of the music he would convey that sentiment to the musicians by saying: 'Mr Goody [referring to Goodall] said it's not working, try something else.' This seemingly insignificant anecdote provides some indication of the complexity of relationships between creative, technical and financial entities in Jamaica, representing a significant difference from recording practices of Europe and North America. It also demonstrates that financiers of recording sessions like Dodd could play a creative role in the recording process, even if only under the under the guise of the audio engineer's authority.

There is evidence to suggest that Dodd recognized the authority of the audio engineer in the Jamaican music production model and after building his own recording studio, Michael Veal claims that he, along with Sid Bucknor and Goodall, performed audio engineering duties (2007 p. 96). However, Veal goes on to state that Sylvan Morris, (trained by Goodall) joined Dodd's Studio One as the principal audio engineer and musicians such as 'Jackie Mitto, Leroy Sibbles, Richard Ace and Robbie Lyn [sic] arranged music, ran sessions and functioned with Morris as de facto producers' (ibid., pp. 96–7).

Goodall's work in Jamaica during this period is significant because he not only brought focus to the importance of recorded sound and its potential as a creative tool, but he demonstrated a willingness to share and disseminate that knowledge, which had a direct impact on the development of the music that would emerge in Jamaica during the following decades. It is significant that the first generation of Jamaican audio engineers – most notably Byron Smith and Sylvan Morris – trained under Goodall's guidance. They would later became the respective audio engineers for Duke Reid's Treasure Isle and Coxsone Dodd's Studio One.

These studios in particular set the standard for a new era in JPM and the respective works of Smith and Morris are both significant in their own right. In Michael Veal's book, entitled *Dub*, Morris describes Goodall as a mentor who 'Brought me into the recording field, to get familiar with the studio equipment and console and everything – he sort of schooled me there' (2007, p. 96). Goodall was, therefore, simply the right person, with the right skills and right attitude, in the right place, at the right time, who left an indelible mark on Jamaican studio culture. As an audio engineer, Goodall had a significant influence on the development of JPM and the emergence of Khouri's Federal Recording Studio as a premier regional recording facility. Goodall and Khouri would design and create a template for recording in Jamaica that would act as the foundation for others to build on.

Chapter 4
Establishing a Jamaican Sound

While Graeme Goodall was recording 'Boogie In My Bones' in 1958 at the RJR studio, Ken Khouri had already initiated plans to build Federal Records, which opened in 1959. Federal would become the first purpose-built, popular-music production studio in Jamaica that was capable of routinely producing recordings with the 'foreign sophistication' discussed in the previous chapters. However, the significance of Federal was not its ability to replicate a North American sound but the fact that it initiated a process of developing a Jamaican recorded sound. This chapter therefore considers the recording practices established under Khouri's guidance at Federal and the impact this had on the development of JPM. Federal not only established a modern Jamaican sound but provided training for the next generation of audio engineers who took that sound to new levels at Coxsone Dodd's Studio One and Duke Reid's Treasure Isle respectively. The chapter also focuses on the production of emphasized bass, as an aesthetic that emerged from the sound system but was integrated at Federal into the music production process. It represents an important element in JPM and the origins of the sound and its pathways of development are considered in detail.

Birth of the Modern Jamaican Recording Industry

Ken Khouri is a notable figure in the development of JPM because his influence ranges from the first mento recordings to the rise of reggae as a popular music genre. Khouri is distinguished by his broad range of recording industry experience, having been involved with studio design and construction, audio engineering, production, record manufacture, mastering, distribution and his role as a record company executive. In Daniel Neely's assessment of Khouri's work he acknowledges that he 'deserves broader recognition' but characterizes him as 'part of the "old guard" of Jamaican businessmen whose importance came into question after the political cultural changes that accompanied the independence movement' (2007, p. 2). Neely's claim seems inconsistent with the actual consolidation of Khouri's 'importance' and the rise in his fortunes, which occurred after Jamaica's independence. It should also be noted that Khouri's Lebanese heritage would have significantly reduced his appeal with the eurocentric '"old guard" of Jamaican businessmen' and I have not been able to find any evidence to suggest that Khouri was anything less than enthusiastic about the 'independence movement' and the 'political cultural changes' that it promised, and in which he played an active role.[1]

Although Neely documents some of Khouri's early achievements his description of him as a man 'whose ego would get in the way of the facts' (2007. p. 2), is in sharp contrast with Graeme Goodall who claims: 'If there was one person, if you like, who is the keystone of that whole surge, that trend away from mento music into popular music, it was Ken Khouri and nobody else.' Goodall's description is supported by Graham Dowling, who in *Wake The Town and Tell The People* discusses the importance of Khouri's studio stating 'Federal was the key to the whole record industry, everything evolved around there' (Stolzoff, 2000, p. 61). There is therefore clearly a need to understand the role that Khouri played in the development of JPM and the way in which he directed Federal to respond to the needs of the sound-system operators and establish a new range of recorded sounds and music products at the start of the 1960s.

Graeme Goodall met Khouri in 1954 and witnessed the expansion of his various music-related enterprises throughout the 1950s and 1960s. Goodall not only became a friend of Khouri but also played a strategic role in the development of some of these enterprises. He describes Khouri as a 'dreamer', a man who was passionate about music and recording. Goodall makes the point that in hindsight, it is easy to characterize Khouri as an opportunist who profited from local music. However, at the end of the 1950s, there was no indication that Jamaica had the potential to develop a vibrant recording industry, which could compete on the international stage. According to Goodall, it was Khouri alone who recognized this potential and saw the sound system as a critical element in the development of this area.

In addition, and perhaps as a product of his audio engineering background, Khouri was uniquely able to understand that the potential of the sound system could only be unleashed if local recording facilities could routinely match those available in North American. Moreover, Khouri understood that there was also a need to build a studio around progressive audio engineering and production approaches that were responsible for the new sounds emerging from North America. However, there were significant challenges to overcome, which included a lack of local specialized skills needed to design and maintain a modern recording facility and the difficulty of formulating a recording method that offered international recording standards at a price point that was commensurate with the limited budgets that sound system owners could justify investing in restricted recordings. Most importantly, Khouri was the only individual willing to financially invest his personal wealth in addressing these challenges, with the belief and hope that they could provide a profitable return.

------

[1] See Balford Henry's (2003) article in the *Sunday Gleaner*, where it notes of Khouri: 'In 2001, he was one of 25 Caribbean persons inducted into the Hall of Fame of the Caribbean Development for the Arts and Culture at its "Awards of Excellence" ceremony at Kings House in St. Andrew.'

Federal Recording Studio

The development of Federal as a regional and international recording centre should be considered within the context of changes that were made to its physical structure. While the Federal studio is often referred to in the literature as a single entity, it in fact represents two distinct recording studios that functioned independently and for a short period operated side by side. I refer to these recording spaces as Federal One and Federal Two respectively. Federal Two continues to function in 2013 and is presently owned by Bob Marley's family and now operates under the name of Tuff Gong. However, this studio was built by Khouri in the mid-1960s and was housed in a much larger purpose built structure on the Foreshore Road (now Marcus Garvey Drive) property. The focus of this chapter is on Federal One, where the seminal ska recordings of the early 1960s were made but also part of the sound track for the James Bond film *Dr. No* (United Artists, 1962).

Federal One was initially wired, set up and serviced by Gene Finzi in approximately 1958 with Goodall acting as an informal advisor to Khouri on the design of the rooms while still working for RJR. Goodall suggested that Khouri build the recording room with a dimension ratio of 4:3:2, the largest dimension being approximately 18 feet. This offered a room large enough to achieve good instrument separation for a popular music group, with a volume of approximately 2000 cubic feet, well within accepted industry standards and able to minimize the effect of unwanted standing waves.[2]

The new studio was initially equipped with an Ampex 351, one-track tape machine, a small Altec four-channel broadcast mixing console and a Neumann AM131 disc-cutting lathe. The studio began operating in 1959, with Khouri acting as the principal audio engineer; however, it underwent a major upgrade in May 1961.

At that time Khouri employed Goodall to assist in aligning the studio with international recording standards and to assume the position of Federal's chief engineer. Goodall explains that in order for Federal to achieve Khouri's goal, there was a need to construct Jamaica's first purpose-built reverb chamber.[3] During this period, multi-channel mixing consoles, designed specifically for recording music, were not commercially available, and it was common for recording-studio owners in the USA, to acquire a radio broadcast console and modify it. Goodall was able to perform these modifications to Khouri's console, expanding it to seven input channels. Six of these were for microphone inputs, three of which were provided with a send control, which allowed the audio engineer to add reverb to the respective channel input. The seventh channel was used as the reverb return

---

[2] A standing wave is generated by the reflection of a sound between two solid surfaces such as walls. The distance between the surfaces determines the resonant frequency and is therefore a critical element to be considered in the design of a recording room.

[3] Goodall claimed that the reverb chamber was based on a design he had seen while working with IBC in London.

channel, which controlled the overall level of reverb being heard. In addition, Khouri purchased a selection of what was considered the best professional recording equipment of the period, including a Neumann U47, RCA 44BX and RCA 77DX microphones. He also purchased a variety of dynamic microphones and an Altec monitor loudspeaker, driven by a McIntosh tube amplifier. The upgrade of Federal allowed the studio to routinely function at a technical and sonic standard that was comparable to that of North American recording facilities.[4]

I asked Goodall if he could provide a sense of how he and Khouri approached the ongoing development of the sound with which Federal would become associated. Goodall explained that Khouri was intent on providing a premium product for his recording clients, and based on his practical understanding of audio engineering, he encouraged Goodall to find ways to modify, improve and refine the recording process. When asked for an example, Goodall described Khouri's approval for the modification performed on Federal's mastering cutting head. He explained that through Federal's association with Tom Dowd of Atlantic Records and George Peros at A&R Records, he received informal advice on a variety of recording and mastering practices. Peros suggested that Goodall could improve the quality of Federal's mastering process by pre-heating the Grampian cutting head before cutting a disc. This was intended to loosen the magnets inside the head, but the warming-up process was not recommended by the manufacturer and could potentially damage this sensitive and costly sapphire-tipped piece of equipment. In order to avoid damage, Peros advised modifying the head by disposing of the Grampian-specified fluid, used to lubricate and cool the mechanism inside the head, and replace it with automotive brake fluid.

According to Goodall, this resulted in a significant sonic improvement, because it '[f]reed it up and gave it [the cutting head] a better top end response'. Goodall describes the modification as a harrowing experience, because he had to drill a small hole in this expensive piece of equipment without any of the waste material entering the head and then replace the fluid using a hypodermic needle. This anecdote supports Goodall's claim that Khouri was determined for Federal to function at a high sonic standard that was based on the 'best practice' of North American recording studios but it also suggests the existence of a recording philosophy where equipment and technology were in the service of musical creativity and at times had to be stretched in the interest of discovering new sonic territory. This approach was in line with a new range of recording strategies, which began to emerge in North America during the 1950s and significantly offered Jamaican music producers a progressive approach toward recording practice. I contend that Federal, under Khouri and Goodall's guidance, established the foundation of a recording culture in Jamaica that was passed on through practice and training and would have a long-term impact on the Jamaican recording

---

[4] This represents a crucial point because successful audio engineers such as Sam Philips also modified a broadcast console to function at the Sun Records studio and Tow Dowd constructed Atlantic Recording Studio's first mixing console.

industry. In effect, Federal provided the sound system with sound recordings that could compete sonically with North American imports and therefore elevated restricted recordings from their novelty status to locally produced music that had the potential to replace foreign records as the staple of the sound-system play-list.

According to Goodall, Khouri tailored the operation of Federal to meet the demands of sound system clients. This included the purchase of acetate discs in 'massive quantities', in order to lower the unit cost, but he also established a block-booking system for regular clients such as Coxsone Dodd, Duke Reid and King Edwards with discounted rates and a credit system that matched the cash flow of the sound-system's earnings.[5] The process of block booking the studio allowed the sound-system operators to negotiate discounted rates from creative talent such as session musicians, a practice that was facilitated by the absence of a proactive musicians union.[6]

In the production and exploitation of a recorded product not intended for commercial release, maintaining a low average cost per recording was a critical consideration for sound-system operators, which Khouri was clearly sensitive to. Goodall claims that Khouri sought to establish Federal as a hub for local music production and encouraged musicians to gather on the studio premises and offer their services to recording financiers. Goodall explains that each day, at about 11am, musicians would gather under the Guinep tree next to the studio in the hope that a 'producer' might call them to play on a session.[7] The influence of Federal was therefore significant because it offered a range of contemporary recording practices and available talent, at a cost and payment structure that was tailored to meet the limited budgets of sound-system operators.

By highlighting the importance of Federal but also the work of Goodall and Khouri, my intention is not to dismiss the contribution of others who played equally important roles in the development of JPM as the 1960s progressed. However, Khouri's intimate understanding of audio engineering and production concepts and the needs of the sound system through his relationship with Dodd, enabled him to devise a contemporary recording facility, which with the expertise of Goodall, was nothing less than revolutionary at the start of the 1960s. In Goodall's view, Khouri's Federal Records acted as the catalyst from which contemporary

---

[5] In American and British recording studios recording sessions were controlled in predetermined blocks of time. Musicians' unions established payment structures for these sessions, but this system would have been costly and restrictive for the production of exclusive recordings in Jamaica, with limited economic potential. It is not clear what role, if any, Jamaican unions played in the establishing of the economic structure for the local recording industry.

[6] Although it is not the focus of this study, I contend that this early formation of cost structures had important repercussions for the development of the Jamaican music industry, where recording would evolve from exclusive recordings to mass-produced records and eventually the production of records for international distribution.

[7] The Guinep is a large fruit tree in the soapberry family found in the American tropics with thick leaf cover that provides shade.

JPM emerged and available evidence tends to support this claim. Although the literature places emphasis on the actions of the sound system owners it is important to recognize that it was Khouri alone who envisioned a recording environment that was tailored to local needs and fostered the creation of a music production complex from which the sound-system operators would emerge. Donald Hendry, who knew neither Khouri nor Goodall, sums up the significance of Khouri and Goodall's work at the start of the 1960s by saying: 'Federal basically was regarded as the one with the skills and popularity.'

A Federal One Recording Session

It was important to establish how an early recording session at Federal was conducted and to obtain a sense of how the role of recording participants contributed toward the music production process. Goodall explained that in the early 1960s, the sound-system operators made up about 90 per cent of Federal's studio clientele and the type of product they demanded had an impact on the way in which the recording process was developed. According to Goodall, Coxsone Dodd and Duke Reid each block-booked Federal for one day a week and the other days were divided between smaller sound-system operators or independent music producers. Goodall claims:

> It was quite the norm that we put out 10 sides [songs] in an afternoon ... If you didn't get 10 sides Duke Reid or Coxsone would say 'what's going on, are you guys goofing off'? If I went to a third take, I'd say something's wrong; [Goodall] I'd go up to Coxsone and say it's not going anywhere, it's a B side, let's go on.

Dennis Sindrey is a guitarist who at this time worked with The Caribs and was employed by Coxsone Dodd to work on many of these early sessions at Federal. In a 2006 interview, Sindrey provided a detailed account of a typical recording session for Dodd at the Federal One studio. He describes the recording process from the perspective of a session musician during which Goodall acted as the audio engineer and claimed: 'Sessions were organized on a conveyer-belt system', using singers that Dodd had previously auditioned. Dodd decided on the choice of musicians for the session and negotiated fees directly with them. Once the band was set up in the recording studio and instruments were balanced by the audio engineer, the first singer would be brought in and the piano player would establish an appropriate key and chord progression for the proposed song. The rhythm section would then create an appropriate song arrangement and rhythmic groove while the horn section composed a series of lines that complemented the vocal arrangement.

Goodall states that every song was a 'head-arrangement', meaning that scores were not provided, and so musicians were required to create and then memorize the harmonic progression and form of the song. This was performed spontaneously, with musicians varying and embellishing their instrument part as the arrangement evolved, or as required. Goodall makes the point that although some musicians were self-taught, many had received formal music training, could read music, were typically competent jazz players and included exceptional musicians such as Ernest Ranglin, Monty Alexander, Don Drummond and Tommy McCook.[8]

Sindrey explained that the spontaneous nature of the writing and performance represented an environment that was often tense but also exciting. He, in part, attributes the vibrant sound of these recordings to the methods employed for their creation. Sindrey claimed that each musician was paid 10 shillings per song and so were anxious to record as many songs as possible. Both Goodall and Sindrey describe a music-production process tantamount to an efficient production line, the use of which possibly predates Motown records, where Moorefield notes that 'Gordy cultivated an assembly-line approach to making music' (2005, p. 21).

Informants such as Goodall and Sindrey describe the development of a music-production and studio-performance culture at Federal that was focused on the demands of sound-system operators. There was a need to create and capture performances quickly and efficiently, but also ensuring that musical arrangements were catchy and, most importantly, danceable. The evolution and design of this recording methodology was based on spontaneity, employing a three-take strategy as a general guide, initiated, overseen and administered by Goodall as the audio engineer.

This production process contrasts sharply with trends in North America, where Millard explains that, 'By the late 1960s a pop record might represent over 100 hours of studio time' (1995, p. 299). The recording model developed at Federal seems to have focused on a recording strategy that avoided the 'Constant playing and replaying of a piece of music. But after the second take of the same song, the decline in musicianship sets in as boredom takes over' (ibid., p. 305). Later chapters will explore this theme in more detail, but my informants suggest that the spontaneous recording process was centred on the audio engineer and musicians. They assumed responsibility for the creativity embodied in performance and sound, evident in the earliest mento recordings, but formalized into a contemporary music production system at Federal, which catered to the sound system. The audio engineer played a critical role in maintaining spontaneity as a creative force and the three-take strategy, described by Goodall, must have been an intimidating prospect for any recording artist or session musician.

Goodall's description of the development of a recording method that was based on spontaneous writing and performance techniques is significant because it was out of sync with popular music production practices generally employed in North America and the UK. The emergence of this practice, where musicians spontaneously composed music for an existing melody and lyric, was in part

---

[8] Ranglin was voted in the polls of the *Melody Maker*, a prominent British music periodical, as the best guitarist in the jazz category for 1965.

tolerated on the basis that these music products were not initially intended for mass production but also because Jamaica's copyright laws did not adequately protect intellectual property. Furthermore, participants were often unaware of their rights and the fact that they were entitled to part ownership of the music they were creating.

Based on the information from my informants it would appear that during the course of these early Federal One sessions most participants were not thinking beyond the immediate product of the recording session. In the case of the studio, audio engineer and musicians, this meant payment for their respective services, and in the case of the sound-system operators it meant thirsty patrons who would be queuing up to hear their latest creations. However, these economic incentives, which all participants shared in no way marginalizes the intense creativity and ingenuity that is evident in these recording sessions. While Goodall makes no claim to have invented the music production system being employed at Federal, it is a distinctly Jamaican production methodology that is rooted in the spontaneous creative authority of the audio engineer and musician. With origins that go back to the mento sessions described by Hendry, Goodall and Khouri built on this approach with an exploratory attitude toward sound creation, representing a music production system that is still much in evidence in 2013.

Emphasized Bass as a Recorded Sound

Throughout this book I argue that sound and sound creation processes represent a critical element in popular music that are much in need of investigation. In the case of JPM, the emphasis of low frequency came to represent a recording aesthetic that by the mid 1960s was uniquely associated with Jamaican music production. Although the origin of the sound is rightly attributed to the influence of the sound system, to date, the pathway of the sound's development and its transfer to the recording process remains largely undocumented. The sound of emphasized bass therefore provides an opportunity to assess how the audio engineer acts as a sonic mediator between the sound system and recording studio, influencing not only the recording process but also the way in which music is created, captured and consumed.

In any discussion of emphasized bass it is important to recognize a distinction between analogue vinyl records and compact discs. The physical mechanism of cutting grooves into vinyl and the mechanical limitation of a needle vibrating in accordance with them, represents the extent to which dynamics, frequency and especially low frequency can be reproduced. The compact disc, by contrast, exhibits significantly fewer limitations and, as digital media, dynamics and frequency are stored in the form or ones and zeros with a range that is limited only by the bit rate and sample frequency of the system's design. In the case of commercial compact discs, the internationally agreed standard for music reproduction of 16 bit/ 44.1 Khz has the potential to far exceed the performance of the average vinyl record. While the debate regarding the aesthetics of analogue and digital continue, the ability of digital media to outperform vinyl in the reproduction of dynamic and frequency range is not in doubt.

The significance of this point is that many forms of post-1980s music and pre-1980s music remastered for release on compact disc demonstrate an increase in the level of low frequency, which would not have existed on vinyl. While I make no attempt to decipher or trace the acceptance of emphasized low frequency in digital media, it is fair to describe it as an aesthetic, to the best of my knowledge, was first explored, developed and embraced by the sound system in Jamaica. While Goodall's description of modifying the Federal cutting head is a prime example of one way in which 'sound engineering technologies ... have taken their current shape in the context of western musical and social history, and they are coded with a logic that reflects this history' (Greene and Porcello, 2005, p. 5), the development of emphasized low frequency as a Jamaican sound aesthetic seems to challenge this claim. It suggests that the 'current shape' of sound technologies and the sonic textures they create might have more complex origins that move along pathways of influence, which at times are difficult to detect. The deciphering of these sonic characteristics therefore represents an important element in the study of recorded popular music, which represents the underlying focus of this book but is also an area in much need of further study.

The Origin of Emphasized Bass

There is a consensus of opinion that the early development of the sound system was driven by what Bilby describes as sound-system operators trying to provide what 'their patrons wanted to hear: the hot African American rhythm and blues' (1995, p. 156). However, what made the sound system different from other contemporary forms of music reproduction were the mechanisms it employed to encourage the listener to dance. Jah Vego, in a discussion with Lloyd Bradley, describes the importance of low frequency, because 'We dance down there with our waist and hips [Vego jumps to his feet and nimbly win's up his waist] we need bass. The music have to hit you down there and for that we need the big bass' (2000, p. 118).[9] Although it is not clear where the need for emphasizing bass in reproduced sound originated, it had become imbedded as a significant part of the sound system experience by the late 1950s.

Norman Stolzoff argues that the dancehall, and therefore the sound system and JPM, are deeply rooted in the folk traditions of Jamaica and its African heritage.[10]

---

[9] The word 'win's' is more commonly spelt 'wine's' and is a colloquialism derived from winding as in winding a clock. On the development and growth of sound systems in the UK, see Bradley's discussion with Vego (2000, pp.117–18).

[10] Stolzhoff (2000). The Jamaican 'dancehall' is closely associated with entertainment for the lower socioeconomic groups in Jamaica's society and offers evidence of what Braithewaite (1971) terms the 'creolization' of Jamaica.

Monica Schuler identifies an important strand of that heritage with a renewal of African influence in Jamaica when approximately 8000 African manual workers were transported to Jamaica after emancipation in the mid-nineteenth century, as indentured workers.[11] Helen Myers sees this as a significant influence in Jamaica because: 'Many Africanisms of contemporary West Indian cult music were introduced by free blacks who came to the islands in the second half of the 19th century' (1993, p. 464). Kevin O' Brien-Chang and Wayne Chen imply that these immigrants brought a strong cultural identity in the form of music and dance through their religious practices, which revitalized many of the underlying African traditions in Jamaica.[12] This view is supported by Edward Seaga's anthropological research into revivalism in the 1950s; there is no definitive evidence that yet connects emphasized bass, as a reproduced sound, to the sounds that emerged from the Afro/Jamaican folk tradition.[13] For the purpose of this discussion, emphasized bass therefore refers specifically to the electronic intervention of sound through the medium of sound reproduction and/or recording, but cultural and social values undoubtedly played a part in this process and represent an area in urgent need of further investigation.

Interestingly, the presence of emphasized bass is noted on the opposite side of the Atlantic by Louise Meintjes, who documents the complaint of a South African mastering engineer during the 1990s who was encouraged to master records with so much bass that the manufactured records would jump – 'Boy! If the record jumped, it was a sure fire seller' (2003, p. 115). This complaint might be considered an echo of Paul Khouri (son of Ken Khouri), the owner of KK Mastering in Kingston, Jamaica. During an interview in June 2002, he described a similar scenario as described by Meintjes, where throughout the 1980s and 1990s producers wanted so much bass on their records that the size and depth of the grooves cut into the vinyl went beyond what a domestic turntable needle could accommodate and resulted in the record jumping. However, Khouri understood this to be a local value, which he acknowledged and tried to accommodate. Unfortunately, Meintjes does not explore this phenomenon or offer an explanation for the practice, but implies that emphasized bass defined a cultural difference in values of sound that existed between black South African musicians and white

---

[11] See Schuler (1980).

[12] See O'Brien-Chang and Chen (1998, pp. 10–11).

[13] Edward Seaga documents the 'Great Revival' of 1860–61 in which he claims there was a substantial rise in the membership and popularity of revivalist cults (1969). Schuler's study was not available at the time of Seaga's research, but it is interesting to note that revivalism is based on the practice of polytheism and African forms of ancestor worship. Seaga's research, therefore, supports the claim that there was a renewal of African values during this period. Music and dance played an important role in these religious practices and it therefore seems reasonable to assume that JPM has been influenced by these traditions, but the route, extent and nature of those influences are difficult to identify accurately or substantiate without further investigation.

South African audio engineers. It is not clear if this phenomenon originated in Africa or was because 'Reggae began to influence global popular music' (Wallis and Malm, 1990, p. 179), in what these authors term a 'transcultural' process: 'First the Africans were brought as slaves to the Americas [... and then] during the forties and fifties, records with Caribbean music found their way back to Africa' (ibid., p. 174). Although a deeper analysis of the connections between emphasized bass and culture are beyond the scope of this book, it represents an area in much need of further research.

Emphasized Bass and the Sound System

Glen Whitter is an audio engineer who has worked in the Jamaican music industry since the mid-1960s and developed a close interest in sound reproduction and sound systems from a young age. Since the 1970s Whitter has owned and operated Sound Specialists, which offers public address systems for rental, primarily for the reproduction of live music. According to Whitter, Sound Specialists was one of the first companies to offer this type of service in Jamaica, which included the sound-system aesthetic of emphasized bass for the reproduction of live music. Whitter had previously worked at Dynamic Sounds recording studio as an audio engineer during the 1960s, and is familiar with a variety of technical aspects related to the fields of recording and sound reproduction.

In April 2007 Whitter explained that emphasized bass was first achieved by sound-system operators using a simple tone control, as found on a turntable preamplifier, similar to those used on domestic hi-fi systems. He explained that bass represents the hardest frequency range to reproduce in an amplified music system and therefore the undistorted reproduction of low frequency is an attribute of a sound system that Jamaicans associate with 'quality'. Whitter and other informants expressed the view that a 'good' sound-reproduction system should be capable of producing bass that can be physically felt as well as heard. In an environment of competing sound systems, emphasized bass became a critical indicator of a sound system's worth.

As the design of sound systems became more complex, Whitter explained that multiple speaker arrays and crossover networks were incorporated into their design. Sound-system builders started to split the audio signal, prior to amplification, into three or four frequency bands using a 'crossover'.[14] Each band of frequencies then ran through its own respective amplifier and tuned loudspeaker cabinets. The balance of the frequencies could then be manipulated by increasing or decreasing the volume of each frequency band's amplifier and this became a process through which bass could be emphasized.

---

[14] A 'crossover' is an electronic device that is able to divide an audio signal into selected bands, which typically can be adjusted and calibrated to function with the amplifiers and loudspeaker system.

According to Whitter, many sound-system operators purchased multiple 18-inch loudspeakers to reproduce the lowest frequencies on their respective systems, a practice that was not generally employed for music reproduction in North America or Europe during the 1960s. According to Whitter, these loudspeakers were designed and manufactured to be used predominantly in movie theatres and he describes a conversation with a Goodman's loudspeaker representative in the UK who asked: 'Why do you have so many movie theatres in Jamaica?' The representative was surprised at Whitter's description of their intended usage because, at the time, a typical music reproduction system in the UK consisted of a 100 watt amplifier driving two columns of four, 12-inch loudspeakers.

It was not uncommon in Jamaica to find a sound system employing custom-designed tube amplifiers and multiple frequency-range cabinets that totalled 1000 watts and more. Much of that capacity was needed to reproduce and emphasize low frequencies.[15] Whitter also explained that these systems had to be run directly from the electrical provider's overhead power lines, not because this was a source of free electricity but simply because the amperage consumption of the amplifiers far exceeded what was available from a non-industrial electrical supply.

During an interview with Michael McDonald in June 2008, he referred to the 18-inch loudspeaker cabinet as a 'house of joy', providing a sense of their size and a sentiment for how low frequency was locally perceived. These descriptions cannot provide a definitive measure of the sound system's impact but they do offer a sense of how sound reproduction values were distinct in Jamaica. I contend that some of the derogatory comments made in reference to JPM by British media personalities such as Tony Blackburn, were in part due to the fact that the average radio station or domestic music reproduction system in the UK could simply not reproduce the low frequency content that represented a significant element of JPM. This led to an unjustified label of JPM suffering from 'low production standards', when in fact, they were simply different production standards that some foreign aural palette's could neither comprehend nor accommodate.

Glen Whitter's testimony suggests that the design of many Jamaican audio systems between the 1950s and 1980s pioneered a progressive movement in the development of sound reproduction, but he also points to a difference in the sonic value systems of Jamaican and UK audiences, most noticeable before the introduction of the compact disc. The sheer musical power of the sound system became an important feature, along with the ability to produce what Jahn and Weber describe as, 'Low end so potent it felt like an earthquake' (1998, p. 9). Engineered sound therefore became the basis for creating a unique entertainment system that focused on dance but appealed to a range of human senses.

---

[15] In this comparison, the reader should bear in mind that the sound-system dance catered for crowds that would typically number in the hundreds. Thus, despite the massive size of these systems they were intended to provide music for relatively small audiences and would be perceived as very loud.

According to Dennis Sindrey, emphasized bass represented a tool used by sound-system operators to entertain their patrons and demonstrate their system's physical prowess. Sindrey explained that two selectors would compete against each other to see who could select and play the record with the most bass. The winner was the first selector to vibrate a beer bottle off the low-frequency speaker cabinet. Sound engineers where therefore involved in the constant and ongoing improvement of sound systems and, in particular, the reproduction of low frequency, seen as a potent performance indicator that could be felt as well as heard and appears to have deep cultural roots that are in much need of study.

It should be added that the use of massive amounts of volume and low frequency were in part the result of sound systems performing outdoors with few physical restrictions in regard to walls that would reflect sound waves. A noticeable feature of these outdoor performances with elevated bass levels is that from any location in Kingston, during the evening and especially on the weekends, the distant low frequency rumble of multiple sound systems cannot be escaped. Low frequency therefore becomes a mechanism for advertising where dances are being held and the sound of low frequency emanating from multiple sound systems is a memorable element of Jamaica's distinct evening soundscape.

The eventual integration of emphasized bass into the recording process led to a change in the way that foreign records were received locally. These records increasingly sounded lightweight and thin by comparison to locally produced recordings, when played on a sound system. Graeme Goodall offers evidence of this by describing how the song 'My Boy Lollipop' (1964), recorded and mastered in London, had to be re-mastered by Goodall in Jamaica, specifically so that low frequency could be added, allowing the record to be played on the sound systems, without sounding weak and insipid.

It is also interesting to note that a widely acclaimed popular song like The Beatles' 'Oh-Bla-di-Oh-Bla-da' (Apple, 1968) based on an interpretation of a ska rhythm, had limited impact on the local Jamaican market. Although it is difficult to be certain why this song was largely ignored in Jamaica, its relative lack of low-frequency content would have made the record difficult to place in the music programme of a sound system, despite being performed by the most popular music group in the world, at that time, and the song's clear tribute to Jamaican music. Up to the end of the 1990s, the sound-system playlists continued to be dominated by local music, with the exception of some American popular music that was typically presented early in the evening's entertainment programme as a sonic entrée, leading to the main course of local music.

The Sound System's Distribution of Recorded Music

The transfer of emphasized low frequency from the sound system to the recording process is closely tied to the development of the sound system owner's recorded products and the transition from using restricted recordings that were not shared or distributed to exclusive recordings, which while strictly controlled, were sold to smaller non competing sound systems. Graeme Goodall describes the way in which recordings at Federal were made on tape and then transferred to acetate disc at the end of the session. As a first-generation copy of the master recording, the sonic quality of these copies or dubs would have been good but, as previously discussed, they deteriorated quickly and, in the case of a popular recording, the disc would need to be periodically replaced. For the sound-system operator, the mass manufacture of records was at odds with their need to be in control of the public's access to their recorded catalogue, which, in the case of Dodd and Reid, was growing by an average of 10 sound recordings per week.

Goodall explains that as the sound-system catalogues grew it resulted in a growing demand for studio time, but increasingly this was for making new acetate copies of existing recordings. Goodall states that Khouri recognized a need to facilitate this copying process and to make it both efficient and cost effective for his sound-system clients. He therefore set up a dedicated copying room at Federal with a disc recorder and two tape machines used for the copying of sound recordings onto acetate disc.[16] Khouri also suspended normal recording services at Federal on Fridays, so that Goodall could conduct or oversee the copying process.

Goodall confirmed that some of the bigger sound-system operators began to request extra copies of acetate discs, which they sold to smaller sound systems. He explained that large operators such as Edwards, Dodd and Reid developed associations with smaller sound systems, usually located outside Kingston. These sound systems were not considered competitors, and so offering them the opportunity to purchase acetate discs of established popular songs represents the first form of distribution of sound-system recordings. Goodall stated:

> The sound-system operators, yes they wanted one or two copies for themselves, for their sound-system dances; but it was amazing, there was an underground there, that the other sound-system operators heard something and said 'yeah the public like this particular tune', or like a couple of tunes. So the next week they would come in and say to Coxsone, Edwards or Duke Reid, 'I want that tune', and so they would cut them and sell them for anything up to five pounds for four cuts on a single 10-inch disc. But Coxsone was very, very smart. He would never sell it to anybody, shall we say, who was going to play around the corner from him.

Goodall explains that Dodd and Reid would send their most trusted assistants, known respectively as Bim-Bim and Cuttings, to Federal on Friday morning with their master tapes and a list of dubs to be cut. Even smaller operators would come into Federal and have dub-plates made, which they would sell and then return to Federal, with the proceeds, to order additional discs. This piece of information

---

[16] Goodall explained that Khouri purchased two tape machines for dubbing so that as one disc was being cut, the next song was being lined up on the second tape machine.

suggests a growing trend in the distribution and sale of dub plates as their popularity as exclusive recordings began to decline.

I asked Goodall if he could provide any sense of the number of discs that were cut on a typical Friday. Goodall explained that the weekly numbers varied, but said:

> I could get four tunes on one 10-inch soft wax [acetate disc]. Ken Khouri charged 30 shillings if you put two tunes on it and 35 shillings if you put four tunes on it. Monday, Tuesday, Wednesday, Thursday was for recording but Friday was dub-day ... I remember one Christmas Friday, I cut 185 double-sided ten-inch records [acetates].

Although these figures represent the output for a Christmas week, and would have therefore been above average, they provide a sense of how dynamic the trade and usage of acetate discs was (see Figure 4.1). Goodall's testimony provides a sense of the way in which Khouri and Federal catered to the needs of the sound-system industry during a period when sound recordings were still exclusive products with restricted distribution.

Figure 4.1   An acetate disc or dub-plate. From the author's archive

Introduction of the Blank Label Disc

During my interviews with Goodall he explained that during the early 1960s, Khouri expanded his record manufacturing and studio operation by purchasing the equipment needed to perform mastering services and the manufacture of vinyl record stampers. This represented two processes that up to that point had only been available overseas, and their introduction to Jamaica allowed Federal to offer the entire range of recording services from recording, to the preparation and manufacture of records on-site, within a number of days as opposed to weeks.[17]

With this new production capability, Khouri and Goodall developed a specialised product in the form of a 45 rpm vinyl record that was aimed specifically at sound-system operators whose distribution of acetate discs was continuing to grow and assumed ongoing recurring costs. Khouri established a price structure for production runs of 50 or 100 vinyl 45 rpm records, inclusive of mastering and stamper manufacture, which made the cost competitive with the long-term copying of acetate discs. Khouri in effect offered Dodd, Reid and Edwards the opportunity to employ vinyl records instead of acetate discs, with much longer rates of usage and this significantly represents the first sound-system music product that was suitable for domestic consumption. In order to maintain the lowest possible cost structure for these vinyl discs, Khouri offered them with a blank white label to avoid printing costs (see Figure 4.2). This new form of sound-system media became known as a 'blank-label'. The introduction of the blank-label disc by Khouri is significant because it underwent a mastering process, which Goodall explained played a key role in the transfer of emphasized low frequency from the sound system to the recording process.

Emphasizing Bass in the Recording Process

When Ken Khouri established Jamaica's first record-mastering service at Federal, he selected two critical pieces of equipment, which at the time represented the best available technology in sound processing. Khouri purchased a Fairchild 660 mono limiter to control dynamics, and a Pultec EQP-1A equalizer to fine-tune frequency content during mastering. In 2013 these particular pieces of equipment remain highly sought after and are still considered a standard to which later equipment design is compared. In a 1996 issue of *Mix* magazine, Fletcher (the author uses only one name) describes the Fairchild limiter saying it: 'must be heard to be believed! It's like adding the in-your-face fatness you have always craved with the thickest, most controlled bottom end you have ever experienced, and with a high end that just shimmers and dances to your delight' (Fletcher, 1996). Khouri's selection of these tools once again demonstrate his commitment to providing

---

[17] Prior to this, mastering and stamper manufacture was available in Miami. See details regarding stampers below.

Figure 4.2   Blank label 45 rpm vinyl record. From the author's archive

his recording clients with the 'best' of what was available. It is all the more surprising given the fact that Federal had no local competition during this period and that Khouri's primary clients were producing music that was not intended for commercial release.

Graeme Goodall describes the new process of mastering, which Federal introduced and was necessary for the manufacture of vinyl records including blank labels being offered to the sound-system operators. Although mastering involves initially transferring a sound recording from the master tape to acetate disc, it includes modifications to the dynamics and frequency content of the sound. The modification is intended to follow specifications established by the RIAA to ensure that commercial records comply with the limitation of domestic record players and/or commercial radio stations. However, the vast majority of Federal's clients during the early 1960s were sound-system operators and their recordings were not intended for commercial distribution, and therefore the RIAA specification had limited significance.

Goodall explained that mastering in North America and the UK was typically a specialist process performed in a dedicated studio. However, at Federal, mastering was conducted in the recording studio control room and Wednesday mornings of each week were reserved for this process. Consolidating mastering and recording into the same space allowed for the Fairchild Limiter and Pultec equalizer to be employed during recording as well as mastering. In addition, Goodall now assumed responsibility for every aspect of recording process, from the placement of microphones and balancing of instruments to mastering, which in North America and the UK was typically performed by separate audio specialists.

Goodall explained that when mastering he initially emulated international mastering standards, adjusting the frequency response and the dynamics, to comply with the RIAA specification. Goodall described how this approach was not well received by Coxsone Dodd, who voiced concerns regarding the sound of the vinyl blank-label discs compared to non-mastered acetate discs. In the interest of trying to please one of Federal's main recording clients, Goodall attended a dance where Dodd's sound system was playing, so that he could hear for himself how the blank-label discs sounded and to try and identify the cause of Dodd's concern. Goodall explains:

> I managed to get a pretty good sound and I tried to understand what they wanted to put down, and I wasn't getting anywhere … So I went down to see Coxsone at one of his sound-system dances … Coxsone's assistant Bim Bim came up and said Mr Dodd wants to see you … Coxsone bought me a beer and my wife who was totally pregnant at that time, she had to take a back step because the bottom end (low frequency) was vibrating the baby. I listened, then I realized what they were trying to get on to a 45 so that it sounded right in these sound systems … I figured out that what I had to do was augment the bass, keep the mid range up there because this is driving with the rhythm, vocals were important but not all that important, it was the driving rhythm because this worked the sound system, this got the people dancing, this got them moving, this made them hot, this made them thirsty, hello, they bought more beer. That's what it was all about. The sound system dances were not designed for the music as such … they were designed to sell liquor and the major sound-system owners and promoters had liquor distributorships. I had to capture that and get it reproduced as they wanted it and that was the secret, and that's what started it all because later on I found out that you had to tune your ear; it was almost like building a 1/3 octave equalizer into your brain and not have it in front of you on a panel.

Goodall points out that although he had been recording music to be played on a sound system, he had, up to this point, never heard how his recordings sounded on this medium. After attending Dodd's dance, he realized that although a mastering process was necessary for the manufacture of blank-label discs, it could not be applied in the same way as mastering for the domestic markets of the UK or North America. Goodall had to devise a mastering strategy that ignored the need of domestic record decks and commercial radio, bringing the sound of vinyl closer to the unmastered sound of a fresh acetate disc. He sums up that realization by saying:

> My concept was, these people want to dance to this music they don't want to hear absolute 100% clarity on a vocal … they want a driving music to dance to and this was in their soul and it was my job to somehow or other capture that in

the studio put it on the tape yes, but then transport it onto an acetate, to make a
master, to press it and then when it played back on the sound system something
to drive them

Based on this experience, Goodall modified his approach to mastering and sonically
tailored the sound of blank-label discs to the sound-system aesthetic, emphasizing
the low frequency content and rhythmic components of the sound recording.

The above description by Goodall marks a defining moment in the development
of JPM because it represents the creation of a new recorded sound specification
that the audio engineer introduced, as a characteristic of locally made vinyl discs,
with the potential for mass production (see Figure 4.3). Goodall claims that up to
that point, he had considered the voice to be the central focus of a popular record,
but he moved that focus to the rhythmic components in the music, representing
a radical new interpretation of recorded sound to meet a specific local value.
The process of creating an enhanced vinyl disc, tailored for the sound system,
provided new technical challenges for Goodall, but the resulting product proved
very successful with sound-system operators and their patrons. The new mastering
standard implemented by Goodall would have a far-reaching influence, not only
on the sound of recorded JPM, but also on a trend in the evolution of the music and
the way in which performers responded to that trend.

Figure 4.3   Two 45 rpm metal stampers manufactured in Jamaica. From the
             author's archive

I asked Goodall to describe what difficulties he encountered when trying
to establish this new approach to mastering and how the new sound influenced
the recording and music-production process. Goodall replied, 'Anybody can
put it down on tape ... It's a little more tricky to put it onto a 45 rpm record or

a 33 1/3 record where you're cutting grooves and there is a physical limitation.' He explained that in order to contain the low frequencies that he now wanted to put onto disc, he had to widen the grooves of the cutting head to 110 lines per inch, to physically accommodate the increase in low-frequency content. Goodall calculated that when mastering with this increased groove width one side of a 45 rpm record would be limited in duration to 2 minutes 45 seconds. However, because Goodall acted as the audio engineer and mastering engineer at Federal, he was able to insist that musical arrangements conform to this time limit. With recording and mastering being conducted in the same location the control and adjustment of sound became a continuous process from its capture to the final dynamic and frequency adjustments made during mastering, all performed by Goodall. As a result, songs were now rehearsed and recorded with Goodall using a stopwatch to ensure that they did not exceed the emphasized bass time limit.

By installing the Fairchild limiter and Pultec equalizer in the recording studio, Goodall was also able to use these devices while recording. He developed a method of equalizing the kick drum and bass so that their respective frequency bands were adjusted into two distinct sonic spaces, a technique known as 'shelving'. This allowed the kick drum to sit above the bass, enhancing the clarity and definition of the low-frequency content of the recording. The Fairchild limiter was sometimes used on the bass during recording to improve the dynamic consistency of the performance. Goodall made no mention of radically changing his instrument and vocal balances during recording, but preferred to subdue the vocal track and accentuate the rhythm during mastering using the Pultec equalizer. Goodall went on to explain that the overwhelming acceptance of the new vinyl disc sound ensured the continued use of emphasized bass in the production of local music and the ongoing development of ways to employ, expand and exploit its usage.

Ken Khouri's Legacy

The significance of Ken Khouri is easy to overlook in the development of JPM because his greatest achievements were grounded in the use and adaptation of technology, making it locally available as a platform for others to work from. His success during the 1960s and emergence as Jamaica's first music industry mogul during that decade makes him an easy target for stereotypical views of class and race, perhaps fuelled by resentment for his success and the political polarization of the 1970s. Acknowledging Khouri's achievements does nothing to devalue those of Dodd, Reid, Edwards and many others who played an equal or greater role in the development of JPM. It strikes me that many of these early music industry participants shared a real passion for music but they were also financially astute and at times capable of being ruthless in order to protect their respective business interests.

Based on the testimony of Graeme Goodall and other informants, it becomes evident that Federal played a critically important role in the emergence of the modern 'Jamaican sound'. While not the sole achievement of Khouri, he undoubtedly played a central role in establishing this new sound aesthetic and making the recording process accessible to the sound-system operators. Goodall sums up the significance of Khouri by saying 'try to imagine a Jamaican music industry without Federal?'. He claims that while other investors in the record industry tried to emulate Khouri's success, none had his broad understanding of the recording process and local need, or his foresight and commitment that made Federal the music production powerhouse that it became.

This chapter has shown that Federal was the only location where popular music could be routinely and effectively produced at the start of the 1960s in Jamaica. It embraced the audio engineer-/musician-directed recording approach, first seen in Motta's studio and the multi-microphone recording model used by Goodall at RJR, and turned them into a vibrant music production-line mechanism that served sound-system owners in particular. The recording approach that was formalized at Federal perhaps also assisted in the development of a mechanism for locating musical excellence with a focus on 'groove'. I contend that any musician who could survive a 10-song work day at Federal, working without scores and under the pressure of Goodall's 'three-take strategy' was exceptional. Any player who could emerge from this work environment with a request from Dodd or Reid to come back the following week was, by definition, gifted in the art of spontaneous musical creation and groove playing. The hit musical products that were churned out from Federal during the early 1960s consolidated spontaneity as a critical component of the local musical engine, still evident in Jamaican studios today.

Other recording studios would assume a position of leadership during the 1960s and 1970s – Treasure Isle, Studio One, Dynamics, Randy's, Aquarius, and many others who all made contributions toward the Jamaican sound – but Federal represents the root from which they all emerged. At the start of this chapter Goodall is quoted as describing Khouri as a 'visionary' and perhaps the best support to this claim is Khouri's building of the Federal Two studio. Goodall described how Khouri not only envisaged Kingston as a recording centre for the region, but Federal Two was designed and built as a regional sound stage and recording facility that could accommodate large orchestras and was intended to service the regional movie, advertising and recording industry. Although this part of Khouri's vision was never fully realized, in 2013 Federal Two still represents one of the best regional recording rooms and continues to be in demand with both local and foreign clientele.

Goodall describes with a sense of irony how 'Dodd and Reid wouldn't use the big studio if you gave them for free', much preferring the sound of Federal One and increasingly the work of Byron Smith, who Goodall admits with some pride 'got a better drum sound than me'. I asked Goodall how he accounted for this difference in their respective interpretation of rhythmic sound; he responded, 'His genes vibrated different to mine.' Goodall describes Federal Two as having a 'cleaner more defined sound', evident on Desmond Dekker's '007' (Beverly's, 1967), which contrasts sharply with Derrick Morgan's 'Forward March' (Beverly's 1962) recorded at Federal One. Both recordings were produced by Leslie Kong and were engineered by Goodall, but they represent different branches of the Jamaican sound.

While the sound of both studios are grounded in local sensibilities, Federal Two was moving towards narrowing the difference between a foreign and local sound while Federal One and its forebears, in the form of Reid's Treasure Isle and Dodd's Studio One, maintained and continued to develop a sound aesthetic, which might be described as more 'guttural' or 'raw' – remaining inspired and driven by the sound system. Khouri's Federal therefore not only established the foundation for the Jamaican sound but through Goodall's training of Byron Smith and Sylvan Morris ensured that a progressive approach toward audio engineering was passed onto the next generation of recordists who would take local music to new levels of achievement. Goodall also acted as an informal advisor to both Reid and Dodd on the design and equipping of their respective studios, and his impact on the early development of JPM is therefore crucial.

The testimony of Graeme Goodall and other informants in this chapter suggests that JPM developed with the audio engineer performing a key role in recording and mastering, where local values were absorbed via these technical processes, and through creativity and ingenuity were translated into new sounds that assumed a Jamaican identity. I contend that the absence of large record corporations, A&R (artists & repertoire) men and publishers aided this process and fostered a recording environment that was, at the time, unique. In the new Jamaican recording model that emerged from Federal, the audio engineer performed a wide range of duties that included roles that in North America and the UK were the responsibility of the producer. Although the combination of multiple recording roles is commonplace in 2013, it represented an uncommon approach towards recording in 1962.[18] Study of Jamaican recording-studio culture and local popular-music recording practices, of which Goodall might be considered a founder, provides a deeper understanding of why, as noted in the introduction to this volume, Wallis and Malm state, 'It is only in the sophisticated recording studios of Kingston that the reggae sound the world has learned to recognize is created' (1990, p. 167).

It is interesting to note that the audio engineers Sylvan Morris, trained by Goodall, and Errol Brown, trained by Byron Smith, recorded the majority of Bob Marley's music in Jamaica. However, as Hebdige points out, 'Blackwell considered it a little too heavy for the white audience, so he remixed it in London. [Using non-Jamaican audio engineers.] He brought Marley's voice forward and toned down the distinctive bass' (1987a, p. 80). Significantly, Hebdige thus identifies an exact reversal of the sound-modifying process that Goodall had devised at the start of the 1960s, in response to the needs of Coxsone Dodd's sound system and passed on to both Smith and Morris. The critical point to make here is that the music of Bob Marley was created in response to, and integrated with, the sound

---

[18] See Cunningham's discussion on the changing role of the producer (1996, pp. 378–84).

of emphasized bass, which by the mid 1970s had become an indelible part of the Jamaican musical identity; however, its roots unquestionably originate at Federal.

From the perspective of the twenty-first century, it is perhaps difficult to appreciate the significance of an engineered sound such as emphasized bass and the challenge that its creation and production presented to audio engineers such as Goodall in the pre-digital era. Since the introduction of the compact disc, we have seen a steady increase in the low frequency content of many styles of recorded music. The practice of 'Pumping the shit out of the low end' and ensuring that 'The bass drum is the loudest thing on the record' (Rose, 1994, p. 76) is a record-production practice now widely associated with rap music. However, the originators of this genre include Kool Herc, a Jamaican who had moved to New York and, as Hebdige notes, 'Knew the Jamaican sound system scene and ... By 1973 Herc owned his own system. This was much louder and more powerful than other neighbourhood disco set-ups, and it had a much fuller and crisper sound' (1987a, p. 137). The influence of the Jamaican sound system and the emphasized bass of Jamaican records is therefore far-reaching and yet to be fully assessed. While the analysis of harmony, melody and rhythm provides important information, an understanding of the sound-system aesthetic interpreted through the audio engineered processes of Khouri's Federal Records is vital for a thorough understanding of JPM and the forces that directed its evolution and development.

Chapter 5

The 1970s–80s:
A Period of Dramatic Change

During the 1960s, Kingston saw a significant expansion of the local music industry and a number of new recording studios appeared, including Coxsone Dodd's Studio One and Duke Reid's Treasure Isle. Both would emerge as new epicentres for JPM production, a position that would later be challenged by studios such as Randy's, Joe Gibbs, Dynamic Sounds, Aquarius, Harry J's and Channel One. The 1960s and 1970s are considered by many to be the 'golden age' of JPM and although recording practices did change with the introduction of multi-track recording, the multi-microphone recording model, discussed in the previous chapters, remained firmly in place. Recordings continued to be based on the group performance of a rhythm section to which vocals and other instruments were added in a process of overdubbing; only limited by the available number of recording tracks. Perhaps the most significant development of this period was the expansion and increasing complexity of mixing, as an independent post-recording process and the resulting emergence of dub and version B sides, notably discussed in Michael Veal's *Dub* (2007).

As highlighted earlier, these developments are certainly worthy of discussion but in my assessment, there is a pressing need to address gaps in the literature concerning changes that occurred in the recording and production of post-1980s music in Jamaica. The new music to emerge from this period became known as dancehall music, embracing a new recording model, methods of composition, and modes of performance and music arrangement predominantly based on the use of riddims (reusable backing tracks). While 1980s dancehall music has attracted significant scholarly attention, some of the emerging narrative is in conflict with my own experience as a working musician, as well as my academic research. In light of this, a critical evaluation of the literature, specific to the music of this period and the technology used for its creation and production seemed not only necessary, but long overdue. This chapter therefore sets out to establish a sense of how music-making and recording practices changed in Jamaica during the 1980s and how a new music-production methodology centred on riddims emerged.

Dancehall Music

There is consensus that dancehall music emerged from the political, economic and social turmoil that marked the 1970s and 1980s. Although initially sharing many of the melodic, harmonic and rhythmic elements that were evident in reggae, the new music quickly developed unique writing, performance and production traits that set it apart from existing genres. It is not apparent why the name 'dancehall music' was adopted for this particular style, as previous styles of JPM were just as prevalent in the dancehall. However, Donna Hope speculates that 'the proliferation of stage shows and other staged events backed by the sound systems resulted in dancehall's identification as a music that is tied to a space and place' (2006, p. 26). My observations as a working musician during the 1980s is consistent with this view, where the sound system appeared to be reenergized by performers such as Yellowman, and a new generation of music consumers who embraced the dancehall as a vibrant music arena.

In 2013, a range of local music continues to be loosely described as dancehall music and this genre, in terms of longevity, might be considered the most successful local music to date. It has proved to be especially adept at absorbing new technologies and continually reinventing itself while maintaining a strong dance and deejay aesthetic, firmly rooted in local values and the dancehall/sound system culture of Jamaica.[1] The development of dancehall music therefore offers an ideal opportunity to consider the way in which music-makers and recording participants were influenced by changes in technology that occurred during the 1970s and 1980s and, most importantly, how that technology was adapted to meet local need.

Despite the apparent success and international recognition of dancehall artists such as Shabba Ranks, Super Cat, Shaggy, Beenie Man, Sean Paul and Damien Marley, Jahn and Weber note that during the 1990s 'you could hardly open a *Daily Gleaner* without reading about the harmful effects of DJ music' (1998, p. 19).[2] That trend has continued and in a *Sunday Gleaner* article dated 27 December 2009, the front-page headline reads: 'Shut em up! Too much freedom in the name of creative expression', referring to the lewd and violent lyrics often associated with dancehall music. These comments not only highlight the complex relationship between Jamaican society and the new music, but they also represent the existence of an unusual alliance between conservative voices and the reggae establishment who appear to find common cause in the rejection and de-legitimization of dancehall music.

The 1970s and 1980s represent a volatile period in the development of Jamaica, and the dramatic social and political changes that took place during this period are well documented.[3] During the 1970s there was a polarization of politics when elements in both main political parties were involved in arming their supporters, leading to an escalation of political violence, and a wave of skill and capital flight from the island. The era also resulted in the intertwining of politics

---

[1] See Cooper, (1993, 2004); Stolzoff, (2000); Hope, (2006, 2010); Stanley-Niaah, (2010) and Brent Hagerman, (2011).

[2] The deejay (rapper) is considered synonymous with dancehall music.

[3] See Stone (1989); Panton (1993); Gunst (1995); Manley (1990); and Seaga (2009).

and organized crime, still much in evidence as the BBC's online news service on 23 June 2010 describes how Christopher Coke (a.k.a. Dudus), 'A drug lord whose activities span the Caribbean, North America and the UK', brought Jamaica to a standstill under a government-imposed State of Emergency. This took place after 'The Jamaican government bowed to heavy US pressure and announced in May that it would extradite Mr. Coke', which, according to the BBC report, 'enjoyed substantial protection from the ruling Jamaican Labour Party and Prime Minister Bruce Golding'.[4]

High levels of crime, violence and corruption have undoubtedly had an impact on Jamaican society and the creation and production of JPM. Much of the existing literature emphasizes the connection between the development of local music and political ideology, and Lloyd Bradley voices a common view that 'by the late summer of 1971 politics began to involve itself with music with a hitherto unheard-of enthusiasm' (2000, p. 280). In *My Life and Leadership*, Edward Seaga, leader of the Jamaica Labour Party (JLP) from 1974 to 2005 and prime minister of Jamaica from 1980 to 1989, confirms Bradley's claim, writing: 'Music is indispensable to Jamaican political campaigns as singing is used to build up the participation and spirit of the crowds' (2009, p. 208). However, while the exploitation of popular music by politicians in Jamaica is prevalent, it should not be assumed that politics directs music production.

David Panton notes that, in the early 1970s, The People's National Party (PNP), led by Michael Manley, brought unprecedented social, political and economic change to Jamaica through a programme of reforms, based on 'The PNP's formal declaration of democratic socialism in 1974' (1993, p. 35). Although the majority of Jamaicans, from all classes, initially supported Manley and acknowledged the need for social change, mismanagement of the economy and the gradual polarization of politics along socialist and capitalist lines proved to be divisive and destructive.

Norman Stolzoff claims that 'In the 1980 national elections, marred by nearly "civil war-like" political violence that claimed the lives of more than 800 people, Jamaican society underwent a transformation from the socialism of Manley and the PNP to a new era of "free-market"' (2000, p. 99). When Seaga was elected in the landslide victory of 1980, the JLP immediately moved the country into a political and philosophical U-turn, realigning Jamaica with American interests and a capitalist, free-market system. The new government encouraged foreign investment and trade instead of stressing the themes of nationalism and self-reliance that had marked the policies of the previous administration.[5]

Although the 1970s saw an alignment of the PNP's political agenda with some aspects of Rastafarian rhetoric expressed through music, both political parties adopted the use of existing popular sound recordings, sometimes with the open support of the recording artist. Kenneth Bilby notes how themes of national

---

[4] See http://www.bbc.co.uk/news/10146172 (accessed 20 September 2010).

[5] See Levi (1989); Manley, (1990); Panton (1993); and Gunst, (1995).

identity, class consciousness and the Rastafarian's emphasis on the majority's African ancestry and cultural roots had become popular during the 1970s as 'the voice of the downtown "sufferer" now came to the fore. Reggae recordings regularly and openly contested the gap between rich and poor' (1995, p. 165).

This period, therefore, provides a rich source of material for political, social and cultural commentators, but their observations, in regard to the development of JPM, need to be considered in the context of musical products that first and foremost represented a commercial commodity, driven by an incentive for monetary profit. Although it is possible to find associations between lyrical themes in popular music production and political ideology, their connection needs to be explored in the context of the commercial impetus to which these creative works were responding. In my view, this fundamental facet of commercial music production, as its primary driving force, is all too often ignored.

Locating the Values of Dancehall Music

Dick Hebdige provides an early commentary on the transition from reggae to dancehall music during the 1980s. In a chapter entitled 'Slack Style and Seaga' Hebdige states that: 'In Seaga's Jamaica Inc, sex, money, flash and nonsense have tended to become the new religion of the airwaves' (1987a, p. 125), seemingly singling out Seaga's government as the harbinger of dancehall music's suggested values of consumerism and low morals.[6] Paul Gilroy echoes this theme claiming that 'the largely Rasta-inspired singers, songwriters and dub poets who had guided the music to its place as a vibrant populist force in the society were brushed aside', and 'Under Seaga, the singers' and songwriters' influence faded and they retreated from the revolution which their Rasta language had demanded' (1987, p. 188). Lloyd Bradley provides a musician's view of the 1980s in a chapter entitled 'Kids Play', quoting Dennis Bovell who claimed: 'When computers came in, that's when the amateurs took over'. He goes onto say that 'you didn't have to take a group into the studio, or get yourself a riddim track or anything, just buy a Casio, plug it in the studio and chat what you wanted to chat' (2000, p. 501).

The above comments represent a range of views and although they vary in focus, they demonstrate an alignment of perspectives that are disapproving of dancehall music; rejecting it as the legitimate successor to reggae. This and subsequent chapters challenge Bovell's criticism of a production methodology, employing riddims and deejays, which in fact were introduced as elements of reggae music production. In addition, Bovell's reference to the 'Casio' (keyboard), widely associated with the production of the song entitled 'Under Mi Sleng Teng' (Jammys, 1985); the implied flag bearer of the 'amateurs' will be assessed in

---

[6] In Chester Francis-Jackson's (1995) *Dancehall Dictionary: A Guide to Jamaican Dialect and Dancehall Slang,* 'slackness' is defined as 'vulgarity'.

the context of actual production practice where sometimes amateurs and non-professional instruments play a vital role.

Gilroy's 1987 assessment of dancehall music, suggesting that it was less of a 'vibrant populist force' than reggae, is in hindsight, clearly flawed. However, it would also be accurate to point out that 'the largely Rasta-inspired singers, songwriters and dub poets who had guided the music to its place as a vibrant populist force', did so by 'brushing aside' the clean-cut tunesmiths of ska and rock-steady at the close of the 1960s. This rise and demise of popular music genres represent an ongoing act of renewal in an industry that is significantly driven by record sales and not underlying political or social agendas.

Hebdige's dismissal of dancehall music and the connections he makes between the policies of one political party and 'sex, money, flash and nonsense', the suggested values of the new music, is tenuous at best. Seaga responded to this claim during an interview I conducted with him in February 2008, saying: 'I am not aware of any direct links between the policies of my government during the 1980s and the changes that took place in popular music'. However, Seaga did point out that the themes of the 1970s, such as self-reliance, embraced by Rastafarians and other policies of the PNP administration had failed and resulted in the near bankruptcy of Jamaica by the end of the 1970s. According to Seaga 'this failure left many Jamaicans with a sense of scepticism and a cultural void that was filled by the deejays and dancehall music'. The continued growth, success and dominance of dancehall music during subsequent PNP governments, from 1989 to 2007, supports Seaga's claim and suggests that the new music was merely reflecting the changing values of society rather than conspiring with politicians to bring about change.

Kenneth Bilby also challenges Hebdige's assertion, noting that the 'slack style' associated with dancehall music, has a long tradition with an 'emphasis on bawdy or suggestive lyrics acquired by mento' (1995, p. 155), evident in songs such as 'Big Bamboo' and 'Naughty Little Flea'. These represent some of the earliest Jamaican commercial recordings made during 1950s.[7] Daniel Neely notes the national outcry in 1956 to Ken Khouri's release of 'Night Food', which prompted a motion in the House of Representatives and the introduction of 'a restrictive set of ideas known as the 'Calypso Morality Code' (2007, p. 10). In addition, Donald Hendry confirms that recordings made at Motta's studio during the 1950s were vetted before final selection and inclusion on MRS albums. This bawdy lyrical tradition continued in the 1960s with Max Romeo who sang 'lie down gal mek me push it up, push it up' (extract from the song 'Wet Dreams' (1969), banned from the BBC play lists) and General Echo a.k.a. Ranking Slackness, who 'was the first to challenge the predominantly "cultural" approach of the majority in the mid to late 1970s' (Larkin, 1994, p. 99).

---

[7] See The re-released compilation album of various artists entitled *Boogu Yagga Gal: Jamaican Mento 1950s* (Heritage Music, 2002).

There is clearly a need for a dispassionate assessment of dancehall music, one that avoids the imposition of values and judgements of a creative process that appears to be based on nostalgia for the 1970s. There is a need to recognize that JPM, irrespective of its genre or lyrical theme, is the product of an industry that is primarily driven by economics and constantly seeks to reinvent itself, in direct response to the demands of those who pay to consume it. From my perspective, these commercial forces do not undermine the potential for musical creativity or the ability of artists to make political or social statements; they simply represent a consistent driving force that acts as the primary arbiter of the resulting music. There is therefore a need for ongoing study that seeks to objectively unravel the complex array of forces that have influenced the development of dancehall music and the demand of music consumers to which it responds.

A number of more recent studies have made significant inroads in this regard providing sociological, cultural and anthropological perspectives on the forces that not only respond to, but also direct the phenomenon of the Jamaican dancehall. Carolyn Cooper, (1993, 2004), Normon Stolzoff, (2000), Donna Hope, (2006, 2010), Sonja Stanley-Niaah, (2010) and Brent Hagerman, (2011) offer a broad range of perspectives on the cultural milieu from which dancehall music emerges and the values it represents.

Despite these diverse avenues of investigation, the national debate that surrounds dancehall music continues to focus on the lyrical text, but Susan McClary and Robert Walser remind us that 'many analyses of popular music rely too heavily on lyrics' (1990, p. 285). While not disputing the significance of the lyric, I contend that it is important to acknowledge that 'it is not at the service of the text that much popular music is constructed' (ibid., p. 285). This is especially true of dancehall music where the creation of lyrics and music are often achieved independently as two distinct creative works. The content of this and subsequent chapters therefore seeks to build on these recent studies adding specific details regarding the production of dancehall music, the use of riddims, the mechanisms that are employed to create them and the musical process from which they emerge.

The Introduction of Digital Technologies

Existing musicological and ethnomusicological perspectives confirm that dancehall music of the 1980s assumed a characteristic that was radically different to pre-existing genres, commonly attributed to its embrace of and dependence on digital technology.[8] However, Curwen Best notes 'the effect of digital technology on Caribbean music in the last two decades of the twentieth century was indeed

---

[8] The term 'digital' is used here to describe a technology that is able to store sound and MIDI information in the form of data files, consisting of 1s and 0s. The same term can also be applied to the processing of sound as a data file.

unprecedented' (2004, p. 6), confirming the existence of a trend that was in fact not limited to dancehall music or Jamaica.

Best makes a critical point because digital technology was in fact introduced with the production of reggae during the late 1970s and its integration with Jamaican music-making and production practice represents a gradual and selective process that continues in 2013. I contend that an accurate assessment of the influence of digital technology on JPM is long overdue. From my perspective as a working musician, terms such as 'digital' and 'computerized' first emerged during the early 1980s but were coined as derogatory comments by some commentators, intended to stigmatize particular examples of dancehall music.

In a 2006 interview with James Peart, an established studio and touring musician who is not limited to working in any single music genre, he claimed that the vast majority of post-1980s Jamaican popular music production, irrespective of genre, employed the drum machine, synthesizer and the use of riddims.[9] However, Peart suggested that music performed by deejays tended to be singled out by some and interpreted in a predominantly negative light. He claimed that 'dancehall music is more times referred to as fast food, bubblegum music, digital, computerized and boogu-yagga music'.[10] These terms imply that dancehall music is synthetic, disposable and inconsequential, lacking finesse. Peart suggested that these sentiments tended to be expressed by those who could not relate to the new music and often appeared to be based on a preference for singing. Peart claimed: 'When Beres [Hammond] records a song on Pro Tools using drum machines, samplers and digital keyboards, with a dancehall riddim, no one refers to it as digital, computerized or boogu-yaga music yet a deejay recording on the same equipment is salt; worse still, the same Beres riddim with a deejay on it can go from being great reggae music to fool-fool dancehall music'. Peart highlights what appears to be a prejudice by some individuals towards deejays in particular but emphasizes that in his opinion, 'good and bad music has nothing to do with genre'.[11]

In light of this, it is surprising that terms such as 'digital' and 'computerized' have assumed what appears to be a literal interpretation by the academy, nowhere more prevalent than in the discussion of 'Under Mi Sleng Teng'.[12] Kenneth Bilby points to the pivotal status of this sound recording stating that, 'the year 1985 is generally regarded as a turning point in reggae. In that year producer Prince

---

[9] Peart has toured and recorded with an elite group of JPM artists from Alton Ellis and John Holt to Shabba Ranks and Dianna King.

[10] The term 'boogu-yagga' is a common Jamaican term defined in Chester Francis-Jackson's (1995) *Dancehall Dictionary* as '1. An unattractive person. 2. Of coarse or common behaviour.'

[11] Peart confirmed that his example of Beres Hammond was based on his intimate knowledge of Hammond's repertoire, having worked for a number of years as his musical director.

[12] See Hebdige (1987a); Bilby (1995); Stolzoff (2000); Bradley (2000); Katz (2003); and Veal (2007).

Jammy (now known as King Jammy) released a song by Wayne Smith called "*Under Mi Sleng Teng*" [sic]' (1995, p. 173).[13] For Bilby, '"Under Me Sleng Teng" ushered in the "digital revolution"' (ibid. p. 175), a view that Norman Stolzoff appears to support, claiming: 'What was new about Smith's song is that it used a drum machine and synthesised instruments as the backing track' (2000, p. 106). More recently, Michael Veal asserts 'Jamaica would change dramatically in 1985, when seemingly out of nowhere the music suddenly went digital' (2007, p. 12), representing a widely repeated claim that incorrectly connects 'Under Mi Sleng Teng' to the introduction of new technologies in Jamaican music-making practice.[14]

I contend that the above claims need to be carefully considered in the context of the instrumentation and production techniques that were being employed prior to the creation of 'Under Mi Sleng Teng'. I draw on the testimony of informants, including Noel Davy, one of the creators of this musical work who were active music-industry participants during the 1980s. They offer accounts of actual music production practice that dispute the above claims.[15] The information these informants provide not only suggests that the significance of Smith's song has been misinterpreted, but that our attention has been diverted away from other significant developments in the production of JPM, and dancehall music in particular. It is therefore appropriate to assess what part digital technology and computers played in the development of JPM through two distinct paths:[16] the practice of recording and the use of new musical instruments.[17]

Digital Recording Technology in Jamaica

In order to gain a recording studio perspective on the introduction of digital technologies during the 1980s, I interviewed Errol Brown in January 2008. Brown is eminently qualified with a distinguished career that began during the 1960s and is considered to be one of Jamaica's foremost audio engineers. He claimed that digital technology was first introduced into Jamaican recording studios in the

---

[13] The term 'Sleng Teng' is one of many local Jamaican/English terms to describe marijuana.

[14] I conform to the spelling: 'Under Mi Sleng Teng', which is consistent with the writing of Jamaican/English. Some authors use 'Under Me Sleng Teng' or even 'Sleng Teng'.

[15] This includes a range of discussions with Peter Ashbourne, Peter Couch, Robbie Lyn, Sly Dunbar, Cleveland Browne, James Peart, Noel Davy, Errol Brown and Jeremy Harding concerning the first introduction of digital technologies.

[16] The term 'digital', here refers to the process where sound is created in or converted to a binary numeric form for storage and manipulation before being converted back to an analogue form that can be heard.

[17] For the purpose of this discussion it is important to acknowledge a distinction that had existed between musical performance on a musical instrument and the recording process used to capture the musical performance. There would be an eventual merging of these two previously distinct aspects of music production, discussed in the following chapters.

form of outboard effects units that acted as direct replacements for analogue units, at the close of the 1970s. The digital units typically had improved specifications and performance over their analogue counterparts, but performed the same basic functions with similar control layouts. Brown claimed that examples included the Lexicon 224 reverb unit and the Deltalab Effectron Digital Delay. These units replaced analogue devices, such as the EMT plate reverb and Roland space echo, performing digitally on integrated circuits what had previously been achieved using audiotape and mechanical reverb plates or springs.

By the mid 1980s, digital audiotapes (DATs) made their first appearance in Jamaican recording studios such as Couch Recording Studio, owned and operated by Peter Couch. I conducted an interview with Couch in February 2008 during which he claimed that the first DAT machines to be imported into Jamaica cost approximately US$2500. They slowly gained popularity as a replacement for the two-track analogue recorder, as their price decreased. By the start of the 1990s, most Jamaican recording studios employed DAT as a cheaper and more reliable medium for recording and storing mixes but their introduction had limited impact on the music production process.

According to Couch, the first popular multi-track digital recorder to gain acceptance in Jamaica was manufactured by the Alesis Corporation, known as the Alesis Digital Audio Tape (ADAT), introduced in 1992. This recording system used affordable, super-videocassette tapes as a recording medium, and although it became popular in home studios and small recording facilities at the start of the 1990s, the system never gained acceptance in larger production studios.[18] The big studios such as Tuff Gong, Dynamic Sounds, Mixing Lab and Music Works considered the recording format cumbersome and unreliable.[19]

During the 1990s, the international recording industry transitioned to a number of competing proprietary and non-proprietary-based, computer-recording systems, from which the Pro Tools recording system emerged as the new recording industry standard, slowly replacing analogue multi-track tape.[20] However, Jamaican professional music-production studios remained firmly entrenched in analogue recording technology going into the new century, and gradually made the transition to the Pro Tools system after 2000. My informal survey of the main Kingston recording studios in 2006 suggested that Pro Tools had become the standard recording medium for many but for most represented a recent addition,

---

[18] Digital recording systems such as the Fairlight and Synclavier, although available and brought into Jamaica to be used by foreign producers such as Steve Lavine in the early 1980s were never offered as a local recording format.

[19] A similarly configured system was offered by Tascam but based on a different storage medium. ADAT became established in Jamaica as the most widely used modular digital recording format.

[20] See further details regarding the first computer recording systems in Jamaica in Chapter 6.

and many studios still offered 24-track, analogue tape-recording services.[21] It is also interesting to note that many recording studios integrated Pro Tools into their recording set-up as a replacement of the 24-track analogue tape recorder. Local recording process was often based on recorded tracks being routed and mixed on the analogue-mixing console, as opposed to the digital-mixing interface, which the Pro Tools software provides.

Therefore, in regard to the recording practices of Jamaica during the 1980s, the song entitled 'Under Mi Sleng Teng' and the majority of JPM produced up to the end of the twentieth century, are more accurately described as being 'analogue', because they were recorded using analogue microphones, analogue mixing consoles and multi-track analogue tape recorders. Digital technology, if present in the recording chain, played a relatively small role in the functions of the recording studio and their influence on the process of recording was therefore limited.

Digital Instrument Technology in Jamaica

The terms 'digital' and 'computerized' more readily describe a new range of musical instruments that became available during the early 1980s, but their usage and impact needs to be considered carefully. In November 2009 I interviewed Sly Dunbar, a prominent session musician who claimed that he acquired his first Oberheim DMX digital drum machine in 1983, but by that time Willie Stewart and Cleveland Browne were already recording regularly with this instrument.[22]

According to Dunbar, Bob Marley's bass player, Aston Barrett (aka Family Man) had been recording with drum machines since the mid 1970s. This claim was supported by Cleveland Browne, who in a July 2008 interview stated that he played live drums on a Bob Marley session over a pre-recorded analogue drum machine for the song entitled 'So Jah Say' (Island Records, 1974). The song was released on the album *Natty Dread* and the sound of the drum machine is clearly evident. Dunbar adds that, prior to 1985, he used the Oberheim DMX drum machine on songs such as 'Taxi Connection' and 'Triplet', although he was unsure of the commercial release date of these recordings. These claims are further supported by David Katz, who notes Marcia Griffiths's description of the production for 'Electric Boogie' (1982), recorded using only drum machine and synthesizer (2004, p. 335).

In an interview with Robbie Lyn, one of Jamaica's prominent keyboard session musicians, in 2006, he confirmed using an Arp Pro Soloist synthesizer from the mid 1970s. Lyn describes how he used synthesizers while working with Peter

---

[21] Studios contacted included Tuff Gong, Music Works, Grafton, Studio 2000, Joe Gibbs, Harry J, and Mixing Lab.

[22] Willie Stewart was the drummer for the reggae group Third World and Cleveland Browne is a prominent local musician who at that time had had significant commercial success with The Browne Bunch and the reggae artist Freddie McGreggor.

Tosh between 1978 and 1982, acquiring a Korg Poly 6 synthesizer in 1981 and his first digital synthesizer, a Yamaha DX7, in 1983. Lyn confirms that new digital instruments such as the DX7 became popular in Jamaica, primarily because of their ability to produce convincing imitations of existing instruments used in reggae, such as the acoustic piano, Fender Rhodes electric piano, Hohner D9 clavinet and Hammond organ. However, the DX7 also offered a wide range of synthesized and acoustic instrument sounds, including bass, which would increasingly be explored during the 1980s. According to Lyn this particular instrument proved to be extremely flexible, compact and portable, significantly expanding the range of the keyboard player's influence in JPM.

The testimony of these informants confirms that drum machines and synthesizers were being employed in JPM a decade before the recording of 'Under Mi Sleng Teng', but digital drum machines such as the Oberheim DMX and digital synthesizers such as the Yamaha DX7 were commonly being used in Jamaican recording studios, primarily to record reggae, at least two years prior to 1985. In addition, these informants describe how the Simmons Drum and Syn Drum, both synthesized percussion instruments were commonly featured on reggae recordings of the early 1980s, representing a transitional technology between the acoustic drum kit and the DMX drum machine. Why this information has not more readily surfaced is unknown, but the above testimony firmly establishes the fact that 'Under Mi Sleng Teng' was not responsible for a sudden or revolutionary transition to digital technology nor was it responsible for the introduction of the drum machine and synthesizer.

Noel Davy's Sleng Teng Riddim

'Under Mi Sleng Teng' is perhaps the most widely discussed sound recording in JPM studies and is coincidently cited as the epitome of the degrading of JPM by the reggae establishment. It therefore seemed appropriate to interview Noel Davy, the owner of the Casio keyboard on which the 'Sleng Teng' riddim was created and discuss his development as a musician and the circumstances surrounding this important riddim's creation.[23] I first became acquainted with Davy in 1993 when we were working for different groups on the annual Sunsplash world tour that took place over a period of 12 weeks.[24] I interviewed Davy in January 2006 and asked

---

[23] Despite the prominence of 'Under Mi Sleng Teng' in the literature and acknowledgement of Davy's role in its creation, Davy claimed that he not been previously interviewed with regard to the making of the riddim or the sound recording other than by the local media.

[24] During this tour I was playing with the group that provided backing for Marcia Griffithes, Freedie McGreggor, Barrington Levy and Shinehead while Davy was playing for The Mystic Revealers, but Davy has also worked for extended periods with Black Uhuru and Damien Marley.

him to provide a description of his background and musical training. Davy grew up in the Waterhouse area of Kingston and enrolled at Excelsior College in the early 1980s to study piano with Jon Williams.[25] Davy claimed that he was initially self-taught on the piano but was intent on becoming a professional musician; however, the only instruments that Davy owned were an acoustic piano and a melodica. He explained that outside playing in church, his lack of ownership of a synthesizer was the main obstacle that restricted him from finding performance or studio work in the popular music field.

Davy confirmed that by the time he was trying to gain entrance to the music industry, session-group recording was on the decline and work opportunities were typically for keyboard players who owned their own synthesizer and could 'build riddims'. Davy eventually saved some money and asked a friend travelling to the USA to purchase an instrument on his behalf. However, he could not afford a Yamaha DX7, which represented the latest professional synthesizer that had been introduced to Jamaica, and so Davy instructed his friend to purchase the best instrument that his budget allowed for.

The instrument purchased on behalf of Davy was a Casio MT40, a small, 37 key, desktop keyboard instrument designed for domestic use. During a discussion with Jeremy Harding in January 2008, he made the important point that instruments such as the Casio MT-40 were what he termed an 'electronic keyboard', distinct from a synthesizer because they lacked the ability to modify and edit built-in sounds. This type of instrument often provided built-in loudspeakers and sequenced pieces of music intended for the user to play along with. Davy confirmed that this particular instrument differed from professional instruments such as the DX7 in that the number of available sounds was limited and they were only available in presets. In addition, the instrument lacked the facility for editing sounds and many of the existing sounds were generally considered sonically inferior to professional instruments and were not considered appropriate for performing or recording reggae.

Davy explains that he had a wide range of musical influences that included jazz and rhythm and blues; however, he was also influenced by the music he heard in the dancehall and was a regular attendee at dances where King Tubby's Hi-Fi provided the sound. Davy described with great enthusiasm the impact that deejays such as Yellowman, performing live over version B-sides, had on him as a developing musician. He confirms that by the early 1980s, there was a growing trend for musicians to 'build riddims', meaning, to programme a drum machine and then perform and record keyboard-derived arrangements over the drum pattern, one track at a time.

---

[25] Williams is a well-known classical and jazz teacher and performer who works in the Kingston area. Waterhouse is considered one of the inner-city garrison communities of Kingston – heavily politicized and prone to low levels of economic development and high employment.

Davy was therefore inspired to imitate this newly established music creation method, but had to do so within the technical limitations of the Casio keyboard. Davy describes how he then located writers or performers who could compose lyrics and melodies that were adapted to these riddims. The results were recorded onto an audiocassette and played to potential recording financiers who, it was hoped, would pay for the riddims and vocalist to be recorded in a professional recording studio with professional instruments and released as a 45 rpm record.[26]

Although Davy was unable to programme his own drumbeats on the Casio MT40, he was able to imitate the practice of building a riddim by employing pre-existing music presets found in the Casio's permanent memory. Davy experimented with different presets using a variety of harmonic progressions employing a piano sound. It was through this process that Davy would create the musical structure that later become known as the 'Sleng Teng Riddim'.[27] Although not the first song to be recorded on Davy's Casio-derived riddim, the song entitled 'Under Mi Sleng Teng' was the first commercially successful song to be recorded over it and the riddim therefore assumed this name. Davy explained that the riddim originated as a sequenced two-chord, one-bar rhythmic vamp that came with the Casio MT40, stored in the instrument's memory, under a 'rock' heading. He tried experimenting with the preset and found that 'When I slow it down, the bass line start to fall on the one drop.'

An Internet search for the technical specifications of the Casio MT-40 produced the following information, which had been contributed anonymously to the website: 'The MT-40 had a built-in pattern based on the Eddie Cochran song "Something Else". Because of this, a synthesizer version of the song's bassline [sic] ended up as the basis of one of the most popular dancehall music riddims of Jamaican music – the Sleng Teng riddim which started the "Digital Reggae" revolution in 1985' (http://en.wikipedia.org/wiki/Casio_MT-40 (accessed 25 August 2008)).[28]

Davy said that, after adjusting the speed of the preset, he experimented by playing additional instrument parts, such as a piano 'bang' on top of it, and then asked some aspiring deejays to try voicing different songs over the riddim.[29] Davy recorded these performances onto an audiocassette tape, and it was one of these recordings that eventually found its way to the sound-system owner and audio

---

[26] Davy applies the term 'build' to describe the process of creating a riddim, which is significant because it denotes the process of creating music in a linear fashion, one track at a time, analogous to building a wall one brick at a time.

[27] I am using the term 'musical structure' as opposed to 'composition' because even though Davy is credited as a one of the authors of the riddim, he confirms that it was based on a pre-existing piece of music and authorship is therefore uncertain.

[28] This reference is one of several that are located using the name of the song in the Google search engine (2008). While acknowledging that this is less than an authoritative source, it is interesting to note that it confirms Davy's claim that the riddim was based on a preset while repeating claims found in the academic literature that generally describe the song as starting the 'digital revolution' in Jamaica, which are inaccurate.

[29] See the definition of 'bang' in Glossary, Appendix B.

engineer/producer Lloyd James, a.k.a. Prince/King Jammy. After hearing the riddim, James invited Davy to record it in his studio. According to Davy, James acted as the audio engineer on the recording session, recording the Casio preset onto a multi-track analogue tape in its slowed-down form. However, there were no individual instrument outputs available on the Casio and so drums and bass were recorded as an integrated stereo track.[30] James then recorded the deejay Wayne Smith who provided a suitable lyric and vocal performance. Tony Asher, who owned a programmable synthesizer, was then employed by James to perform additional keyboard parts consisting of a piano bang and a synthesized horn phrase. The completed riddim was then mixed by James, copied to an acetate disc and played on his sound system. The enthusiastic response of the audience led James to release the song commercially as a 45 rpm single and, although the song was successful, it was ultimately the underlying riddim that would resonate with Jamaican audiences and achieve unprecedented success.

Davy's description of his development as a musician is not unusual in the sense that there is a need to gain experience from professional environments, but this often entails the use of instruments and knowledge that are less than ideally suited to the task at hand. Davy describes the difficulties he experienced acquiring a synthesizer, which by the early 1980s was considered a prerequisite for a working keyboard player, but these instruments were expensive and not readily available in Jamaica. Davy's ambition and resourcefulness in spite of the Casio's limitations reflects a quality that permeates every level of the Jamaican music industry and undoubtedly plays a role in it being able to compete in an intensely competitive international music arena. I contend that Davy's account of acquiring the Casio keyboard and its role in the creation of the 'Sleng Teng Riddim' does not constitute a lowering of musical standards as Bovell suggests. It represents a continuation of an existing approach toward music production in Jamaica where fresh ideas are injected, often by 'amateurs', but there is also a need to use creativity and 'tun han mek fashion' (do not let the limitation of available resources undermine ambition) in the spontaneous process of making popular music.

Evidence of this approach to music production can be found in the comments of Bunny Lee, who I interviewed in 2006. Lee described the recording session for the song entitled 'Bangarang', commissioned in 1969. As the financier of the sound recording, Lee explained that, at the time, he could not afford to pay established professional musicians and so 'I hired some little inexperienced amateur guys'

---

[30] In 'Solid Foundation' (Katz, 2004), it is claimed: 'Smith took the concept to Jammy who got session player Tony Asher to construct the rhythm with drum machines and synthesizers using the pre-set melody for the bass line.' An analysis of the original 'Sleng Teng Riddim' suggests that Davy's account regarding the use of the Casio is correct because the sounds are very similar in timbre and quality to those associated with the Casio, but, in addition, the drum and bass play as a continuous loop. If the instruments had been recorded individually, as Katz claims, it is unlikely that the drums and bass would always be heard together.

(musicians) which included the brothers Carlton and Aston Barrett. According to Lee, 'the song was based on a jazz tune called "Bongo Chant"', but 'the musicians couldn't manage the chords'. Lee states that the harmonic progression and rhythm of the original song was simplified to accommodate the musicians' playing ability. In spite of this, the song became a significant local hit-record and the Barrett Brothers went on to become the core of Bob Marley's rhythm section and created many of the rhythmic structures that underpin his seminal reggae recordings.

In the case of the Barrett brothers, it is not clear if they ever learnt the jazz harmony associated with the song 'Bongo Chant', but few would contest the creative impact that they had on popular music through their work with Bob Marley or find fault with their inability to play the original harmony of 'Bongo chant'. I therefore contend that the integration of amateurs into the production of JPM and a willingness to try new and unconventional approaches to music production is a tried and tested method of adding vigour and vitality to sound recordings. As such, Davy and his 'Sleng Teng Riddim' do not represent a revolution but a well-established music-making tradition that was and continues to be practised in Jamaica.

The 'Sleng Teng Riddim' Legacy

Based on the evidence provided in this chapter, it seems apparent that 'Under Mi Sleng Teng' did not mark a digital revolution in Jamaican recording practice. Moreover, it was far from being the first song to employ drum machine and synthesizer in Jamaica, despite claims to the contrary. The perplexing debate that has surrounded the production of Davy's riddim has only further been exacerbated by erroneous assessments of its musical function, for example: Dick Hebdige claims: 'Wayne Smith made a record called "Under Mi Sleng Teng". It has been estimated that by October 1985, no less than 239 versions of this tune had been made' (1987a, p. 12). While Hebdige correctly points out the importance of the number of derivative sound recordings, he mistakenly cites the 'tune' entitled 'Under Mi Sleng Teng', which was in fact only recorded once by Wayne Smith. The number '239', represents the number of times that the 'Sleng Teng Riddim, as an autonomous piece of music located by Davy, was commercially released as the backing track for 239 independent and unique tunes, each written or adapted for the purpose of being recorded over this one riddim.

I therefore contend that the significance of this musical work is that it marked an unprecedented public acceptance of a riddim-based music production system that displaced the 'song' in favour of the 'riddim' as the central creative focal point. Although initiated for the production of reggae, riddim-based music production found relevance with what would become dancehall music and the deejay. The success of the 'Sleng Teng Riddim' therefore marked this transition in a way that was unequivocal and undeniable. For many established music practitioners the massive popularity of the riddim represented a seismic shift in creative forces that left no room, or significantly reduced the relevance of established music-making practice and recording craft.

The importance of the 'Sleng Teng Riddim' is therefore not found in the technical means of its production but in the massive, unprecedented commercial success that it came to represent as a piece of dancehall music. Even to Jamaican audiences, familiar with the concept of hearing single riddims used for multiple songs, the success of the 'Sleng Teng Riddim' was on a scale that had not been previously seen and this had a substantial impact on the production and consumption of JPM. The 200 plus songs that were recorded on the riddim are proof that a massive realignment of public support had occurred that, in effect, opened a flood-gate of imitators, in the form of financiers, producers, musicians, audio engineers, singers and deejays who all rushed to emulate and cash-in on the the Sleng Teng phenomenon that Davy, James and Smith created.

If a revolution took place in JPM in 1985, it was in the form of a perceived wholesale move of the local music industry to the creation of riddims that increasingly featured deejays and with a focus on creating what might fairly be described as, the 'hyper riddim'; one piece of music that could be used for hundreds of different songs and therefore generate massive monetary rewards for its owner.

In my view, the 'Sleng Teng Riddim's' creation, using a domestic keyboard, was incidental although this fact has further incensed the reggae establishment who suggest that the keyboard's lack of professional pedigree is proof of the resulting music's illegitimacy. However, it is important to note that the popular music industry has a long tradition of incorporating unconventional, domestic and non-professional instruments in music production. Examples include not only the rhythm box employed by Bob Marley, noted above, but also David Bowie's use of the Stylophone on his massive international hit Space Oddity (1968) and the seminal instrumental recordings of Pablo Moses using the Melodica.

The chapters that follow provide a detailed analysis of how the new instruments of the 1980s were specifically incorporated into and influenced music creation and music production techniques. These were initially employed for the production of reggae but were adopted and adapted by dancehall music practitioners. By analysing the roles of recording participants and production practice we are better able to understand why dancehall music was perceived as making some aspects of music production easier while bringing to the fore aspects of music-making that became more complex and creatively demanding. In this sense, the following chapters respond to Deborah Wong's assertion that 'technology is a cultural practice and that an examination of technological practices in context is the only way to get at what technology "does" … technology can thus have different applications and/or evocative associations in different societies' (2003, pp. 125–6). With this in mind, the next chapter considers in closer detail the unique way in which technology was adapted to meet the needs of dancehall music and the part that musicians and audio engineers played in that process.

Chapter 6

Drum Machines and Synthesizers: The Serial Recording Model

This chapter sets out to assess some of the critical changes that occurred in Jamaican music production as a direct result of the introduction of new instruments, such as the Yamaha DX7 and Oberheim DMX drum machine, at the start of the 1980s. It provides accounts of how these instruments were introduced to Jamaica and the influence they had on the culture of recording and the roles of musicians and audio engineers. It describes the way in which recording transitioned from a group-based multi-microphone recording model to a serial recording model where instruments such as the DMX drum machine and DX7 synthesizer were recorded one at a time without the need for microphones. The chapter considers the way in which the new recording model influenced creativity, performance and the role of recording participants; challenging the perception that the new instruments made the production of successful commercial music in Jamaica easy to achieve.

The Introduction of Synthesizers

Digital instruments such as the Yamaha DX7, introduced in the previous chapter, are not only significant because of the new sounds that they offered musicians but because they demanded a significant investment of resources and time, if they were to be used effectively. There was in fact a wide range of new instruments that appeared in Jamaica during the early 1980s, reflecting an interest in exploring the new sonic textures increasingly being heard on some foreign sound recordings. Local performers such as Robbie Lyn, Keith Sterling, Tyrone Downie, Handel Tucker and Peter Ashbourne represent some of the prominent users of synthesizers who were active in Kingston at the start of the 1980s. For those who could master the technical demands of the new instruments and employ them creatively, there was an expanding range of recording and performance opportunities; however, the opposite was true for musicians without the capital or inclination to adapt and engage with the new technologies.

To try and assess how the instruments impacted Jamaica's studio culture, I discussed their integration with Robbie Lyn. Having retained a prominent position as a keyboard player in the Kingston studio scene, since turning professional in 1968, Lyn is uniquely qualified to comment on changing recording practice. Lyn has not only attained recognition in all genres of JPM but the majority of his work experience has been as a studio musician. He therefore represents the vanguard of those who embraced the new instruments and played a critical role in their integration, particularly in the newly emerging dancehall music.

I asked Lyn to provide an overview of the change that occurred in the music-making process between the 1960s and 1980s. He explained that, during the 1960s and 1970s, it was important for a session musician to become a member of a studio group in order to obtain regular work, performing and creating backing tracks for recording artists. The creation of backing tracks was often based on a specific melody and/or lyric, in the form of a song provided by a singer. The studio group provided musical performances for which each member was remunerated, but there was an informal understanding with financiers that musicians would also provide writing and arranging services for no additional cost or credit. Lyn states that during his early career, working for Coxsone's Studio One, he and his fellow group members were paid by weekly salary, to provide the above services. The conditions and rates of pay for recording studio services were therefore dependent on the scope of work and the performers' ability to negotiate the rate of compensation in a competitive and vibrant recording industry.

Lyn claimed that by the end of the 1970s that there was a growing demand for the synthesizer in Jamaica, but the dominant keyboard instruments found in most recording studios were still acoustic and/or electric pianos, and a Hammond or similar electronic organ. Recording practitioners were increasingly looking for ways to exploit the growing number of available recording tracks and Lyn states that synthesizers were increasingly being heard on records originating in North America and Europe, which had an influence on local recording trends.

In a July 2008 interview with Peter Ashbourne, a prominent musician and keyboard player, he claimed that the Putney, Arp 2600 and Mini Moog synthesizers were purchased by Federal, Dynamic Sounds and Tuff Gong studios respectively, during the 1970s. However, Ashbourne points out that whereas the piano and organ were well-established instruments that were relatively easy to operate, the same was not true of these synthesizers. As a result, they received limited usage because most piano or organ players were not familiar enough with the instruments to operate them effectively. Ashbourne explained that mastery of the new instruments was difficult to achieve without private ownership, but Jamaica's depressed economy of the 1970s and foreign exchange restrictions, made purchase difficult.

During the 1980s, although the Jamaican economy did show some signs of growth, an exploding national debt, declining value of the Jamaican dollar, foreign exchange restrictions and high import duties continued to make private ownership of the new instruments difficult and beyond the means of musicians who were not touring internationally. Robbie Lyn confirms the difficulties associated with purchasing the latest instruments and offers the example of the Emulator II sampler, which in 1986 cost US$8000, representing a significant investment but also requiring the additional purchase of a sample library in the form of floppy discs, each disc containing one or more instrument samples.

In addition, the new instruments required the user to provide private transport to and from the studio at a time when the Jamaican government heavily restricted the importation of motor vehicles. Cars could only be purchased through a licensing system and the cost of a local vehicle was between two and three times greater than the same vehicle in North America. In addition, the new instruments demanded that the user had proficient literacy skills and the ability to interpret the often complex user manuals that were provided with the instrument. Lyn explained that there was a need for the users of the instruments to have a good understanding of their design, the MIDI technologies around which they were based, and the evolving recording processes that were being employed to capture and mix the new sounds.

Lyn describes a scenario where he was not only required to perform, create and arrange music as a studio musician, but was now required to invest significant sums of money in acquiring his own instruments, provide transport for them and become a proficient operator, able to interpret and adapt their sonic capabilities to meet local needs. Lyn emphasizes that the transition to analogue and later digital synthesizers demanded a considerable adjustment in playing technique, creative approach and understanding of the recording process. He notes that this change was reflected by the fact that he was referred to as a pianist during the 1960s but by the end of the 1970s he was typically referred to as a keyboard player.

Lyn pointed out that the new keyboard instruments such as the DX7 had a significant impact on his role as a session musician because they allowed him to quickly run through a library of sounds while rehearsing the part to be played on a song. He was now able to play piano on a backing track and use the same instrument to then add organ, strings, tuned percussion, brass, woodwind and a wide variety of other synthesized or sampled sounds. There was no need for the session to be stopped while the audio engineer set up additional instruments, microphones and then create an appropriate sound. Many recording practitioners therefore embraced the speed and flexibility of new instruments such as the DX7 because they encouraged spontaneity in a way that had not previously been possible, while providing realistic substitute sounds for established analogue instruments such as the piano, organ and clavinet. The new instruments also had the potential to reduce the amount of time needed to make a sound recording while also offering an expanded sound palette of sounds not typically heard in JPM. The keyboard player could now audition a wide range of instrument parts and sounds as the song was being played, which proved to be an efficient method of enhancing spontaneity during recording. However, this also demanded that the creative process was open to the influence of sound and timbre, which could now influence the creation of melody, harmony and rhythm.

Lyn's testimony is consistent with Théberge's claim that 'With the expansion of sonic technologies, the musician is able to engage with the micro-phenomena of musical sound itself, and such an engagement often forces a reassessment of the role of more traditional categories of musical practice' (1997, p. 186). These comments are certainly true of JPM and what we see during the 1980s is a broadening but also shifting of roles in the recording studio and the need for recording participants to develop a new sensitivity toward sound and music creation within the context of new methods of recording.

The Sound of a Different Drum

Many of my informants, who worked in Jamaican recording studios prior to the 1980s, including Robbie Lyn, Sly Dunbar and Cleveland Browne, point to the digital drum machine as a catalyst of change in the production of JPM. They suggest that the spontaneous group writing, arranging and performance, which had dominated the 1960s and 1970s, simply became redundant when working to a set drum programme provided by a drum machine. It was impossible for the drum machine to interact with the small deviations of pace and dynamics that naturally occurred during the spontaneous performance of a live rhythm section.

Although the 1980s saw a gradual and steady trend of session groups being replaced by one or two musicians/programmers in Jamaican studios, Robbie Lyn states that the style of arranging and instrumentation initially mimicked group performances and remained focused on the production of reggae. As noted in the previous chapter, the drum machine was introduced at a time when reggae was still the predominant genre of locally produced music. While the new digital instruments could reproduce the traditional rhythm-section sounds associated with reggae, Lyn pointed out that the sound quality of the new instruments were different and had what he described as 'a clean sound'. In the case of the drum machine this included the production of consistent dynamics and timing that for many recording participants of the period represented desirable attributes in the production of popular music. However, the significance of the drum machine was that it encouraged the use of what I term a linear recording model, where the drum machine programme is captured and other instruments are then added to the sound recording one at a time.

Errol Brown provided an audio engineer's perspective on the transition to the new linear recording model, pointing out that the reason for the perception of the sound being 'clean' was in part because the drum machine did not require the use of microphones for the capture of drum sounds. Professional drum machines such as the Oberheim DMX provided an independent output for each drum sound, which could be connected directly to the mixing console and then directed to an independent track on the tape machine. Significantly, this meant that drum sounds were no longer coloured by microphone selection, placement and the sonic characteristics of the recording room but, most importantly, there was an absence of microphone leakage on individual instrument tracks.[1] In addition, the drum

---

[1] 'Microphone leakage' refers to where the capture of a sound using a microphone often includes the unavoidable capture of other instruments that are also being played during the performance. This is most noticeable on the drum kit where a microphone placed in front

programmer was now positioned in the studio control room and worked alongside the audio engineer.

The absolute isolation of individual drum sounds coming from the drum machine is a crucial development, which in conjunction with the transition in modes of musical performance, opened up new opportunities for mixing. Drum isolation encouraged and expanded the practice of using single backing tracks over which multiple songs, in the form of vocal performances were recorded. This meant that drum sounds could be captured individually on tape and then radically rearranged during mixing, representing a process that was not feasible with live drums. Although live drums had previously been recorded using multiple microphones, with the assignment of one microphone to one drum or group of drums, it was impossible to avoid the resulting leakage where each microphone inadvertently captured the unwanted sound of other drums and possibly other instruments also playing in the studio.

The first routine musical rearrangement of backing tracks, which multi-track recording and post recording mixing made possible, was heard in dub and version B-side mixes. These began to emerge with the introduction of multi-track recording at the close of the 1960s and as derivative works of an A side, set out to explore and locate new sounds. Evidence of microphone leakage is readily heard on many dub and version B-side mixes of the 1970s, before the drum machine's introduction. For example on King Tubby's 'Soundboy Massacre' (Delta Music, 2000), a compilation of Tubby's dub mixes from the 1970s, the organ, piano and electric rhythm guitar are muted at 0.14 yet the guitar continues to be faintly heard because although the guitar track is muted, its sound was also captured by the microphones placed on the drums and/or bass.

In these dub mixes the rearrangement of musical parts during mixing was limited by the extent to which microphone leakage was considered acceptable.[2] The drum machine and synthesizer therefore removed restrictions on the rearrangement of drum and instrument parts. In addition, the absence of microphones meant that recording could be moved from the studio to the studio control room, where instruments were now captured serially one at a time.

Changes in Performing Practice

The perfect timing of the drum machine was seen as a positive attribute in the recording process however; drum beats became static and very different in feel

---

of the kick drum will inadvertently capture the sound of the other drums being played but at a reduced level.

[2] A device called a noise gate could be added to each recorded track and acted as an automatic mute switch, muting the track if the sound fell below a set amplitude. However, although these devices were available in many Jamaican studios, to place them on each drum of a drum kit was time consuming and rarely produced perfect results.

to that of live drums. Reggae up to the start of the 1980s had often employed a fluid approach to time and pace with nuanced fluctuations that were directed by the drummer and bass player. In an interview with Michael Fletcher, I asked how the drum machine influenced the feel of music for him as a bass player. Fletcher described how 'drum machines removed some of the push and pull of reggae's feel', where tempo, but also, emphasis and dynamics are subtly changed during the live performance of drum and bass'.[3]

This aspect of instrumental performance is not unique to JPM and is noted by Charles Keil and Steven Feld in the discussion of what they term 'vital drive': 'Charles Mingus bassist extraordinaire, and Danny Richmond, drummer, have been known to create a number of vital drives within a single piece' (2005, p. 66). Vital drive was considered a critical element in the performance of reggae that the drum machine appeared to remove. However, Fletcher notes that despite the loss of the live drum and bass feel, it did not result in an absence of 'feel', which other instrument parts were now often required to compensate for.

The increasing popularity of the drum machine and ultimate decline in group-based recording meant that specialist instrumentalists, such as drummers, bass players, guitarists and pianists were replaced by a new type of studio musician. These musicians were not only required to perform serially, one instrument at a time, typically using a drum machine and synthesizer but they were also required to think serially, in terms of the musical arrangement. The sound recordings that emerged during the early 1980s appear to demonstrate a general trend toward the simplification of musical elements in reggae and the newly emerging dancehall music. This was in part the product of musical arrangements being 'built' one part at a time using the serial recording model but there was also an increase of what might be termed the 'hunt and peck performer'.[4]

The term 'hunt and peck; is not intended as a derogatory description but simply describes the way in which both established and emerging music practitioners approached the use of the drum machines and the synthesizer that were increasingly dominating music production in Jamaica. While working in Jamaican recording studios during this period it was common to see this 'hunt and peck' approach representing a practice that was facilitated by the design of the instruments, the sounds they offered, the new linear recording model and the fact that the multi-track tape machine could seamlessly punch in and build a single composite music track out of many disparate instrument performance segments. However, I would like to stress that the absence of traditional keyboard performance skills should not be interpreted as an indication of diminished musical creativity or ingenuity.

---

[3] Michael Fletcher was a member of the Dean Fraser led 809 band during the late 1980s and early 1990s but is best known as the musical director for Shaggy.

[4] The term 'hunt and peck' was coined to describe typists who are unable to touch type but use two fingers; although typically creating text at a slower pace the technique does not negatively influence the creativity embodied in the text.

Although it would seem that established keyboard players would have a distinct advantage in the new keyboard-dominated recording paradigm, many established piano and organ performers could not adjust to the new instruments and creative process. These increasingly demanded an intimate familiarity with the technology and the adaptation of musical sensibilities to serve the changing demands of a new generation of music consumers. There was also a tangible rejection of the complex instrument textures and musical arrangements that had come to epitomize the international reggae sound of Bob Marley and others, now increasingly rejected by Jamaica's youth. Like the British punks of the 1970s the newest generation of music consumers in 1980s Jamaica 'seemed to challenge capitalist control of mass music – there was an emphasis on do-it-yourself, on seizing the technical means of music production ... punk raised questions about musical meaning, it suggested new sounds, new forms, new texts.' (Frith, 1981, p. 158). In this environment the 'hunt and peck performer' found relevance, and their simple melodic and harmonic structures provided focus for the intense rhythmic structures increasingly found in the drum programming and deejay vocal performances of dancehall music. Although ridiculed by the reggae establishment, these new exciting sounds resonated with local audiences and were widely embraced.

This and subsequent chapters offer evidence of the way in which the serial recording model evolved and the complex creative and technical process that underpinned its success. Despite the crude appearance of the two-fingered 'hunt and peck performers', their musical products were often vibrant examples of popular music that not only appealed to local audiences but by the late 1980s had begun to establish an international presence through performers such as Shabba Ranks. James Peart, a keyboard player who began his professional career at the start of the 1980s, describes the environment as: 'People were tired of the same old, same old [sic] [meaning ska, rock steady and reggae] and looking for something new.' The new dancehall music that emerged during the 1980s was largely a response to that sentiment. It offered music consumers a range of fresh musical ideas, captured using new instruments, sounds, performance techniques and production methodologies, which despite being ridiculed and scorned by the establishment, represented a breath of fresh air and sense of rejuvenation.

Robbie Lyn is part of an elite group of musicians who were able to transition from reggae to dancehall music and adapt their performance and musical approach to meet the demands of the new music and changing technology. Lyn describes a local recording industry that was in a state of flux as changes in the recording industry gathered momentum at the start of the 1980s. However, although we see dramatic change in many areas of music performance and recording practice, the spontaneous creation of instrument parts during the recording session was maintained as a central core of the JPM aesthetic. In order to understand how the new serial recording model functioned, it is important to consider how the DMX drum machine influenced musical structure, instrumentation, performance, arrangement and recording process.

I asked Lyn to provide a musician's perspective regarding the way in which the drum machine was integrated into recording sessions and how this altered the process of recording. He stated that initially drum machines were adapted to the composing and recording of reggae. So, for example, the recording session typically began with connecting the drum machine and keyboard to the mixing console so that they could be heard through the control room loudspeakers. The song to be recorded was identified and an appropriate key, harmonic progression and tempo were selected. The drum programmer then created drumbeats for each section of the song and these were placed in a programmed song arrangement, stored in the machine's memory. The complete drum programme was then recorded to tape as a rhythmic template that all additional instrument and percussive parts were recorded to, in a process of building up the musical arrangement, one instrument at a time. This description is consistent with my own experience and in 1984 I acted as the creative producer for an album project recorded at the Music Mountain recording studio where drum programming was provided by Cleveland Browne (a drummer) and Danny Browne (a guitarist) respectively, employing this song programming approach on the DMX drum machine.

The above testimony of Browne and Lyn is significant because although they were still hired for recording sessions, primarily as musical performers, their success and popularity as session musicians in the new linear recording model was based on a number of other attributes that included:

- the number and type of 'new' instruments owned;
- the ability to read and comprehend user manuals that provided access to the new instrument's potential;
- the technical proficiency needed to navigate the features of the new instruments, including the selection and editing of sound;
- the ownership of a library of unique sounds;
- the ability to compose multiple instrument parts in a linear process of recording;
- the ability to collaborate and work in close proximity with the audio engineer.

While musicians and audio engineers were grappling with the integration of drum machines and the creative challenges that they posed, financiers of recording were largely receptive to a range of benefits that the new technologies offered. For example, the rental of recording studios with a large recording-room, a well-maintained drum kit, acoustic piano, electric piano and organ, a wide selection of microphones and an experienced audio engineer, skilled in the art of choosing, placing and balancing microphones, became unnecessary. One or two musicians/ programmers, employing the new instruments, captured by an audio engineer versed in only basic microphone usage and multi-track recording, could now create a recorded product that competed sonically with the big established commercial studios. In addition, financiers could now negotiate session fees at a discounted rate because the musician(s) were employed to perform multiple parts, often working for a 'per riddim' fee irrespective of the number of instrument parts created and recorded.

Another perceived advantage of the new recording model was that the drum machine not only offered the programmer the standard drum kit sounds of kick, snare, hi-hat, hi- tom, mid-tom, low-tom, ride cymbal and crash cymbal – but also a selection of sounds listed by instrument category, available from a built-in sound library that included light percussion. Individual drum sounds could also be tuned across a range of pitches and the general sense was that the drum machine negated the hours of studio time typically spent at the start of recording sessions trying to achieve a 'good' drum sound. Moreover, the drum machine provided a wide range of percussion instruments, which could be programmed and integrated into the drumbeats, removing the need to hire a percussionist. The new linear recording model was therefore not only faster and cheaper, but opened up a new adventurous approach toward the creation of drumbeats and musical parts, now only restricted by the musician/programmer's imagination.

The New Challenge of Working with Drum Machines

Cleveland Browne, with not only his broad range of musical experience but also significant success as a dancehall music producer, is uniquely qualified to comment on the demands of dancehall music and the creative and technical resources that were needed for its production. I asked Browne to identify the greatest challenge of working with drum machines during the 1980s. Browne reaffirms an earlier comment of Errol Brown regarding the way in which recorded sound changed after the drum machine's introduction. Browne states:

> I think we have lost the uniqueness and unique qualities, acoustic properties of various studios. Back in the 60s and 70s you could identify a studio from the sound, you could hear the room, the reverb units they used, [and] the micing techniques the engineer used.

Browne suggests that prior to the introduction of digital instruments, the sound of a song was dependent on the quality of the instruments, the available microphones, the audio engineer's choice and placement of those microphones, but also the acoustic characteristics of the room in which the recording took place, and the sonic characteristics of the studio equipment. He suggests that popular Jamaican recording studios such as Federal, Treasure Isle, Randy's, Aquarius, Studio One, Joe Gibbs, Dynamic Sounds and Channel One all established signature sounds, located mostly in their live drum sound but this characteristic was lost with the introduction of the drum machine. By the end of the 1980s, live drums were being used in relatively few commercial recording sessions and many of the established studios were using their recording rooms to record only voice or the occasional acoustic instrument.

During Errol Brown's interview in 2008, he pointed to a less obvious impact that the drum machine had on JPM, claiming that it changed the technical demands on the next generation of audio engineers. Brown claimed that recording live drums 'represent[s] a real test of the audio engineer's skill', in terms of aural analysis, translated through the choice and placement of multiple microphones in close proximity to each other. Brown explained that live drums represent an instrument, which produces sounds with a wide dynamic and frequency range coming from multiple sources. The audio engineer is required to assess the drum sounds but also the playing style of the performer and the recording room's influence on the sound of the instrument. In addition, there are issues such as drum separation, the proximity effect and phase of microphones that need to be considered.[5]

According to Brown, 'If you can record drums, you can record anything.' I asked Brown if this meant that the younger post-1980s engineers, not well versed in recording drums, were less qualified than those who were trained to record live drums. Brown responded, 'No, but their focus was different', meaning that drum sounds no longer provided an opportunity for the audio engineer to stamp their mark on the recording.

> I think the engineers lost that skill to define sound based on their own interpretation ya know, although you could do a little still, but you're getting the sound straight out of the drum machine through a wire.

Both Cleveland Browne and Errol Brown concur that while the drum machine had many positive attributes, one of its limitations was that sound recordings began to sound the same, despite the fact that they were recorded in different studios by different audio engineers. In addition, Cleveland Browne points out that live drums had allowed for the unique interpretation of established drum beats such as the One Drop, now largely missing as a result of quantized drum programming.[6] Therefore many records shared the same generic drum beat, resulting in a growing demand for drum programmers to find ways of exploring the technical resources of the drum machine, which included changing the characteristics of the machine's factory sounds and/or locating new beats.[7]

---

[5] 'Microphone phase' describes the phenomenon when two microphones pick up the same audio signal, but the phase of one microphone diaphragm is opposite to that of the other resulting in sound cancellation. Instrument separation is the art of selecting and placing microphones so that they produce the desired characteristic of the individual instrument they are set to record while rejecting the sounds of other instruments.

[6] It is important to point out that most drum programming was performed using one finger on each hand to perform the drum parts, which meant that accomplished drummers had a relatively small performance advantage, if any, over those who did not play drums.

[7] 'Factory sounds' is a term used to describe the stock sounds that drum machines are manufactured and sold with.

According to Cleveland Browne, there was a common perception that the drum machine made music production simple, based on the fact that it removed the need for an operator with specialized performance skills. Drum programming appeared to be accessible to anyone who could read the instrument's instruction manual. In addition, drum machines could be set up in the studio and recorded very quickly compared to live drums. As previously mentioned, the new instrument significantly reduced the amount of studio time needed to make a commercial sound recording.

Browne confirmed that, although the drum machine had many positive attributes, it also brought a distinct set of problems to the creative recording process that could not be solved using established musical approaches or music-production practices. He explained that although recording sessions could be completed quickly, their duration no longer reflected the amount of labour that was invested in the creating and capturing of a sound recording. For example, the 'When Riddim' (1992), created and recorded by Steely and Clevie for a song of the same name, became a massive Jamaican hit and went on to be used as the riddim for a substantial number of other hit songs. Browne claimed:

> We did a song like 'When' for instance with Tiger, it won 'Song of the Year' at the JAMI awards, it's a song we did in half an hour, we didn't spend much time on it, but it was minimalistic, drums driven.[8]

Browne explained that the apparent ease and speed at which riddims such as the 'When Riddim' could be recorded is deceptive, highlighting the fact that there was a substantial amount of pre-production work from which the riddim benefited, but this took place outside of the recording studio.[9] In addition, the 'minimalistic', music arranging strategy that is identified by Browne, represents a complex process of instrument reduction, based on experimentation and market analysis that riddim creators such as Steely and Clevie engaged in. Browne describes a music production process that was very dynamic, constantly undergoing modification and fine-tuning to suit the perceived needs of a range of consumers but particularly those who consumed music via the sound system.

Browne explained that working with dancehall music demanded the ongoing creation of new sounds and imaginative ways of incorporating them into riddims, a responsibility now largely assumed by him in the role of musician/programmer. This process was conducted in a pre-production environment, driven by the fact that dancehall music had a strong rhythmic emphasis, and riddims were increasingly employing sparse musical arrangements that featured drums. According to

---

[8] Tiger is the name of a popular deejay from the late 1980s and early 1990s.

[9] The term 'pre-production' refers to preparation work that is conducted before going into the studio and suggests work for a specific music project, but can also include a general development of sound creation and rhythm manipulation strategies and experimentation. Pre-production covers a range of functions, including the establishing of tempos and keys, as well as consideration of music treatments and sound references.

Browne, sound and rhythm were therefore key elements in establishing a riddim's unique identity and would hopefully allow it to achieve hyper riddim status.

The process of utilizing sound described by Browne was not unique to Jamaica, and Paul Théberge states that, 'most manufacturers of digital instruments recognized that the production of sounds had become essential to the success of their products' (1997, p. 77). The sound-crafting process therefore represents a significant development in popular-music production, which Théberge confirms, 'has become increasingly dependent upon the technologies of audio production and reproduction, ... there has been a corresponding importance attached to "sound" – as both an aesthetic and commercial category' (2003, p. 94).

In the context of JPM, the responsibility for sound creation had traditionally been assumed by the audio engineer but Browne described a transition of that responsibility, increasingly assumed by the musician/programmer. Browne claimed that although instrument manufacturers, such as Oberheim, eventually recognized the need to expand their sound libraries, new sounds coming onto the market were available to everyone. There was therefore a need for programmers to invest a substantial amount of time and resources into creating personalized sounds and finding unique ways of using the existing sounds of instruments such as the DMX drum machine. Part of this process involved being well informed about the latest developments in musical instrument hardware, software, sound design and new recording technologies. As a result, Browne's contribution to the production of a riddim could no longer be fairly assessed on the time spent in the recording studio, now representing just one part of a much wider music production process.

I asked Browne if he could provide examples of the way in which he located sounds that were used in his dancehall-music productions during the 1980s and a broader sense of the type of tasks that he, as a programmer, now performed. Browne explained that during the early 1980s he purchased an Oberheim DMX drum machine that stored drum samples digitally on EPROM chips.[10] One EPROM chip stored one set of sounds, such as bass drums, that was fitted to the corresponding bass drum slot in the drum machine. According to Browne, each EPROM slot on the drum machine contained electronic filtering, which was designed to enhance the general sound characteristics of the samples contained on the corresponding chip.

Browne described how he inadvertently discovered that this offered an opportunity for creating new sounds. He tried changing around the EPROM chips, placing them in the incorrect slots, recalling: 'I would take like an 808 [Roland 808 drum machine] cowbell and put it in the tom slot'. According to Browne, this resulted in electronic filtering, which was intended to optimize the sonic characteristics of the tom-tom drum samples, now being applied to the 808 cowbell, in contravention of the manufacturer's recommendations. An Internet

---

[10] EPROM (Erasable Programmable Read-Only Memory) was a memory chip that could store information after the power had been removed from the equipment in which it was used.

search in July 2010 located a user manual for the Oberheim DMX drum machine (Revision 3, 1982).[11] In a section entitled 'The DMX Voices', the manual makes no mention of the possibility of changing EPROM chips, as described by Browne. In addition it makes no mention of an available sound library, where the user can update and change drum sounds. It should be noted that by 1985, with the introduction of the DX (the replacement for the DMX) drum machine, the new manual (Revision 2, 1985), includes a description of how to replace EPROM chips as a way of changing drum sounds and the availability of a growing sound library.[12] Although Browne does not claim to have been the originator of the above sound altering technique, it is evident that he formed an understanding of this technology and was exploring its limitations, apparently before the manufacturer of the drum machine recognized this potential.

Browne was therefore employing unconventional sound-creation methods that might be considered new and experimental, but he also employed unorthodox use of the drum machine's tuning mechanism as a way of creating new sounds and effects. Browne explained that the electronic sweep-tuning feature of the DMX drum machine could be used in two distinct ways.[13] The tuning facility allowed him to create new sounds by dramatically re-tuning certain drum sounds, like the side-stick, or he could vary the pitch of a drum while it was being recorded to tape. For example, Browne would use the pitch control, located on the drum machine, to alter a drum's pitch spontaneously during recording and create a musical effect.

Browne also recorded and edited his own personalized set of customized drum sounds before commercial drum libraries became available to drum-machine users. He notes: 'I remember going to the UK and getting special samples that did not come with the machine ... I had my own sounds made'. Browne explained that this process had to be done in the UK because EPROM blowers were not available in Jamaica at that time.[14]

The sound-altering processes described by Browne are significant because they not only represent the acquisition of sound-creation skills that had previously been the responsibility of the audio engineer, but they also demonstrate how the musician combined musical and technical roles to develop new creative strategies that could exploit the new instruments in the production of dancehall music. In a sense, the process of sound creation had, in part, been transferred from the audio engineer to the musician/programmer, but, in reality, sound creation had become

---

[11] The manual is available online: http://www.electrongate.com/dmxfiles/DMX_owners_manual_rev3.pdf (accessed July 2010).

[12] This manual is also available online: http://www.genericwittywebsite.com/oberheim/Oberheim%20DX%20User%27s%20Manual%20%28Second%20Edition%29.pdf (accessed July 2010).

[13] 'Sweep tuning' did not move the pitch in semitones, but in cents, so a change in pitch during the performance of a sound had a glissando effect of which the speed and range could be altered by manipulation of the rotary pitch control located on the machine.

[14] An 'EPROM blower' is a machine used to record data onto EPROM chips.

a collaboration of the programmer/musician and the audio engineer who was still required to process the sounds and record them to tape. Browne describes a scenario where, in order for him to be successful as a musician, he had to acquire a thorough understanding of the new instrument's technical potential and limitations in the ongoing search for new sounds, textures and new drumbeats.

Browne's testimony is evidence of the ways in which the roles of musicians and audio engineers evolved, suggesting that any fair appraisal of these new production methods could no longer be based on traditional values of musicianship or creative and technical competence associated with older forms of JPM and their respective recording models. This is not to say that notions of musicianship and audio-engineered sound design became obsolete, but as the new approaches and practices developed, established value systems became increasingly redundant in the context of this new music production system.

The Integration of Creative and Technical Roles

While discussing the process of creating new sounds with Browne, it became apparent that although instruments such as the drum machine were perceived as being 'easy' to make music with, the actual process of consistently making successful commercial music with these instruments was complex, time consuming and demanded a new creative approach. In effect, what Browne describes is the amalgamation of sound modification, groove and musical process being intertwined into a skill set that was pioneered in Jamaica through the production of dancehall music. However, reggae and other earlier forms of JPM, which continued to be produced, borrowed from the new production techniques when convenient.

Browne describes an act of music-making where it is difficult to identify where the creation of sound ended and musical conception began. In this sense Browne's testimony does not describe the development of new skills that functioned independently of his musical sensibility, but rather the evolution and expansion of his musical sense, which adopted but also adapted new ideas and concepts. Browne makes the important point that drum sounds no longer simply represented the palette from which he created drumbeats but sound became integrated with the music creation process, significantly influencing the attitude and characteristics of what he programmed or performed and the way in which it was interpreted on the studio's control room loudspeakers.

The claim that the new technology made the creation and production of music 'kids play' is not supported by the testimony of Browne. Although a popular and successful piece of music such as the 'When Riddim' could be recorded in just half an hour, this does not reflect the true extent of the technical and creative effort or experimentation and preparation that went into its creation and production. While Browne's testimony does not reflect the practice of every drum machine user, it does establish the fact that some dancehall-music practitioners engaged in a new range of skills and practices, which have been largely ignored or possibly misunderstood. The amalgamation of traditional audio engineering and musical skills is what set successful practitioners such as Browne apart from their peers.

Browne, Lyn and Brown concur that the role of recording participants and the development of music production was no longer limited to the confines of the recording studio in post-1980 Jamaica. This marks a significant difference between the production of dancehall music and preceding JPM genres, which needs to be recognized and understood, if any accurate assessment of dancehall music and its production values are to be made. In the new dancehall-music production paradigm these informants describe how the musician was now required to be intimately familiar with the new instruments, the technology they were based on and how that technology integrated into the recording process. Moreover, there was a need for the musician to be well versed in the instruments' operation, which included an ability to provide unique sounds or the modification of existing sounds, while providing writing, arranging and performance skills essential for the creation of riddims.

The Audio Engineer as a Source of Creative Inspiration

My informants concurred that the drum machine and synthesizer's new array of sounds influenced how melody, harmony and rhythm were composed and arranged. In this new creative environment, inspiration was increasingly found in the 'vibe' of the recording session, which now became manifest in the studio control room and establishing that vibe was based significantly on sounds, which the audio engineer was expected to provide. The use of sheer volume, but also studio effects and the full frequency range of the control room loudspeakers became tools that a 'good' audio engineer used to inspire creativity and performance, representing a new creative environment for the musician. The often-abstract sounds and balances of the recording room and headphone monitoring system, which demanded experienced session players to obtain an optimal performance and sound was now replaced by the musicians' direct interaction with the existing captured sound, heard via the control room monitors. This allowed and encouraged a new dialogue between audio engineer and musicians, which became intimate and nuanced. Working from the studio control room meant that verbal interaction was unrestricted and even possible during the process of recording, but there was also visual interaction and cues, which replaced the often abstract information that a headphone monitoring system was able to provide.

What we therefore see during the early 1980s is a dramatic change in the music creation process and the way in which inspiration was created in recording spaces. Increasingly, new drumbeats began to move away from the traditional 'one-drop' and 'steppes' beats that had dominated reggae of the 1970s.[15] The drum machine, in conjunction with the new recording participants and recording

---

[15] See the definition of 'steppes' in Appendix C.

model encouraged the exploration of these new beats and sounds that dancehall music proved especially receptive to. An example of this is the Admiral Bailey song entitled 'Punanny' (1987) produced by Steely and Clevie. This particular song was performed over a riddim that became known as the 'Punnany Riddim' and the drum beat, created by Cleveland Browne, was based on a dotted crotchet rhythm played by the kick drum. This riddim would achieve hyper-riddim status and derivative interpretations, employing the same drumbeat would be heard on numerous recordings during the course of the following two decades.

I asked some of my informants to comment on the role of the audio engineer in the new linear-recording model and was interested in discovering what influence the audio engineer had on the process of spontaneously creating riddim tracks. Although the responses were varied, there was a common theme that 'good' audio engineers demonstrated self-confidence and a technical ability to capture musical performances efficiently and accurately. There was also a sense that the audio engineer played an important role in the music production process, by helping to create a 'good vibe'. When informants were pressed to define this term, phrases such as 'hyping the sound [and] niceing-up the sound' were used, suggesting that the audio engineer was responsible for creating a musical balance that inspired creativity.[16] In fact, the term 'vibe' represents a word that has a multitude of applications in the Jamaican vernacular and is employed to describe a wide range of circumstances, situations and attitudes, and is therefore difficult to define. Although use of the term is discussed in a number of contexts in the literature, most notably by Keil and Feld (2005), I am hesitant about drawing parallels between the term's meaning in a Jamaican musical context and the practice of music-making in other locations. Many of my informants hesitated when asked to provide a specific meaning for the term, but when used to describe a positive attribute of a musical context, there was a general sentiment that the term described a sense of well-being, comfort, or, as James Peart said, 'Ya jus feel nice bout the music.' A 'good vibe' was ultimately seen as a critical element in the new spontaneous music creation process where musicians were now required to perform in relative isolation rather than with the interaction of fellow group members.

Both musicians and audio engineers agreed that the new serial recording model resulted in the monitored sound of the recording not only being employed as a technical reference for the sonic characteristics of instruments but also being employed as a tool for musical inspiration and creativity. The studio control room loudspeakers had the potential to bombard the recording participant's senses with a unique range of sonic textures that became an important source of inspiration and played a significant role in providing the essence of a 'good vibe' in a Jamaican recording context. Some musicians had strong preferences for working with

---

[16] Terms such as 'niceing-up' and 'hyping' are best translated as making the mix appealing and compelling to the listener.

specific audio engineers, based primarily on their ability to create working mixes that inspired them to perform in a particular way.[17]

Errol Brown claimed that from the audio engineer's perspective, this new recording paradigm demanded the development of new levels of sensitivity and technical skills on the part of the audio engineer. While ensuring that an effective technical representation of the instruments was being captured on tape, the audio engineer was also required to provide a working mix of the music that encapsulated the vibe and feel that inspired recording participants. However, from the audio engineer's perspective, providing a great vibe and a good technical recording represented two sonic goals that were often diametrically opposed.

Several musicians and audio engineers pointed to Steven Stanley as the epitome of the audio engineer as the 'vibe specialist'. Attributes of Stanley's recording approach during the 1980s and 1990s included high-volume monitoring levels, precise instrument balances and a particular attitude toward the recording process that many found inspirational. Cleveland Browne describes Stanley as an audio engineer with an acute sense of rhythm and groove, able to 'make the riddim dance'.[18] In addition, Stanley is well known for periodically breaking into wild fits of dancing during the recording session interspersed with periods of intense concentration. Based on my own experience, this appeared to be Stanley's way of confirming that the mix was moving in the desired direction but also helped to maintain a studio atmosphere that I would describe as energetic, vibrant and inspirational.

While questioning Gregory Morris, one of the new generation of audio engineers whose work is featured in Chapter 9, I asked him about the audio engineer's ability to create a good vibe during recording sessions. Morris responded, 'Have you ever worked with Steven Stanley?', suggesting that Stanley represents the benchmark of Jamaican 'audio engineering vibe', a position that is perhaps reflected in both Stanley's international and local success, and in his influence on a generation of JPM recording practitioners.[19]

Some informants added that another important attribute of an audio engineer was an ability to make accurate punch-ins and correct any performance errors during the recording process.[20] This ability was identified as important for the

---

[17] I use the term 'working mix' to describe the balance, sound and treatment of instruments and voices that is created by the audio engineer to facilitate the changing needs of the recording process.

[18] The term 'dance' in this context suggests that the riddim compels the listener to move in response to the sound and this is considered to be an important attribute of JPM, particularly dancehall music.

[19] Comments regarding the vibe created by Steven Stanley were also made by James Peart, Robbie Lyn, Peter Ashboune and Cleveland Browne. Stanley is perhaps best known for his work with the group Talking Heads and their 1981 release *Tom Tom Club* for which he is credited as co-producer and co-writer on the song 'Genius of Love'.

[20] See Cleveland Browne's comments in Chapter 7, pp. 00–00.

process of creating and performing spontaneous musical parts, a particularly important attribute from the perspective of hunt and peck performers. The practice seems to have been facilitated but also refined by the fact that both musician and audio engineer were now working side by side and the audio engineer was able to see as well as hear when the punch-in should be performed. Despite the fact that musicians expected the audio engineer to create a 'wicked vibe' in the recording session, he was also expected to make accurate technical recordings and, as Errol Brown notes above, these two goals were often in conflict.

During my interview with Gregory Morris in March 2008, I asked: 'If you noticed your level meters on the mixing console are overloaded, but you are in the middle of recording an instrument or vocal track, what do you do?' Morris answered: 'It depends on the vibe – if a singer is really hyped-up in the middle of a vocal track there is no way you can stop the session to readjust levels unless the vocal track is obviously distorted.' Morris suggested that when trying to create a vibe in the studio, volume levels did sometimes get pushed into the red. It was therefore a question of establishing a good working mix that produced the desired recording atmosphere while ensuring that the recording was free of audible distortion. In Morris's opinion a 'perfect recording is meaningless unless it captures that good vibe'.

The testimony of my informants suggests that both audio engineers and musicians began to assume new roles in music production during the 1980s. Studio musicians identified a growing need for the audio engineer to create good instrument balances, spatial effects like reverb and echo, at the appropriate amplitude and with the appropriate emphasis on low-frequency content as an aspect of the recording process. In the new linear-recording model, the audio engineer now helped to provide the vibe that had previously been produced by multiple musicians performing together as a rhythm section.

This change in the role of the audio engineer during the 1980s established his position as a collaborator, working alongside the musician/programmer in the new linear-recording model. Some traditional audio-engineering tasks, such as the electronic manipulation of instrument sounds, were increasingly performed by the musician, while some musical tasks, such as the arrangement of instruments, were increasingly performed by the audio engineer in the final mix – two concepts that will be discussed in greater detail in the following chapters. The dramatic change represented by the move of the musician from the studio to the control room is perhaps best appreciated by comparing recording practices that predate the introduction of multi-track recording to Jamaica. Edward Seaga is one of the few surviving music producers who were active in the late 1950s.

In my interview with Seaga in 2008, I asked him if musicians played any role in the decision-making process while recording during this period? Were they invited into the control room to listen to the completed recording and asked for their opinion? Seaga pointed out that on the occasions he recorded music, it was the audio engineer and himself who decided when the recording was complete. Musicians were then informed that the session had ended; they were paid but were not typically invited into the control room to listen to or comment on the recording. Graeme Goodall and Errol Brown, during their respective interviews, supported Seaga's claim, but Brown added that musicians started to gain more access to the studio control room with the introduction of multi-track recording and the evolution of increasingly complex over-dubbing strategies, culminated in the linear-recording model of the 1980s.

Informants such as Robbie Lyn, Cleveland Browne, Sly Dunbar and Errol Brown, have provided crucial information in this chapter regarding changes that took place in recording practices in Jamaica during the 1980s, which were particularly prevalent in the production of dancehall music. They speak from a position of authority, as an elite group of music professionals who were not only successful in the reggae genre that dominated the 1970s, but were able to make a successful transition to dancehall music that came to dominate the 1980s, 1990s and beyond. While their testimony confirms that some areas of music production may have been simplified as a result of the new instrument technology, they also suggest that others areas became more complex. There is clearly a need to reassess the roles of musicians and audio engineers in the context of the new linear-recording model that emerged during the 1980s and establish a thorough understanding of a music production process that underwent a dramatic transformation.

Chapter 7

The Riddim Production Method:
The Audio Engineer as Music Arranger

As previously discussed, the 1980s saw a dramatic change in JPM with the integration of new instruments, performance and writing approaches and the serial recording model. In addition, the riddim, as an autonomous backing track over which multiple songs could be recorded, emerged as the central framework for music creation and production, yet the fundamental principles on, which riddims function is yet to be fully assessed. This chapter focuses on a unique characteristic of recorded riddims and the way in which they are interpreted and reinterpreted by the audio engineer through a process of performance-mixing. A detailed description is provided of how the mixing console becomes an instrument for the creation of multiple musical arrangements and the introduction of new musical elements, in the form of engineered rhythms, created by the audio engineer.

A Framework for Assessing Riddims

Any discussion of post 1980s JPM needs to consider the use of riddims and how the roles of recording participants changed. A general categorization of riddim types and their function is also presented here, not as a definitive guide but as a means of assisting the reader to grasp the rationale behind this unique system of producing music. Despite the significance of riddims in post-1980s JPM, they are often discussed in general terms with the notable exception of Peter Manuel and Wayne Marshall's 2006 paper, entitled 'The Riddim Method: Aesthetics, practice and ownership in Jamaican Dancehall'. These authors explore the historical development and use of riddims, documenting many details of the way in which they were employed. This chapter, in part, builds on their work but also diverges from it in a number of significant ways.

Manuel and Marshall describe the use of riddims as part of a 'riddim-plus-voicing' system, where multiple songs can be released on a single riddim but also where 'on occasion, the same voicing may be released with different riddims' (2006, p. 448). I contend that the ability of music creators to move vocal tracks between riddims is generally a product of working with samplers or computer-based recording with audio content stored in the form of data files, often manipulated by the computer's keyboard and mouse. These hardware interfaces, by definition, interrupt the practice of what I term 'performance-mixing', where the audio engineer creates a spontaneous musical arrangement for a sound recording using the mute controls of the mixing console. From my perspective as a music practitioner, the practice of moving audio tracks and sounds in the form of data files implies the use of a distinct recording model where the mixing console is no longer the primary mechanism for altering the musical arrangement.

The nature of recording, based on digitally stored sound files and their inherent ability to be moved, muted, looped, time stretched and pitch-changed, through a graphical and hardware interface is at odds with the general practice of riddim production during the 1980s and much of the 1990s. During this period, riddims are distinguished by their integrated live musical performances, captured serially as analogue recordings, employing the punch-in facility of the tape recorder and the creation of musical arrangements as a product of performance mixing.[1] In addition, the infinite number of recording tracks and non-destructive editing that computer recording offered, removed many of the limitations that had helped to maintain a particular creative path in the creation of pre-computer riddims. Although riddims continued to be employed with the introduction of computer recording, in my view, their usage, production and exploitation is significantly different and warrants a separate discussion, in part, addressed in the following chapter.

Further, I contend that the manipulation of a vocal track between different pieces of music, as suggested by Manuel and Marshall, has an association with 'remixing'. In this process the song remains the central creative element, which the music tracks serve. Riddim production is by definition, the antithesis of this process. I contend that 'remixing', while consistent with a wide range of popular music styles is not typical of dancehall music production during the 1980s and 1990s in Jamaica. In my judgement it represents a foreign music production strategy that should be separated from the general discussion of riddims during this period. As previously stated, Jamaican music production practice during the 1980s is distinguished by a focal point that moved from the song to the riddim, representing a revolutionary change in local music creation, performance and recording strategies. I therefore discuss riddims and their evolution as a distinctly Jamaican music-creation and production system, and the terminology I employ is different from that used by Manuel and Marshall.

Despite these differences, the work of Manual and Marshall is significant and represents the opening of an important dialogue that focuses on riddims and the purpose that they serve in Jamaica. This and the previous chapter, along with Manuel and Marshall's discussion therefore responds to Curwen Best's criticism that Caribbean music research is 'not concerned with going beneath the surface of the finished recorded product in order to interrogate the process of technical construction' (2004, p. 2).

---

[1] I use the term 'integrated live musical performances' to identify a specific form of music capture that is distinct from the 'cut and paste' method of computer recording, which integrates sample loops, all of which can be digitally manipulated and then assembled into various pieces of music. I acknowledge that the line that divides these production methodologies is sometimes hard to define.

Categorizing Riddims

The task of defining and describing different types of riddim is made difficult by the fact that they exist as strands of musical creativity and production practice, woven loosely together, which have the potential to be employed in a complex matrix of music genres, sub-genres and hybrid styles, largely isolated within the realms of Jamaican culture but not isolated from it. With this in mind, I acknowledge that there are significant variations in the way that riddims are created and used, but it is appropriate to define them broadly into three primary groups:

1. **Song-derived riddims**: Riddims that were originally recorded as a backing track for a specific song, such as many of Coxsone Dodd's Studio One recordings. Many of these backing tracks or more commonly, a musical element of their creation, were later used as the basis for what I term 'song-derived riddims'.[2]
2. **Beat-derived riddims**: Riddims that are composed as autonomous music backing-tracks, intended to be used as a template on which multiple songs can be written or adapted to, such as the 'Sleng Teng Riddim', discussed in earlier chapters.
3. **Hybrid riddims**: These riddims are composed to sound like beat-derived riddims, but are created and produced with a specific song or small number of songs in mind. This would include riddims such as the 'Rumours Riddim' used for Gregory Isaacs's song 'Rumours' and J.C. Lodge's 'Telephone Love' (Music Works, 1988), where each vocal track, although performed over the same riddim was accompanied by the performance of unique instrument parts, specific to each singer and song. This group would also include some sound recordings by international dancehall-music artists such as Shaggy and Sean Paul. Although produced to sound like beat derived riddims, their production is often guided by different values and the recording of multiple songs over the riddim is treated as a marketing tool for the primary song.

There is a fundamental distinction that should be made here between the local and foreign exploitation of JPM that employs riddims. Locally, artists commonly record vocal performances over beat-derived and song-derived riddims, which are non-exclusive pieces of music and often have ambiguous creative origins and ownership. This recording practice, with its inherent issues of authorship,

---

[2] An example of a song derived riddim is 'Murder She Wrote' (Taxi, 1992), performed by Chakadimus and Pliers. This song's backing track was based on a riddim derived from the song entitled 'Bam Bam' (Dynamic Sounds, 1966), commonly referred to as the 'Bam Bam Riddim'. Most interpretations of this riddim include the bass line melody, harmonic structure and vocal hooks. However the original song performed by Toots and The Maytals was not created using the riddim production method, as described here.

is generally considered unacceptable by the international recording industry. Therefore, locally produced music intended for the overseas market has largely been based on hybrid riddims.[3] However, beat-derived riddims represent the creative epicentre of JPM and, in terms of the themes discussed in this chapter, are the principal point of focus.

The Origins of Performance-Mixing

The riddim-production method (RPM) is a term I use to describe the process for creating beat-derived riddims, suitable to be used with multiple songs, in the hope of becoming a hyper-riddim and representing the predominant local method of producing JPM between 1980 and 2005. In the RPM, the mechanism for tailoring an arrangement of recorded instrument parts to meet the needs of a particular song and vocal track is achieved through 'performance-mixing'. The RPM therefore describes a specific music creation, recording and mixing system that emerged during the 1980s, based on the following criteria:

- The creation of a backing track intended to be used for multiple songs.
- The use of the drum machine as a template to which instrument parts are performed.
- The use of rhythmic, harmonic and melodic instrument parts in the form of short repetitive phrase, which are repeated but also varied. Although percussive instrument parts were typically created as a sequenced one-, two- or four-bar loop, harmonic and melodic parts, even when repetitive, were typically performed live for the four-minute period, which marked the maximum duration of a popular song. Because of the intentional and unintentional variation that could be included in these instrument parts, I chose not to employ the term 'ostinato' as used by Manuel and Marshall to describe these performances.
- The musical arrangements provided for individual songs and vocal tracks are achieved through the use of the mixing console, using the mute function to add or remove instrument parts.

---

[3] There are examples of song-derived riddims being used in the international market, for example, Dawn Penn's 'You Don't Love Me' (also known as 'No No No') originally recorded by Coxsone in 1967, rerecorded by Steely and Clevie in 1994. This production has been mired in litigation over the ownership of the intellectual rights embodied in the song's backing track. Coxsone Dodd, as the original producer, has claimed ownership along with the musicians who performed on the original recording as well as Steely and Clevie, who created and produced the 1994 interpretation. As a result, foreign record companies are cautious about signing Jamaican artists and productions unless the origins of all the creative aspects of a sound recording are accurately assigned and substantiated.

- The musical arrangements that result are typically a spontaneous creation of the audio engineer, made in response to a vocal track.

The RPM, in part, can be considered a product of the new emerging technology because the digital drum machine, in conjunction with the increasing use of 16- and 24-track recorders, allowed individual instruments, but especially drums to be captured independently, void of microphone leakage, as previously discussed. As a direct result, the audio engineer could alter instrument and drum arrangements, using the mute controls of the mixing console, in a way that was not possible with live drums. The style of dancehall music most commonly associated with, but not limited to, the RPM contains the following:

- A prevalence of the deejay (rapper) as vocalist.
- A repetitive musical structure based on a one-, two- or four-bar sequence.
- A focus on sound and/or drum beats as a featured hook or element, often providing the unique identity for a riddim.
- The exclusive use of electronic keyboards, samplers, synthesizers and drum machines to create all the musical parts.

'Performance-mixing' describes a spontaneous mixing strategy that initially evolved and developed with the creation of dub and version B-sides but was later adapted to the mixing of riddim-based dancehall music. Dub and version B-sides represent two distinct Jamaican recorded-music forms that were typically created as the by-product of an A-side, 45 rpm record. The version B-side is best described as an instrumental mix of a 45 rpm record's A-side, whereas dub involves a dramatic reinterpretation of the A-side, through a process of mixing, where the voice track is muted and the instrument tracks are presented as a new and independent musical work.

The performance mixing of riddims discussed in this chapter differ from the above because it represents a mechanism of extracting multiple A sides from a single backing track (riddim) over which multiple singers have performed different songs. The strategy for the performance mixing of riddims therefore not only demands that the audio engineer demonstrates a musical sense but is capable of musical interaction and the formation of sounds and rhythmic elements that respond to the given vocal performance and the structure of the lyric. This chapter focuses on and explores this phenomenon in some detail.

I asked Errol Brown about the origin of performance-mixing strategies and their link to dub and version B-sides. Brown claimed that he was unaware of these mixing approaches being introduced by any individual but claimed that multi-track recording offered a potential for extracting different interpretations of a recording, which was attractive to the sound system. Brown suggests that these mixing approaches were the product of different audio engineers exploring the new technology in the context of the sound system's needs. Brown trained as an audio engineer working under Byron Smith at Treasure Isle and after Smith's departure assumed full audio engineering duties for the studio. Brown explains that Sonia Pottinger purchased the Treasure Isle studio from Duke Reid in the early 1970s and asked Brown to help find ways of generating income from the existing Treasure Isle recording catalogue. Brown explains that albums such as *Treasure Dub Volume I* (Treasure Isle, 1974) and *Treasure Dub Volume II* (Treasure Isle, 1974) were created in response to this request and represented a method of extracting additional revenue from existing sound recordings with very little additional expense for the owner of the sound recordings.

Brown, as the audio engineer, was given complete control over the selection of material and how it was mixed, but on the condition that the resulting albums were produced when the studio was not otherwise engaged in commercial recording sessions. As such, both dub and version B-sides represent unique and significant JPM products that feature the creative interpretation of existing music tracks by the audio engineer, who acted as the technician, musical arranger and creative performer.[4] This is a significant point because, although dub and version B-sides did not typically have the revenue earning potential of the A-side, from which they were derived, they established the concept of the audio engineer in a new creative role as a musical arranger, able to generate new derivative recorded works from existing sound recordings.

Errol Brown explains that the economic restraints associated with mixing dub forced the audio engineer to explore the technical limits of the recording studio and his own artistic ability. In a 2001 interview with Steven Stewart, a seasoned music professional who has worked as both musician and audio engineer, he highlights the imaginative ways in which audio engineers crated new sonic textures despite having limited resources. For example, some audio engineers achieved punctuation in their mixes by splashing reverb onto the sound of a percussive instrument while synchronizing the physical lifting of one side of the reverb unit and dropping it.[5] This would cause the reverb springs to hit the side of the reverb tank causing an explosive sound that the manufacturers of these units expressly advised against. In the free-form rearrangement of music tracks that characterized the mixing of dub and version B-sides, the audio engineer was able to freely explore these new and often unconventional sounds and resulting musical textures. As such, the audio engineer became a performer, using the mixing console as an instrument to rearrange and sonically reshape pieces of pre-recorded music through the tools that the studio provided.

It is not clear how performance-mixing was integrated into the RPM, but by the start of the 1980s sonic textures associated with dub and version B sides, such as copious use of reverb and echo, were finding resonance with the drum machines potential for allowing radical reinterpretations of recorded music tracks, as

---

[4] See Veal's thorough discussion on the audio engineer exponents of dub (2007).

[5] The term 'splashing' is used to describe the effect when a large amount of reverb is applied momentarily to an instrument. The technique is not intended as a repositioning of the instrument in the sound stage but as a sound effect used for musical punctuation.

discussed previously. In addition, the growing practice of recording multiple songs, in the form of a vocal performance and lyric, over a single riddim, encouraged the use of performance-mixing, as a convenient way of altering the recorded instrument tracks so that they complemented the respective vocal performance. However, whereas performance-mixing for dub and version B-sides was a free-form creative process with no restraints, the same was not true of mixing a riddim and vocal performance which was intended as an A-side of a 45rpm record.

The A-side was the primary musical work from which revenue was derived and as such, the vocal track represented a critical component, which dictated the creative direction of the mix. The recorded instrument tracks that collectively represented the riddim therefore needed to be mixed in a way that related to and supported but also enhanced each respective vocal performance. Performance-mixing therefore employed dub and version B- side mixing strategies but applied them in a new role, helping to integrate multiple vocal performances with a pre-recorded riddim as cohesive pieces of commercial music.

Steven Stewart explained that with the introduction of reusable riddims, applying performance-mixing to the production of A-sides, in the support of a vocal track, introduced a number of challenges for the audio engineer. For example, natural occurring spaces between vocal lines, where previously an instrument phrase might have been performed, now had to be filled by the audio engineer who might add echo to the last word of the vocal line, in effect using sound to compensate for the absence of an instrument part. It should also be pointed out that vocal performers also responded to these perceived spaces by freely ad-libbing vocal sounds as a means of compensating for the absence of arranged instruments that inevitably resulted from the use of generic riddims.

The Mechanism of Performance-Mixing

Before looking closer at ways in which performance-mixing was applied to the production of multiple songs on a single riddim, it is appropriate to consider the primary sound-altering tools at the audio engineers' disposal. The performance-mixing process is dependent on individual instruments and voices being stored on independently recorded tracks, captured serially with an absence of microphone leakage. Each recorded track is fed to an independent channel on the mixing console where the audio engineer can alter the sounds of the respective instrument in a number of ways. Typically this includes:

- Muting: where the recorded track can be switched on or off.
- Level: where the volume of the recorded track can be adjusted with a fader control.
- Pan: this positions the instrument in a stereo field from left to right.
- Equalization: where the sonic timbre of the recorded track can be changed prior to or during mixing.

- Auxiliary send: where a variety of outboard effects such as reverb and echo can be added to the recorded track before or during mixing.
- Group fader: a number of selected recorded tracks can be assigned to a single or pair of group faders and then the above facilities of muting, level control, equalization and applying effects through an auxiliary send can be applied to this group of recorded tracks from the grouped channel(s).

These represent the primary tools found on a mixing console that are employed by the audio engineer to conduct performance-mixing.

The process of mixing represents a complex set of actions that vary according to the material, studio and audio engineer. For the purpose of this chapter my intention is only to provide a broad outline of mixing approaches, as they pertain to performance-mixing and prior to the introduction of computer based recording systems. The following is based on information provided by my informants but also my observations over a 30-year period during which I have witnessed, taken part in and conducted a significant number of mixing sessions.[6]

At the start of a mixing session the audio engineer establishes a principal balance of the recorded instruments that make up the riddim and adjusts the frequency content and dynamics of each instrument. The audio engineers I interviewed had a preference for balancing instruments, starting with the kick drum and bass, paying particular attention to the frequency ranges of these important instruments and the way in which frequency influences the rhythmic pulses contained in the recorded performance. However, the sequence of balancing instruments was largely a function of the material being mixed and could vary accordingly. As additional instruments are added, any perceived issues regarding their sound or unwanted sounds are corrected and they are positioned in a stereo field, using the pan control available on each mixing console channel strip.

When the basic instrument balance and stereo image is established, the audio engineer integrates the vocal tracks treating them sonically with dynamic and spatial processors and frequency filters. On completion of this process the audio engineer will assign a number of outboard effect processors to the auxiliary send/return controls on the mixing console. Typically, these might include a range of reverbs, delays or other effects, which are each assigned to a respective send/return control on the mixing console.[7] This represents the means by which the audio engineer is able to apply sound effects to individual recorded instruments, and allows him to adjust the respective send control on the instrument channel, which increases or decreases the level of the sound effect in relation to the recorded instrument sound.

---

[6] This includes mixing sessions for Bob Andy, Big Youth, Mighty Diamonds, Yellow Man, Toots Hibbert, Richie Stevens and Black Uhuru.

[7] The process of identifying and assigning processing and sound effects can be performed at any point in the mix preparation process and varies greatly depending on the individual preference of audio engineers.

The approach to mixing, commonly found in North America and the UK, was one of slowly crafting instrument parts into a complex collage of layered sound, on occasion demanding that the mix be recorded to master tape, one section at a time, and then physically edited into a composite master recording. The introduction of automation on mixing consoles was a response by mixing-console manufacturers to a demand for increasingly complex mixes, involving multiple pairs of hands rehearsing sonic alterations via the mixing console's controls. The introduction of automation allowed alterations in the mix to be made one at a time and stored, providing the audio engineer with the potential of building up and creating a complex mix that could be accurately recreated and recalled at a later date. This allowed and perhaps encouraged mixing to be conducted over an extended period and was both time consuming and expensive.[8] However, this approach was largely rejected in Jamaica and was at odds with the mixing process as a live performance.

The Audio Engineer as Music Creator

In the RPM, performance-mixing became the mechanism for not only creating the final balance of instruments and applying effects, as described above, but was also used as a method for spontaneously arranging the musical instruments, as an improvised accompaniment for a specific vocal performance. However, the mixing console's mute controls were also employed to create entirely new audio-engineered rhythmic structures. These new rhythmic elements were derived from the sound of existing instruments and are locally referred to as a 'mix', but for the purpose of this discussion, I will refer to them as an 'engineered rhythm'.

Engineered rhythms are not only unique to JPM but epitomize the significance of the audio engineer and the unilateral freedom that he enjoyed as a musical auteur. Engineered rhythms are created by the audio engineer turning on and off the mute controls of all, or selected, recorded instruments, treating them as a single sound element used to create a new rhythmic phrase. The switching process is performed by the audio engineer with a rhythmic structure that synchronizes with the tempo of the recorded instruments. By creating these engineered rhythms the audio engineer applies a secondary level of musical interpretation, strategically altering the sonic texture of the sound recording, with the ability to introduce tension and release that help to define the riddim in relation to the vocal track.

Use of engineered rhythms became so popular in the mixing of dancehall music during the 1980s that musicians were required to replicate the effect during live performances. Based on the testimony of my informants as well as my own experience, a backing group would typically agree on a palette of engineered rhythms (mixes) to employ during a live performance and then, under the spontaneous direction of the group's musical director or vocalist, would perform those engineered rhythms in imitation of how the audio engineer employed the

---

[8] See discussions in Cunningham (1996) and Warner (2003).

mute controls in response to a vocal track during performance-mixing.[9] This has also resulted in the recording of imitated engineered rhythms, performed by the musician when recording music tracks and, as such, represents a complex relationship between live musical performances and performance-mixing that remains largely undocumented. This process represents an ongoing exchange of creative ideas between musicians and audio engineers, which is not unique to Jamaica but is uniquely manifest in the RPM.

The application of engineered rhythms during performance-mixing is the product of the audio engineer's assignment of individual instruments to grouped channel on the mixing console. For example, all of the drums except the hi-hat might be grouped together. This allows the audio engineer to not only mute individual drums from their individual channel strip, but to also mute all of the drums, with the exception of the hi-hat, using a single mute switch on the grouped-drum channel. The audio engineers that I interviewed confirmed that the main purpose of grouping instruments was to provide dramatic changes in the musical arrangement and for creating engineered rhythms.

Most informants did not subscribe to any set system for grouping instruments and suggested that each decision was made intuitively, at the start of the mix. Decisions were, however, based on the audio engineer's assessment of what function the grouped instruments should provide within the riddim, how this related to the vocal track, and what the feel and vibe of the song seemed to dictate as dance music.

The mixing strategy for dancehall music was therefore typically a process of balancing the recorded instruments and voices, selecting sound effects and assigning them to send/return channels, and assigning specific instruments to grouped channels. Performance-mixing was then undertaken, primarily based on the manipulation of the mute and send/return and fader controls as the recording was being played. This was captured as a two-track master on analogue tape or DAT. Although the final mix might be rehearsed a number of times with the audio engineer trying different combinations of instruments, engineered rhythms and effects, my informants emphasized that their manipulation of the controls of the mixing console remained largely spontaneous and improvised, described by Errol Brown as: 'It's a vibes thing' (a process based on vibe). My analysis of the examples, offered below, and the testimony of my informants were consistent with what Michael Veal describes as the audio engineer's use of 'the mixing board as

---

[9] My performance experience includes the 1992 and 1993 world tour for the Reggae Sunsplash franchise working with Papa San, Barrington Levy, Carlene Davis, Marcia Griffiths, Freddy McGreggor and John Holt, other international touring experience, and local performances with Tiger, Wayne Wonder, U Roy, Dennis Brown, Maxi Priest, Richie Stevens, Beenie Man, and Bounty Killer. It is interesting to note that even though some of the above artists are not considered exponents of dancehall music, they employed and encouraged the groups I worked with to include engineered rhythms in their performances, apparently as a means of helping their material appeal to younger audiences.

an instrument of spontaneous composition and improvisation' (2007, p. 78), in his discussion of dub.

Performance-mixing is therefore not only a device where the audio engineer creates the music arrangement for an array of songs and vocal tracks, recorded over a single riddim, but also the process by which he creates and introduces new musical elements in the form of engineered rhythms and this has had a significant influence on the development of JPM.

The Analysis of Performance Mixing

Michael Veal's book *Dub* provides an important contribution to the study of Jamaican audio engineers and their impact on JPM. Veal extracts information from a number of dub mixes through a process of musical analysis and textual description of the sonic elements located in sound recordings. Although Veal provides an invaluable insight into the world of dub using this methodology, I have selected an alternative approach for the analysis and comparison of performance-mixing, which could also be applied to the analysis of dub. I have designed a method for analysing performance-mixing in the context of, and with consideration for, how the RPM is enacted.

In this analysis method, the riddim, as a repetitive musical sequence is broken down into its component instrument parts and scored using standard notation, which acts as a general reference for the individual instrument parts, which in practice could include variation. I have chosen to represent the performance-mixing arrangement in the form of a graphical grid, employing a timeline measured in beats and bars and list of instruments on the two axes. In the analysis of the recording, I notate on the grid where and when each respective instrument is audible or muted; this traces the audio engineer's manipulation of the mute controls on the mixing console.

I have chosen to limit the grid to the display of the muting of musical instruments by the audio engineer, although it could be adapted to include perceived changes in individual instrument levels and the use of effects. My intention is to provide a clear sense of the audio engineer's creativity and musicality rather than an exhaustive discussion of performance-mixing, which would go far beyond the limits of this chapter. The grid is a representation of the way in which audio engineers appear to conceptualize music and provides a graphical overview of the engineered musical arrangement and application of engineered rhythms. These can then be assessed and compared in the context of the different vocal performances that they serve.

The graphic interpretation therefore provides a clear sense of how the audio engineer relates to the mixing console as a musical instrument, and the mute controls as the keys of that instrument. The audio engineer conceptualizes the mix in sound textures that are made up from a single or sub-groups of instruments, and the application of muting is typically not sensitive to the musical phrasing of individual instrument parts. Although sound effects such as reverb and echo are applied to individual instruments and voices to provide the spatial characteristics of the sound recording, they are also employed during performance mixing to create new textures and musical punctuation.

The sound effect elements have not been included in the following examples, which focus on demonstrating how engineered arrangements and engineered rhythms are applied to a single riddim. I reason that standard music notation would be an ineffective and potentially misleading method for representing performance-mixing, because of the way in which it often ignores the structure of musical phrases, with the muting of some instruments occurring mid-note. In addition, engineered rhythms create new rhythmic parts from existing rhythmic structures, as described above, which from the audio engineer's perspective are treated as a sound generator without rhythmic form.

The point I wish to stress is that whereas the musician is sensitive to phrasing and rhythmic connection of individual instruments within the musical form, the audio engineer is focused on groove, sound and the way in which these elements connect to the vocal performance. The audio engineer in the creation of engineered rhythms shows no hesitation in discarding notions of individual instrument phrasing if the sound of the resulting engineered rhythm is considered pleasing.

The recordings and riddim chosen as a subject for study are taken from an album entitled *Sleng Teng Resurrection: Various Artists* (VP Records, 2005). It is not clear, based on the album credits, if the compact disc employs the original recording of the 'Sleng Teng Riddim' (made on analogue multi-track tape), part of it, or a re-recording of the riddim on a digital recording system. The recording does appear to employ the Casio MT-40 keyboard, which has a particularly distinctive bass sound. During analyses of the various mixes that make up the compact disc, the bass sound and drum sound were consistently heard together. This suggests that the original Casio keyboard and its inability to separate drum and bass sounds were employed.

The album features 17 different songs, the first of which is Wayne Smith's song 'Under Mi Sleng Teng' but featuring the deejay Bounty Killer. The other 16 songs on the compact disc each feature different singers, performing different lyrics and melody over the 'Sleng Teng Riddim'. The authorship of each composition on the album is credited with the music writers 'L. James Snr/I. Smith/N. Davy' and then the respective name of the lyricist for each song. There are no credits listed for the musicians who performed and programmed the riddim or the audio engineer who mixed, and therefore musically arranged, each song. However, the mastering engineer is listed.

I have selected two songs for analysis: The song entitled 'High Grade' by the singer Taz, which features the deejay Marvellous, and the song entitled 'Dancehall Style' by the singer Luciano. For the purpose of this study, only the first 16 bars of each song are compared. The basic instrumentation includes: drum machine, (kick drum, snare drum, hi-hat,) synthesized bass, synthesized piano playing a bang figure, a synthesized pad sound and synthesized horn sound, muted throughout these two examples.

The 'Sleng Teng Riddim' is based on a one-bar, two-chord repetitive vamp in the key of D major.[10] The tempo is approximately 86 bpm but the pitch of each song on the compact disc was 50 cents sharp of concert pitch.[11] There are a number of possible explanations for this, including the possibility that the speed of the master recording was increased or decreased to create a new tempo or that the electronic instruments were not calibrated to concert pitch. The musical parts are as shown in Example 7.1.

The 'Sleng Teng Riddim' is a good introductory example of performance-mixing because the drums and bass are tied together on a stereo track and therefore limit the amount of possible variation using the mute controls that the audio engineer can perform. For these particular examples the audio engineer is controlling only four different mute switches on the mixing console, but this is unusual and typically all of the drums and bass would be recorded on independent tracks. The mixing-derived musical arrangement is laid out for the following examples in a grid of blocks, each block representing one crochet beat in common time. Each grey-tone represents one recorded track on which an instrument or group of instruments are recorded. Each recorded track is fed to a channel of the mixing console with the facility to mute or un-mute the track, as described above.

An absence of shading indicates that the track is muted, whereas shading indicates that the track is un-muted and audible. It is also appropriate to note that, in 'Dancehall Style', the kick drum, snare, hi-hat and bass tracks are highlighted in bars 3 and 4. This tone of shading indicates that an engineered rhythm is being performed by the audio engineer, as described above.

The following analysis grids provide a clear indication of how the audio engineer employs a musical sensibility to rearrange the musical components of the riddim, spontaneously muting and un-muting them in response to each vocal performance. These are rearranged to meet the demands of each respective song and vocal track, manipulated as blocks of sound (see Figures 7.1 and 7.2). These examples are not intended to provide an in-depth analysis of performance-mixing, but to demonstrate the musical creativity and sensibility that audio engineers were required to develop in the mixing of dancehall music. Analysis of the recordings from which the above grids are made indicates a creative and imaginative use of the mixing console's mute switches by the audio engineer. The physical dexterity and sense of timing that are employed within the confines of an existing rhythmic

---

[10] It should be noted that the key might be interpreted as modal and mixolydian with the presence of a C major chord. However, Jamaican musicians, including Noel Davy, refer to the riddim as being in the key of D major, and treat the C major as a passing chord that emphasizes the use of the flat 7. Some vocal melodies conform to the mixolydian mode while others employ D major and avoid the C♮ or C♯ in their melody structure.

[11] The mechanism for establishing tempo was noted in Chapter 1. Pitch was established by loading the song into a waveform editor and the pitch was digitally adjusted until it was consistent with concert pitch. The difference between the original and new pitch was then measured and I estimate is accurate to within ± 10 cents.

Example 7.1   The 'Sleng Teng Riddim'

a) Drums

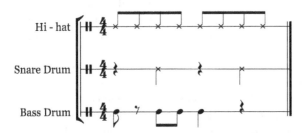

b) Bass

c) Piano bang

d) Synthesizer pad

structure have much in common with the performance of a musical instrument. The analysis grid clearly demonstrates how the audio engineer shapes the sound of a recording through the manipulation of recorded instruments and the creation of engineered rhythms, performed by turning the mute switches on and off in synchronization with the timing of the recorded music.

The use of muting and un-muting becomes an effective tool for creating tension and release in the above examples. In Figure 7.2, bars 11 and 12 mark the end of the first chorus leading into the first verse at bar 13. To emphasize this transition the audio engineer mutes the drums and bass, leaving only the piano bang and synthesizer pad audible, creating a sense of tension. That tension is increased for

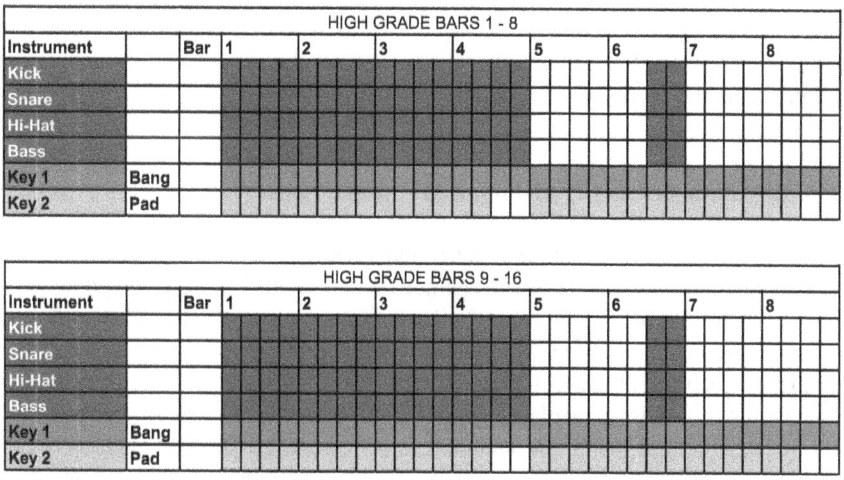

HIGH GRADE BARS 1 - 8									
Instrument		Bar	1	2	3	4	5	6	7	8
Kick										
Snare										
Hi-Hat										
Bass										
Key 1	Bang									
Key 2	Pad									

HIGH GRADE BARS 9 - 16									
Instrument		Bar	1	2	3	4	5	6	7	8
Kick										
Snare										
Hi-Hat										
Bass										
Key 1	Bang									
Key 2	Pad									

Figure 7.1   The 'Sleng Teng Riddim': 'High Grade'

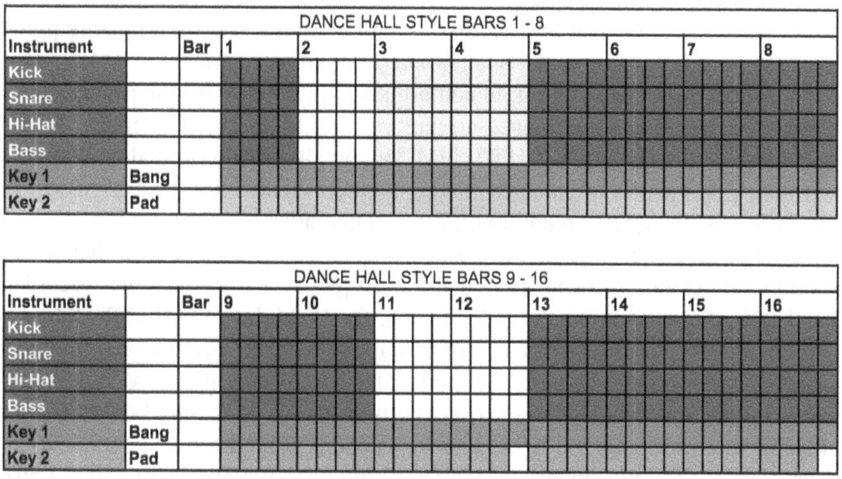

DANCE HALL STYLE BARS 1 - 8									
Instrument		Bar	1	2	3	4	5	6	7	8
Kick										
Snare										
Hi-Hat										
Bass										
Key 1	Bang									
Key 2	Pad									

DANCE HALL STYLE BARS 9 - 16									
Instrument		Bar	9	10	11	12	13	14	15	16
Kick										
Snare										
Hi-Hat										
Bass										
Key 1	Bang									
Key 2	Pad									

Figure 7.2   The 'Sleng Teng Riddim': 'Dancehall Style'

the last beat of bar 12 by the muting of the synthesizer pad, leaving only the piano bang audible. A distinct sense of release is then achieved and coincides with the start of the first verse at bar 13, as all the instruments are un-muted by the audio engineer.[12] A significant point to make here, is that the audio engineer mutes the

---

[12] The term 'hook' is used here to indicate a phrase or section of an instrument or vocal line that is intended to be catchy and memorable to the listener.

drum and bass after they play the first beat of bar 11, imitating how musicians might perform that transition, rather than muting at the conclusion of the musical sequence on the fourth beat of bar 10.

The Rhythmic Sensitivity of Jamaican Audio Engineers

I asked Cleveland Browne what performance-mixing represented to him as a dancehall music producer. Browne claimed that the control of the mixing console's mute switches, in particular, were similar to playing a percussive instrument, and accurate control demanded a musician's sensibility, especially evident in the control of recorded live instruments. These live instrument performances tended to sometimes anticipate or play behind the beat as a way of creating tension with the sequenced drum parts and included small variations. Browne suggested that Jamaican audio engineers had acquired a highly developed and precise sense of rhythm that was needed to work effectively in performance-mixing, and this is especially apparent during the mixing of a recording that includes both sequenced and live instrument parts.

Browne also pointed out that the audio engineer needed to have a considerable amount of self-confidence to perform these mixes, not dissimilar to that required by an improvised instrumental solo, where in addition to technical and creative competence, there is a need for an authoritative attitude toward the performance. Browne stated that performance-mixing represents a critical element in the commercial success of post-1980 JPM, but it also demonstrated a rhythmic sensitivity on the part of Jamaican audio engineers that is not always evident in the work of their American and European counterparts.

I asked Browne if he could describe any personal experiences that might support this claim. Browne offered the example of a song that was recorded for the North American singer Billy Ocean, for which he and Wycliffe Johnson had been contracted by Ocean's record company to write, perform and produce. Browne explained that he and Johnson had been booked into a New York studio to record the vocal for the production and were therefore required to work with an audio engineer from the USA. Browne explains that after the vocal track had been recorded and the singer had left the studio, they noticed a distracting noise between two words, positioned close together, on the lead voice track. Browne instructed the audio engineer to use the record function on the multi-track tape machine to erase the sound between the two words. However, this would have required that the audio engineer punch in and out of the record mode very quickly and precisely to ensure that the vocal part was not damaged.[13] Browne claims that despite authorizing this action, as the producer, the audio engineer insisted that

---

[13] Punch in or out is the term used to describe the process of starting or stopping recording, typically used during the crafting of a musical performance where one musical phrase might be poorly executed and needs to be replaced.

the punch-in was not possible, claiming that it would damage the lead voice track. The audio engineer suggested correcting the problem by bringing the singer back into the recording studio to perform the vocal line again. Browne asked the audio engineer to move from the mixing console and proceeded to perform the punch-in edit successfully, without damaging the vocal. Browne claimed that this type of edit would not have been questioned by a Jamaican audio engineer, and was made possible by an acute sense of timing that Jamaican audio engineers seem to acquire working with dancehall music.

Browne claimed that this ability was based on a highly developed rhythmic sensitivity that many Jamaican audio engineers acquired as part of their day-to-day functions, working with JPM and performance-mixing in particular. The demand for musically accurate timing, combined with their comfort in using the recording equipment as a creative performance tool, ensured that audio engineers played a critical role in the creation and production of dancehall music. The ability to perform accurate punch-ins is also an important element in maintaining a spontaneous flow during the recording session and, prior to the introduction of computer recording, represented an essential skill that Jamaican audio engineers were required to develop and master.

In this chapter and, indeed this book as a whole, the arguments I make for recognizing the significance of musicians and particularly the audio engineer's influence on the development of JPM can be best appreciated by comparison of a Jamaican audio engineer's practices with those of his US counterpart. In an October 2001 interview with Roy Halee for *Mix* magazine, Blair Jackson discusses Halee's work with Simon and Garfunkel and Bob Dylan during the 1960s. Halee is asked: 'What was the separation between producer and engineer in those days?' Halee responds: 'The producer calls the shots in the studio. He was running the session, and the engineer followed along. He was considered a good engineer if he didn't get in the way' (p. 34).

This description is clearly at odds with the recording practices described in this and the previous chapters. In the above discussion of performance-mixing, we see that the Jamaican audio engineer assumes a musically creative role through his arrangement of recorded sounds and his creation of engineered rhythms. In addition, he also assumes a production role through his editing of sound and choice of textures that are presented in the final mix, a duty often shared by musicians. These processes clearly represent some of the creative and technical avenues through which the audio engineer has influenced, and continues to influence, the development of JPM.

A Transition in Music Production Financing

The testimony of Cleveland Browne and Errol Brown is significant in this chapter because they describe a music production process in post-1980s JPM where the line that had separated audio engineer and musician becomes harder to define.

The extended responsibility of musicians now included the ownership of new and constantly changing technologies as well as finding creative ways that these technologies could be applied to the production of local music. This new environment not only reduced the cost of studio time but made it increasingly difficult for financiers of sound recordings to maintain the established payment schemes of work-for-hire that had dominated the production of earlier JPM genres. As a result, recording practitioners such as Browne were increasingly tempted to finance, produce and commercially exploit their own music.

I asked Browne to describe his work experience as a musician/programmer before establishing his own production company and how the new linear-recording model of the 1980s influenced his transition from a work-for-hire musician to self-employed producer. Browne claimed that many of the recording sessions on which he worked as a musician/programmer were conducted without a creative producer, and it was often the musicians and the audio engineer who fulfilled the production duties for the session. Browne claimed that this not only meant taking responsibility for creating the riddim but also included directing the singers who performed over the riddim.

In addition, dancehall music, like preceding genres of JPM were created without the use of musical scores and musicians were expected to spontaneously create the musical parts that made up the sound recording. As a result, the production of a record was dependent on the musician and audio engineer's performance and creative abilities. Browne claimed that the audio engineer became responsible for helping to select and capture the appropriate sounds, and in addition to performance-mixing, provided an important, independent perspective for the musical ideas as they were being created in the recording studio control room.

The testimony of Browne reflects a long tradition in the development of Jamaican popular music, which Derrick Harriot notes in his interview with Lloyd Bradley, stating, 'nearly all of them [the producers] were guys with some money and, to be perfectly frank, they hear a song and think that it's a good song but they have no idea what to do. They depended on the musicians to put it all together for them' (Bradley, 2000, p. 230). Although Harriot recognizes the limitations of some Jamaican producers, he makes the common assumption that it was the musicians who, single-handedly, filled that role, with no mention of the audio engineer. Browne also points out that the absence of an active producer meant that most recording sessions were conducted without sound references, allowing the audio engineer a substantial level of freedom regarding his personal choice of recording methods and sound-crafting techniques.[14]

In regard to the production of riddims, Browne describes a growing alliance between musician/programmer and audio engineer who jointly filled the role of producer but were typically unaccredited for their effort and continued to be paid

---

[14] It is common practice for the producer to provide the engineer with audio references of the sounds and type of mix that they want to create and use. For example, the audio engineer might be told to replicate the snare or kick drum sound of an existing recording.

on a work-for-hire basis. This system of remuneration evolved from a working practice, previously discussed, where a group of musicians created a spontaneous piece of music during a recording session, which was captured by the audio engineer. The selection of recording participants by the recording financier was, in part, based on their willingness to perform writing, arranging and production services without additional payment or credit. However, in the new linear recording model, creativity was now concentrated in the hands of one or two musicians who also owned the instruments and sounds on which music production depended. It became increasingly difficult for financiers to justify a work-for-hire arrangement where they not only assumed ownership of the sound recording but the intellectual property it embodied and was associated with.

Browne describes an experience after he began working with Wycliffe Johnson and the establishing of their music production team known as Steely and Clevie. During the 1980s they enjoyed considerable success working for a number of producers including Lloyd James (Prince/King Jammy). One of their music productions commissioned on a work-for–hire basis by James was licensed to Walt Disney Pictures and used in the animated motion picture *The Little Mermaid* (1989). According to Browne, he and Johnson were the writers and producers of this piece of music, yet James credited himself as performing these roles. Browne claims that he and Johnson asked James for a share of the performance and mechanical royalties resulting from the international sale of their work, but James refused to comply on the basis that the work-for-hire payment represented full compensation for all creative involvement.

This issue eventually came to a head with James when, at the start of a recording session, instead of assuming the role of music creators, Browne and Johnson asked James, as the 'producer', what he wanted them to play. Browne explains, 'there was a deafening silence', which resulted in the termination of his and Johnson's working relationship with James, and Browne claims that they were blacklisted by a number of other Kingston-based producers. Browne explained that the effort by music financiers to block his and Johnson's attempt to assert their intellectual property rights acted as a catalyst for formalizing Steely and Clevie as a music production company and building their own recording studio. They would become one of the most successful production houses in the dancehall-music genre both locally and internationally during the following decade.[15]

I asked Browne if he thought that the reluctance of producers to acknowledge and provide production and writing credits was on account of them misunderstanding how the international music industry functioned. Browne responded that this might be the case for some producers, but made the point that if a producer has registered an overseas publishing company, it implies an understanding of the

---

[15] Browne pointed out that even though James was an excellent audio engineer, much of his work at Jammy's studio was done with other audio engineers such as Bobby Digital (Robert Dixon). This was because James was increasingly involved in managing other areas of what had become a substantial business.

concept of intellectual property and the respective rights attached to that property. These rights represent the commodity for which publishing companies are set up to administer and trade. Browne offered examples where his own creative work had been appropriated by the financiers of recording sessions who claimed to have written and produced it without, in some cases, even being present during any part of the recording process.

Browne sums up the situation by saying, 'You go into the studio with a blank tape and come out with a piece of produced music on that tape; someone in the studio must have created it'. This is a difficult and contentious problem that not only takes centre stage in any discussion regarding JPM, but also has yet to be critically evaluated as a force that has significantly influenced the way in which JPM was created and developed. The changes in music-making technology and recording practices during the 1980s and 1990s had a significant impact on the way in which JPM was financed, and one of the important bi-products of the new technology, largely overlooked, is that it led to creative participants increasingly retaining part or whole ownership of their intellectual property.

The traditional relationship between music financiers and those individuals who provided the creative and technical elements in Jamaica's recording industry is worthy of closer study. It may help to explain why many recording sessions in Jamaica were organized on an informal basis with an apparent lack of creative preparation or pre-production. Browne added that the traditional dependence on spontaneous creation as a centrepiece of music production in Jamaica has not only forced musicians and audio engineers to evolve in a particular way but also to develop strategies for working under what are often difficult situations, including the ability to 'think out of the box'. He comments:

> The producers leave it up to the engineers and musicians many times, whereas overseas you find that somebody who is given the job to produce, they're on it right through to the final takes, so that freedom given to our engineers may have contributed to that phenomenon, ya know, where the freedom allows you to mess around and create new things.

It is significant to note that many of the new dancehall-music 'producers' of the 1980s and 1990s, not only emerged from a music-performance background, like Browne and Johnson; but also came from the ranks of audio engineers, such as Robert Dixon (aka Bobby Digital), and Dave and Tony Kelly. The new technologies and recording models being employed in Jamaica, in effect, transferred a significant level of control and authority away from traditional financiers into the hands of small groups of recording participants on which the creation and successful production of sound recordings now depended.

Although the roles of recording participants changed along with recording processes, these transitions cannot be fairly described as less demanding or creative than the practices and processes they replaced, although they are certainly different. The fact remains that this transition demanded that musicians and audio engineers expand their creative and technical roles, in a process of informal exchange and sharing, which many established recording participants were simply unable to comprehend or accomplish. Moreover, for those who did make the transition successfully, many failed to establish the level of success they had enjoyed with earlier music production practices resulting in some resentment of the new music. It is therefore understandable that ska, rock steady and reggae are often looked back on with nostalgia, while dancehall music has been routinely maligned.

This and previous chapters have broadened and refined the discussion of JPM during the 1980s, the emergence of dancehall music and its dependence on riddims and a new range of technical and creative roles performed by musicians and audio engineers. The use of the RPM, and performance-mixing are examples of the radical way in which JPM has changed. The next chapter considers how these elements were absorbed into digital recording models and the use of computers for the capture and manipulation of sound.

Chapter 8
Computer-based Recording and the Multi-role Producer in the 1990s

This chapter discusses changes that occurred in JPM during the 1990s. It considers the impact of new technologies and, in particular, new audio recording formats and the way in which they altered established modes of music production in Jamaica. The concept of the multi-role producer (MRP) is introduced through the work of Jeremy Harding, who emerged from this period and had a significant impact on dancehall music and furthering the acceptance of the deejay in the international arena. Harding represents the vanguard of Jamaican recording practitioners who pioneered computer-based digital recording and as such grappled with the issues of adapting this technology to serve local needs. He is therefore uniquely positioned to offer an authoritative account on how these changes occurred and the new potential that they offered local creators of popular music.

The Jamaican Recording Industry in the 1990s

Kingston during the 1980s and 1990s had become a dynamic centre for recording with a prolific output of sound recordings for the local and overseas market but also as a recording location for foreign artists. A number of existing studies have considered the impact of the Jamaican recording industry and the high per capita ratio of recording studios on the island.[1] Kozul-Wright and Stanbury report that Kingston (a city of approximately 1 million inhabitants) was home to 'at least 50 studios of which 20 may be classified as major' (1998, p. 17). In my discussion of the early Jamaican recording industry I have already noted that the primary drivers of local popular music production were located in the sound system and sound-system derived record market. The growth in this vibrant recording community began during the 1960s when it was realized that significant revenue could be earned from both local and overseas record markets.[2]

---

[1] According to data analysed in 2008, Jamaica is a small, heavily indebted, middle-income country: a small island state with a population of 2,804,332 and gross domestic product (GDP) per capita of $7700 (at purchasing power parity (PPP)) and public debts totalling 124.1% of GDP (all 2008 estimates). Source:https://www.cia.gov/library/publications/the-world-factbook/geos/jm.html (accessed July 2008).

[2] See John McMillan's paper on industry clustering and the Jamaican music industry (2005).

It is difficult to obtain accurate statistics regarding the productivity of the Jamaican recording industry because as Kozul-Wright, and Stanbury point out:

> There is no accurate count of the number of players in the industry for example, since many companies are neither legal nor taxable entities, often operating from home rather than an official business address. There is a plethora of Jamaican producers and recording studios. (1998, p. 17)

Although Kozul-Wright and Stanbury refer to the state of the recording industry in 1998, I was not able to locate any information to suggest that these circumstances changed during the first decade of the new century. In addition, it should be noted that this attitude towards business is not limited to the music industry. A 2003 *Jamaica Gleaner* article by Christopher Tufton states: 'The Government study released in July this year concluded that at least 43 per cent of GDP in the year 2001, or $155.9 billion, is explained by tax evaders of registered companies, small unregistered companies, and other forms of illegal activities, excluding the drug trade.'[3]

The available evidence therefore suggests that many of Kingston's recording studios operated in an informal manner, possibly to avoid paying taxes. Despite this, they continued to operate openly, and in many cases showed distinct signs of growth, suggesting that they represented profitable commercial enterprises.[4] By the 1980s, many Kingston-based recording studios offered analogue 24-track recording and mixing services, suggesting the existence of a vibrant and prosperous recording industry. This is also noted by John McMillan, who claimed: 'With more than one new recording each year per thousand people, Jamaica could be, per capita, the world's most prolific generator of recorded music' (2005, p. 2).

The operation and function of these recording studios depended on the availability of audio engineers who, according to my informants, typically acquired their training through a studio apprentice system.[5] Most of the bigger recording studios employed at least one full-time audio engineer who became

---

[3] Christopher Tufton, 'Taxes and the informal economy', *Jamaica Gleaner*, 24 August 2003.

[4] The majority of recording studios are privately owned and were very often secondary businesses for their owners, for example Duke Reid, Coxsone Dodd, Tubby's, Black Scorpio and King Jammy's who all ran sound systems, or Tuff Gong, Aquarius, Dynamics and Sonic Sounds who retailed or manufactured records as their primary business. As an informal, cash-based business, the revenues derived from the rental of studio time is likely to be part of Jamaica's 'shadow economy', a term used by Fredrich Snieder. In his study of this type of economy, Snieder states that Jamaica makes up 36.4 per cent of GDP using the DYMIMIC and currency demand method (Sneider and Klinglmair, 2004, p. 12). Therefore, accurate information is hard to obtain regarding the commercial viability of recording studios but their sheer number suggest the existence of a vibrant and profitable industry.

[5] See the discussion with Gregory Morris, regarding his training in Chapter 9.

associated with that particular facility and the sound it produced.[6] For example, Graeme Goodall had an association with Federal Records; he trained Byron Smith, who was later recruited by Duke Reid and became the principal audio engineer for Treasure Isle.[7] Smith trained Errol Brown, as an apprentice, who was later recruited by Bob Marley and became the principal audio engineer associated with the Tuff Gong recording studio.[8]

In order to establish a sense of the changes that took place in the production of JPM during the 1990s, it is appropriate to consider the function of the new technologies, how they were introduced and their influence on the role of music practitioners and audio engineers. It is therefore appropriate to consider how analogue recording influenced the recording process and what impact the introduction of digital-recording systems had on the recording industry.

The Transition from Analogue to Digital

Analogue multi-track tape machines had dominated the Jamaican recording industry since the mid-1960s. Professional machines were prohibitively expensive for personal or domestic use, requiring daily maintenance and skilled operation. The tape machine's transport system had to be cleaned on a daily basis, but it was also necessary to align and calibrate each recording track, consistent with the tape speed and specification of recording tape being employed. In addition, the recording and playback heads periodically needed to have their azimuth adjusted, and undergo demagnetization to ensure an optimum sound-reproduction quality.[9]

Recording on analogue tape also demanded an understanding of the relationship between instrument sounds, their respective frequency content and manner of performance in relation to their optimum recording level and track placement. For example, the use of high recording levels to achieve tape compression was also likely to cause the recorded sound to bleed onto its adjacent tracks, demanding a strategic placement of the recorded sounds onto the tape. Audio engineers working

---

[6] The term 'sound' is being used here in a broad sense meaning that, traditionally, Jamaican audio engineers have learnt their craft by listening and watching with no formal training system (see Chapter 9). The sounds they help to create seem to be based on common principles and recording strategies that, although not documented in any textbook, are understood and shared as a discipline.

[7] Goodall was the first formally trained audio engineer who came to Jamaica in 1954 (as discussed in earlier chapters). He was a member of the American Audio Engineering Society AES, sponsored by Tom Dowd of Atlantic Records.

[8] The information regarding these connections, in the form of training, was discovered during the interviews with Goodall, Brown and later Gregory Morris who was trained by Brown and is featured in the next chapter. It suggests a lineage of training and process of modification that would be fascinating to trace but unfortunately is beyond the scope of this study.

[9] The 'azimuth' refers to the relation of the physical alignment of the audio tape and tape head, which can have an impact on the quality of the recorded sound.

in analogue multi-track recording formats were therefore required to develop a range of skills concerning the optimization of the sound altering characteristics of this recording format, which were largely absent in the emerging digital recorders.

The new digital recorders, although designed to fit the existing recording model, did not need the complex maintenance procedures associated with analogue recorders. They were also less likely to alter the characteristic of captured sound and in my 2008 interview with Michael McDonald, an audio engineer associated with Big Yard Recording Studio, he claimed, 'digital is easy – what you put in is what you get out'. It is appropriate to note that although analogue recorders tended to alter the characteristics of sound, this was utilized creatively by audio engineers and its absence in digital recorders was initially missed.[10]

The first generation of commercial digital multi-track recording systems to be introduced during the early 1980s were prohibitively expensive compared to equivalent analogue systems, and had little impact on the wider music industry.[11] However, by the early 1990s, a new generation of digital recorders began to appear that were significantly lower in cost when compared to the equivalent analogue machines and they employed low cost storage mediums, such as videotapes. These new systems were modular in design and they dramatically changed the way in which music was created, captured and consumed.[12] A headline in the entertainment section of the *Sunday Gleaner*, states: 'Small Studios force HUGE changes', and Teino Evans goes on to write: 'Large, long established recording studios have had to revamp their operations in order to stay afloat as the demand for studio time has declined due to the rise of individual home-based and artiste owned studios.'[13]

The first widely used digital recording system was the Alesis ADAT recording system, which achieved a 'professional recording quality' at a substantially reduced cost compared with analogue multi-track recorders.[14] At the close of the 1980s

---

[10] The sonic characteristic being described here can be termed 'distortion' and as an inherent characteristic of tape recording was largely accepted and utilized by the popular music industry. We therefore see a variety of judgements associated with the reproduction of sound and a persistent view that even the highest resolution digital recordings are perceived by some as being 'cold' or 'harsh' compared to analogue.

[11] This includes: the Mitsubishi 32 track X800 digital – a 1-inch recorder; the CMI Fairlight; and New England Digital's Synclavier music production system.

[12] Digital technology did not depend on the complex mechanical machinery needed to move 2-inch tape consistently at high speed. The new digital recording technology could utilize existing storage formats and therefore the machinery was relatively inexpensive. For example ADAT recorders employed existing VHS technology, while other systems employed personal computer technology running on established operating systems.

[13] Teino Evans, 'Small studios force HUGE change', *Sunday Gleaner*, 21 May 2006, p. 1A.

[14] According to a Mix magazine, memorial article discussing the achievements of Keith Barr the ADAT's principal designer. <http://mixonline.com/news/keith_barr_obit_2508/index1.html> (accessed 1 November, 2010).

an MCI 24-track, 2-inch tape recorder retailed for approximately US$40,000, which did not include shipping to Jamaica and local import duties. The machine weighed 538 lbs and therefore the cost of purchase, shipping, customs duties and professional installation would be in excess of US $ 50,000.

By comparison, in 1992, 24 tracks of the Alesis ADAT multi-track recording system cost US$12,000 and could be imported into the island as checked on baggage and then installed by the average musician with basic technology skills. Whereas the 24-track analogue machine required ongoing service and calibration, this was significantly reduced on the ADAT system. In addition, the ADAT system could be purchased in eight-track modular units priced at US$4,000 per unit, thereby providing musicians with access to an attractive professional sounding recording system that could be readily expanded.[15] Moreover, the cost of the digital media used on the ADAT system was substantially cheaper than 2-inch analogue tape, with a price/performance ratio of 10:1.[16]

Despite these advantages, Errol Brown claimed that the ADAT digital recorder and other modular recording systems were not considered dependable enough for the industrial demands of the professional recording studio, which operated on a round-the-clock basis.[17] It was therefore the owners of home, or small recording facilities who pioneered the transition to digital multi-track recording in Jamaica during the early 1990s and not the established recording studios.[18] The local

---

[15] It should be noted that it is very difficult to acquire accurate data concerning the purchase of musical and studio equipment imported into Jamaica. One reason for avoiding the discussion of this subject is that local customs duties were often avoided. In a *Jamaica Gleaner* article of 13 May 2009 ('Curbing customs fraud'), Collin Greenland, during an interview with Danville Walker (Jamaica's Commissioner of Customs) claims, 'Tax evasion, for example, involves the innumerable attempts to evade either partially or totally revenues due and payable to the Government. The methods attempted include many under-the-table transactions, underinvoicing, fictitious documentation and alteration of genuine ones, as openly bemoaned by Mr Walker since taking over the department for less than a year. Artificial or shell companies involve the setting up of fake companies for the systematic evasion of taxes.'

[16] The details of costs provided here are supplied by informants such as Peter Couch, but were confirmed through a review of music industry periodicals such as *Mix* magazine and *Electronic Musician*. In addition, I drew on my own experience as a music industry participant who built an ADAT-based recording studio in Jamaica, in 1993.

[17] The Tascam DA88 system was considered by some to be a more reliable system that the ADAT system but it was aimed at the film industry. While some professional studios, such as Tuff Gong, acquired these systems, ADAT's proved to be most popular with musicians and small studios in Jamaica. These modular systems suffered from issues regarding the time it took for two or more machines to establish synchronization at the start of play. Because the over-dubbing process demands the repeated rehearsal and playback of small sections of a recording, the synchronization issues made this procedure cumbersome compared to using 24-track analogue tape.

[18] See Curwen Best, (2004) and his discussion of the impact of modular digital recorders in the Caribbean.

embrace of the ADAT system was consistent with other locations and Théberge notes the pursuit of a design 'that positions this product for the semi-professional and amateur home recording market' (1997, p. 249).[19] However, computer-based proprietary recording systems such as those made by Digidesign, as well as non-proprietary systems made by Steinberg, Sonar and Cakewalk also competed in this quickly expanding recording equipment market.

In Jamaica, the new recording systems were initially embraced by producers of music for the advertising industry or musicians who owned drum machines and synthesizers and sought to expand their involvement in music production.[20]

These new recording formats resulted in a steady growth of music practitioners who now came from a diverse range of backgrounds and experiences, but were able to program and/or perform, record and mix their own music. These changes are noted by Paul Greene who claims that this period produced: 'Digital sound editing, effects processing, multi-track recording and MIDI sequencing, practices that have powerfully impacted musical cultures and soundscapes around the world' (Greene and Porcello, 2005, p. 1). This was certainly true of Jamaica, where a proliferation of home studios resulted in the increased availability and lower cost of recording, most evident in the production of dancehall music. Many of my informants felt there was a connection between the new technology and the proliferation and ongoing demand for dancehall music, which proved to be particularly adept at exploiting the creative niches that each new technology seemed to offer.

It is also appropriate to mention that the growth in small domestic recording studios in Jamaica, coincided with a range of exploratory recordings for what is best described as 'alternative music', which freely drew inspiration from North American and European popular music genres during the 1990s. The resulting sound recordings are not easily classified into any existing Jamaican musical genre and although causing a temporary spike of local interest, proved to be commercially unsuccessful and short-lived.[21] Jamaica therefore continued to be

---

[19] Proprietary recording systems meant that both hardware and software had to be supplied by the same vendor. Non-proprietary systems meant that selection of software and hardware could come from different vendors, yet were compatible.

[20] Evidence of this can be found in the work of Peter Ashbourne, Peter Couch, John Williams and myself, who all established home recording/production facilities initially based on IBM 286 personal computers running Windows 3.1 or Atari personal computers during the late 1980s and early 1990s, running sequencer software. I can add that, in addition to the convenience and long-term cost saving of building a recording studio, a main consideration for me was that, despite the large number of 24-track studios available in Kingston, it was very often difficult to book studio time between 10am and 10pm at short notice. This was inconvenient because many audio engineers seemed to dislike working early in the morning and the high crime rates of Kingston was also a concern for some recording participants and corporate Jamaica.

[21] Groups such as the Jamaican Alternative Music Society Ltd were formed in the 1990s representing and promoting a range of locally produced, alternative music styles that had little commercial success.

dominated by dancehall music throughout the 1990s and in 2013 that is still the case, although the shape and form of dancehall music has dramatically changed during this period.

A New Type of Producer

While the growth in digital multi-track recording systems and home studios represented a worldwide phenomenon noted by Théberge (1997, p. 249), the exploration of this technology in Jamaica assumed a unique characteristic. The local dominance of dancehall music by the 1990s and its embrace of drum machines and synthesized instruments meant that, for many, the move from programmer to studio owner/audio engineer, represented a relatively small transition. The music that emerged from these small recording studios was typically the product of one individual, and although that person was often described as a 'producer', they in fact had very little in common with the typical financier of Jamaican recording sessions referred to in earlier chapters.

Unlike their predecessors the new producers performed most, if not every, aspect of the music-production process. This often included financing; designing and construction of the recording spaces; installation and maintenance of the recording equipment; and, finally, the writing, arranging, programming, performing, audio engineering, producing and distributing of their musical products. I refer to these individuals as MRPs and my research suggests that they emerged predominantly from three distinct backgrounds and can be categorized as follows:

1. **Musicians**: Individuals who entered the music industry as a musician and gradually assumed control over other aspects of the music-production process.
2. **Audio engineers**: Individuals who typically trained through the studio apprentice system and gradually assumed control over other aspects of the music-production process.
3. **Non-specialists**: Individuals who became interested in music production through a wide range of influences and by acquiring musical instruments and recording equipment were able to assume the role of the MRP.

It is the non-specialist category of MRP that becomes the focus for this chapter. Their entrance to the Jamaican recording industry was largely a product of the new recording and instrument technologies that became widely available and affordable at the start of the 1990s. My interest in the non-specialist MRP is also based on the fact that having not emerged through the ranks of musician or audio engineer, their approach towards music creation and capture was unimpeded by established modes of music production. The non-specialist MRP therefore seemed likely to approach the use of music-related technologies from an objective and exploratory perspective, not grounded in any pre-existing music-production practice.

During the 1990s, not only did the methodology of music production change dramatically in Jamaica, but also the titles of recording practitioners seemed increasingly inadequate for describing the roles they now performed. This study makes no attempt to provide definitive descriptions of the complex relationships between recording roles, practices and the new technologies, which remain largely undocumented. In fact, there is a need for caution when approaching the study of recording practices in an environment where the application of technologies blur the lines of creative and technical boundaries.

This issue of music-related titles and roles in Jamaica is made more complex by the fact that recording practitioners, irrespective of their function, work experience or commercial success, increasingly referred to themselves as a 'producer'. While the title was perceived as a role of authority and suggested ownership, it only increased the growing sense of ambiguity that surrounded the process of music production. However, these transitions and phenomenon were not unique to Jamaica and Mark Cunningham notes the changing role of recording practitioners in the UK. He cites George Martin who claims: 'Record production is such a different game now ... I started in the business when there were only about ten people in the country who you could describe as record producers. Walk down the street now and you'll find that one in three is a record producer and it's a different technology, it's a different music' (1996, p. 378).

Cunningham's discussion regarding the influence of technology is instructive because his observations can be compared to the Jamaican experience. Cunningham states: 'Brian Eno believes that as musicians increase their familiarization with studio practices and technology behind the recording process, the traditional producer is gradually becoming a thing of the past. This switch, he says, was triggered by MIDI and is now in an advanced stage' (1996, p. 378). Cunningham claims that Eno cites the importance of MIDI and implied use of sequencing, but this aspect of music technology was largely rejected in Jamaica in favour of using live instruments recorded over a sequenced drum program. Moreover, Cunningham's comments are noteworthy because of the absence of the audio engineer as a factor in the demise of the 'traditional producer'. He claims that while musicians '[i]ncreased their familiarization with studio practices and technology behind the recording process', it appears that audio engineers were unable, or chose not to, '[i]ncrease their familiarization with' music creation practices and, like musicians, assume the producer's role.

These comments highlight a critical difference between the recording cultures of Jamaica and the UK. While the new digital technologies allowed musicians in the UK to assume a production role, in Jamaica, musicians and audio engineers had been the primary architects of music production since the 1950s. Therefore, the introduction of the new music technologies to Jamaica did not change the role of musicians or audio engineers but it provided a mechanism for them to assert their ownership of the intellectual rights contained in their creative work and sound recordings. This represents a critical development given Jamaica's historical attitude towards issues of copyright, the ownership of creative works, sound recordings and the inaccessibility and inefficiency of the legal system. In addition, the new technologies also provided a creative freedom that accompanied the self-financing of music production by audio engineers and/or musicians. The non-specialist MRP, like those emerging from the ranks of musician and audio engineer also enjoyed these creative and commercial opportunities. However, unlike their counterparts, they were not constrained or influenced by trying to select and/or adapt new technology to fit established recording models and practices.

The availability and implementation of the new technology therefore had a significantly different impact on the studio culture of the UK and Jamaica, although, on the surface, they appear to share the same dissemination of recording practice, moving from large studios to personal spaces. Unlike Eno's perception of technologies influence in the UK, it was not interpreted in Jamaica as causing the demise of the 'traditional producer', but as the streamlining of an existing production process that increased the potential for intellectual property to be retained by its author.

It is therefore appropriate to note that although this chapter focuses on the emergence of the non-specialized MRP and the introduction of digital recording technology to Jamaica, this represents only part of a complex chain of events that are not easily placed in a chronological order of development and are distinct from the integration of these technologies in other locations. In addition, my research suggests that the introduction and impact of digital recording to Jamaica was preceded by a range of analogue technologies that became available during the 1980s, specifically aimed at the home recording market. I acknowledge that these analogue home studios represented another base from which the new digital technologies became established and out of which MRPs also emerged.

The impact of the new digital technology was felt in all areas of the music industry but, in terms of recording, it appears that music-making became increasingly accessible to the non-trained participant but the same was not true of audio engineering. Although access to recording systems was increased with a removal of the complex technical maintenance procedures that had been attached to analogue systems, professional sounding recordings continued to demand a fundamental understanding of the principles of sound capture: treatment and balance. The general consensus of my informants was that as the twentieth century came to a close in Jamaica, the titles of audio engineer, musician and producer came to imply an individual who commanded a complex range of skill-sets that no longer emanated from one well-defined discipline. With this in mind, the discussion presented here focuses on the act of music production but is mindful of the fact that aspects of musical performance, programming, editing and music arrangement became intertwined with the methodology of audio engineering.[22] The objective of this chapter is therefore to better understand how these relationships worked in the context of JPM and its transition to digital recording formats.

---

[22] See Théberge, (1997); Lysloff and Gay, (2003); and Green and Porcello, (2005) for a discussion of these themes in a wider context.

Jeremy Harding

Jeremy Harding represents one of the new non-specialist MRPs to emerge during the early1990s, becoming a pivotal figure in the Jamaican music industry through his pioneering use of computer-based, digital recording. He was one of the first Jamaican producers to achieve local and international success employing the new technology and, in a 2009 *Mix* online article, Barbara Schultz describes Harding as: 'Perhaps best known as the manager/producer of reggae/hip-hop star Sean Paul, but like many Jamaican producers, he [Harding] does it all: engineering, producing, artist management, programming and playing.' Harding is therefore uniquely qualified to comment on the themes being discussed here.

Harding agreed to participate in my research through interviews and a series of open-ended discussions. He also allowed me to participate in and observe two recording sessions at his private recording studio, where I acted as his engineering assistant. Therefore, the range of information provided in this chapter creates a real sense of Harding's values, experiences and the way in which he integrates music creation and audio-engineering practice as a successful MRP.

During my initial interview with Harding, he explained that he was born in Kingston in 1970 and grew up in what many would describe as a privileged social and economic setting. His father, Oswald Harding, is a distinguished lawyer, academic and Jamaica Labour Party senator who is well known and respected. Harding describes his childhood as one where he was encouraged to achieve high academic standards and was exposed to a broad range of views and experiences. He attended Priory Preparatory School, a private institute at that time, Campion College high school, a public government school, and completed his high school education at Ashbury College boarding school in Canada. Harding then attended McGill University, also in Canada, where he was enrolled to pursue a bachelor's degree in chemical engineering, but after one year transferred to the Trebas Institute in Montreal. Before returning to Jamaica in 1993, Harding completed his studies in a media arts programme, which included elements that focused on the recording industry and music production.

Harding describes his musical training, which began in Jamaica when he was enrolled in the youth programme at the Jamaica School of Music from 1982, and studied music theory, classical guitar and ensemble performance (this is when I first became acquainted Harding, as his guitar teacher). At home, Harding was exposed to classical music but developed a keen interest in a wide variety of popular contemporary styles and, in particular, heavy metal music including performers such as Eddie Van Halen, Steve Vai and Yngwie Malmsteen.

While attending the Trebas Institute, Harding states that he developed a keen interest in contemporary dance music and became a disc jockey working in clubs in his spare time. He claimed that this experience sparked his interest in what he described as 'The art and craft of making popular-music records', and this experience provided him with a broader understanding of how the North American music industry functioned.

The majority of Harding's work as a music professional has been in the field of dancehall music, but despite this, he maintains a keen interest in guitar playing and continues to be inspired by a wide range of popular music. Harding at the time of his interview was acting as the manager for the international dancehall artist Sean Paul. However, he continues to produce music and is involved in the development of other Jamaican artists. In addition, Harding is pioneering a new type of management service in Jamaica, targeted at MRPs and riddim creators such as Stephen McGreggor, who is described by Vivian Goldman in a 2008 *New York Times* article as, 'One of the hottest producers on the Island', and is now signed to Harding's company.[23]

In 2008, Harding completed construction of a professionally designed and built recording studio, located at his home in Kingston, which is used as his private recording facility.[24] This acts as the base for his record label, 2 Hard Records, and his other commercial music operations (see Figure 8.1). Although Harding might not be considered a typical Jamaican dancehall MRP, on the basis of his socioeconomic background, education and wide musical exposure and interests, he is representative of a significant number of Jamaican music practitioners who

Figure 8.1   The main control room of 2 Hard Records (2010). With permission of 2 Hard Records

---

[23] Vivian Goldman, 'For Him, Reggae is the Family Business', *New York Times*, 21 September 2008, p. AR22.

[24] Harding's studio was designed by the New York based Architectural and acoustic design company F.M. Design Ltd, owned by Francis Manzella and was featured on the cover of *Mix* magazine in their 1 February 2009 edition.

do not fit the stereotypical 'sufferer class'. Debra Edwards notes that, 'Harding has been unnecessarily pinpointed on several occasions as "a politician's kid", and has been ridiculed for, "coming from uptown", highlighting a contentious issue evident in a form of social prejudice that Harding admits to having occasionally experienced.[25]

These prejudices have various strands. One is probably simple jealousy, directed against someone seen as coming from a background of relative privilege who has crossed into a world where street-credibility is important, yet who has been notably more successful than most. The other is a common perception that seems to have gained prominence in the 1970s, where a background of poverty was perceived as a prerequisite in order to qualify as a 'real' or 'authentic' artist. However, the reality is that the Jamaican music industry is made up from individuals who come from a wide range of socioeconomic backgrounds, creating a dynamic that runs beneath the surface of local music production and is in much need of further study.

Conforming to the Jamaican Recording Model

During my interview with Harding, he explained that his formal studies in Canada were based on the practice of the North American music industry. He was taught that record companies financed and contracted a recording artist, songwriter, recording studio, audio engineer, creative producer, arranger and musicians to create and capture a sound recording. The record company then manufactured, promoted and distributed the sound recording throughout a specific geographical region and recouped their investment through the sale of records and by licensing the rights contained in the sound recording to record companies in other territories. Harding claimed that the resulting music produced with this model was designed to work with marketing and promotion systems that largely depended on broadcast and print media. Radio, in particular, demanded that music producers and audio engineers comply with a broadly defined set of transmission standards and therefore the techniques of recording and mixing were tailored to meet and exploit these standards in a process described by Harding as 'making records radio-friendly'.[26]

Harding states that on retuning to Jamaica in 1993, he immediately realized that this record industry model did not apply to Jamaican and states:

---

[25] See *Jamaica Observer*, 18 May 2007, p. 4. Harding confirmed his having experienced a range of attitudes, some of which questioned his authenticity as a dancehall music producer on the basis of his relatively privileged social and economic background.

[26] Before the advent of multi-track recording, audio engineers were expected to achieve this sound as the instruments and voice were balanced during the recording process live to a one-track or two-track tape.

> We don't make records according to, like, this was what's on the radio and this
> is the sound that the label is looking for, because it was never about that. The
> records were being made more for, like, this is how it's going to sound on the
> street corner and early producers had sound systems.

Here, Harding not only points out the differences concerning the basis on which
JPM was commissioned, promoted and consumed, but identifies the sound
system as a primary medium through which records had been and continued to be
promoted and consumed in Jamaica.

Harding discussed the predominance of the riddim-production method in
Jamaica during the 1990s and explained the relationship between this method
and analogue recording practice where 'the amount of tracks on your tape would
dictate creatively what you could do with a record'.[27] He explained that after
recording a riddim onto a multi-track tape, seven or eight free tracks might be left
and the financier of the recording would typically use these tracks to record three
independent vocalists with two vocal tracks being allotted to each respective song.

Harding believes that the riddim-production method primarily evolved as a way
of controlling production costs. He suggests that there is an important relationship
between the cost of recording and the potential profit that could be earned from
record sales in the local market. The financier's ability to establish a hit riddim on
which multiple songs could be recorded was therefore an important consideration.
Harding estimated that, on average, it took about two hours to record the riddim,
and two to four hours to record the voice tracks for each song. 'Anything past
three or four hours, the whole room [the studio control room] is going to say OK
you're taking too long.' Here again we see evidence of a spontaneous production
process, similar to that described by Graeme Goodall, from the early 1960s, where
time constraints serve two purposes. One is the objective of limiting recording
costs while the other is intended to harness a spontaneous performance. Harding
describes a scenario where the profit earned from a successful record would have
to cover the financier's operating and recording costs and the cost of unsuccessful
recordings had to be factored into this economic structure.

This production model was aimed primarily at the local market, but had the
potential to generate significant income if the riddim achieved hyper riddim status
and if any of the resulting records were approved for licensing and distribution in
North America and/or the UK.[28] Distribution/retail organizations such as Jet Star,
Greensleeves and VP Records supplied the foreign ethnic markets with Jamaican
records, and occasionally these companies managed to crossover a Jamaican-
produced record into the mainstream popular-music charts of North America or
the UK.

---

[27] Harding is referring to 24-track 2-inch tape.

[28] The main distributors of Jamaican music in these markets were VP Records in the
US and Greensleeves in the UK.

During my interview with Harding, I was interested in discovering how he assumed the role of MRP, and the importance of audio engineering in the range of tasks that he performed. Although Harding had acquired some audio-engineering training at Trebas, he claimed that this was not a prominent feature of the course in which he was enrolled. I was therefore keen to learn how Harding acquired audio-engineering skills and knowledge outside of the established apprenticeship system in Jamaica.

Harding explained that on his return to Jamaica, he was determined to find some kind of employment that would lead to his involvement in music production. However, there seemed to be relatively few opportunities available and the Kingston recording industry, from his perspective, seemed to be controlled by a relatively small number of people who did not display much enthusiasm for attracting or encouraging the involvement of new and younger individuals such as him. Harding describes the Jamaican recording industry, in the early 1990s as being dominated by what were commonly termed 'producers', but claimed:

> Yes, you have studios with engineers but the producers are really more the executive producer type guys that just pay for recordings, they don't really sit there and craft records necessarily with the engineer side by side.

Harding explains that the primary role of producers was to finance the recording process and then to try and profit from that investment by selling records in the local and foreign markets. According to Harding, the audio engineer was primarily responsible for the capturing and crafting of records, but was typically reluctant to share that knowledge with outsiders. He described a tangible air of secrecy that surrounded the recording sessions that he was able to gain access to, and claims that some audio engineers even concealed the identity of particular pieces of recording equipment:

> It used to be sort of a situation actually, where it was a very guarded dark art as to how the records were made. You walk into a session and they see you as a rival, so as you walk in they hit stop on the tape machine and look at you, 'What's up'? Just passing through, they're, like, 'Yeah man, yeah man, ya know, we're just doing a session here with so and so.' You're, like, Cool, and you get this kind of vibe that OK until you leave the room, we're not going to hit play again! Worse when somebody was mixing.

According to Harding, audio engineers played a key role in the development of JPM because of their ability to create particular types of recorded sound, musical arrangements and to introduce new musical elements through the process of performance-mixing. For many audio engineers this translated into what Harding describes as a 'personalized signature sound'. The equipment or techniques used to create this sound were carefully guarded in order to maintain the audio engineer's control over the sound, and thus allow him to enjoy any commercial benefits from work demands that it offered:

> It was really all about, 'Why are you going to show it to everyone else and everybody else can make the same money?' They want to be the, 'in demand' guy, they want to be the top engineer that everyone comes to all the time

Harding explained that the tight control and secrecy surrounding the work of some recording practitioners, led him to consider funding his own music productions using the existing production model. This would have entailed him renting studio time, hiring professional musicians and the services of an audio engineer. However, Harding reasoned that this would not only be an expensive enterprise, but the sustainability of this practice was dependent on commercial success, which could not be guaranteed. Alternatively, Harding could invest his music-production budget in MIDI instruments and one of the new digital recording formats, providing him with his own basic music-production environment. The quality of his music would therefore be limited by his talent and the amount of time and effort that he could invest in developing his audio-engineering, writing, arranging, programming and general music-production skills.

Owning a recording studio allowed Harding to develop and refine those skills and establish an ongoing recording programme, aimed at producing dancehall music for the Jamaican market. The establishing of proficient audio-engineering skills became a primary objective for Harding, based on trial and error but informed by recording-industry literature, the Internet and developing relationships with established music professionals.

Even though the new modular digital, tape-based recording systems by Alesis and Tascam were gaining popularity in Jamaica, Harding decided to purchase the relatively new Digidesign Session 8 recording system. This was one of the pioneering proprietary hard-disk recording systems, based on an Apple or IBM personal computer and comprising both hardware and software. Harding points out that his decision to use what was then considered an unproven technology, in the form of computer-based recording, was in part based on his lack of familiarity with other systems. Harding reasoned that whatever recording system he purchased would demand the same amount of learning on his part, and so his choice of system was based primarily on the performance of the system and its potential to integrate with other emerging technologies.

Harding claimed that the new computer-based recording systems had many distinct advantages over analogue and modular digital recording systems. The price of the hard-disk system, excluding the purchase of the computer, was comparable to a single eight-track ADAT recorder, but unlike the ADAT system it allowed the integration of a MIDI sequencer. I asked Harding if he therefore recorded instruments to the sequencer, which allowed editing and quantization,[29] instead of recording them live, as described by Robbie Lyn and Cleveland Browne in previous chapters. Harding responded 'it depends on the recording project', explaining that sequencers had dramatically improved since the start of the 1990s and that he now employed a sequencer, but also performed some instrument parts live. According to Harding this decision was based on the groove and feel of the music being recorded.

The Digidesign system, although only having eight inputs and outputs, could store and play back a large number of recorded tracks, typically, only restricted by the specification of the host computer. The Session 8 software allowed for random access editing and provided a graphical interface that emulated the functions of a mixing console, including basic sound effects.[30] Despite these apparent advantages, computer-based recording, according to Harding, was initially treated with scepticism in Jamaica. This was in part because of the software mixing-console that was controlled by a mouse and did not allow performance-mixing. By contrast, the ADAT digital recorder could function with a traditional analogue mixing-console, allowing the use of performance-mixing.

Although Harding's decision to purchase the Digidesign system might be considered a risk, given the growing popularity of modular digital recording systems in Jamaica, it ultimately proved to be an astute choice.[31] Computer-based recording not only increased in worldwide popularity during the 1990s, but the Session 8 system employed a design architecture that would evolve into the Pro Tools recording system. Harding was able to upgrade to the Pro Tools system, which would emerge as a recording industry standard during the 1990s. Harding therefore, represented the vanguard of those who made the transition to computer-based recording systems in Jamaica and seems to have been the first Jamaican producer to employ the Pro Tools recording system, providing him with a distinct competitive advantage over many of his rivals.

Harding points out that one of the advantages of the new computer-based recording systems was that their software-based mixing console allowed the mixing process to be automated, saved as a file, and then updated over the course of a number of recording sessions and recalled at will. According to Harding, the

---

[29] Quantization is the optional process of rhythmically standardizing manual drum programming to a predetermined division of the bar based on standard note durations. The accuracy of the quantization is derived from the pulse per crotchet (ppqn rate), which the design of the sequencer or drum machine provides. Higher ppqn rates provide more possible subdivisions of the beat.

[30] The editor can move between various locations in the sound file without the need to rewind or fast-forward as in a linear editing system such as audiotape. As a data file, random access editing allows the audio content to be manipulated using cut, paste, copy and undo.

[31] The main issue here is concerned with the flexibility of the recording system in terms of outside producers being able to work with Harding's recording format, but also Harding's ability to function and work on his own music projects outside of his own studio.

inclusion of this automation feature in Pro Tools encouraged the crafting of mixes and the move away from the spontaneous process of performance-mixing. In Pro Tools, detailed and refined adjustments could be made to a mix using the computer keyboard and mouse over multiple mixing sessions. Several versions of the mix could now be created, each tailored to the needs of the media on which it was to be played. This facet of computer recording would have been especially useful for an inexperienced audio engineer such as Harding, as he began to record and mix his own music productions. The system's 'undo' function allowed for the correction of mistakes and gradual refining and perfecting of audio engineering approaches. Therefore, computer-based recording opened a new range of creative opportunities and failsafe mixing strategies, which were not available on competing recording systems.

Although the Pro Tools mixing-automation facility was highly valued outside Jamaica, established local music practitioners initially rejected it, in part because it was not suitable for performance-mixing. Harding described a scenario where musical arrangements, achieved through performance-mixing, represented a principal component of the RPM; however, as a spontaneous process, performance-mixing depended on the tactile interaction of a physical mixing console. Harding eventually overcame this difficulty by purchasing a Yamaha 02R digital mixing console, which provided the tactile physical mixing console interface, but operated through the Pro Tools automation system. Harding claims that established audio engineers in Jamaica saw this hybrid mixing system as a poor substitute for the traditional large format analogue mixing consoles that continue to dominate the big established Kingston studios.[32]

The challenge of reconciling computer-based recording with practices associated with the RPM was therefore largely pioneered by Harding. He might be considered the first of a new generation of MRPs who employed music production methods that, for the first time, can be accurately described as 'digital' or 'computerized'. Harding, in effect, developed a hybrid form of capturing and mixing dancehall music using this new technology while maintaining the established local values of 'vibe' and 'feel' on which dancehall music depended. Harding explains that a significant advantage of the Pro Tools automation system was that it allowed him to accurately target specific mixes at different forms of media, such as the sound system, radio or television.[33] This would prove to be an important asset in the changing media market of Jamaica during the 1990s.

---

[32] Mixing consoles, were traditionally designed in what was termed a, 'large format', which allowed a number of individuals to sit comfortably at the console and conduct the mixing process. In addition, the length of fader travel was different, which altered the perceived sensitivity of volume changes. The new smaller consoles, such as the Yamaha 02R, were designed to be used by a single operator, but with the benefit of automation. For audio engineers familiar with large format consoles, the small format felt restricted and uncomfortable.

[33] During the 1990s there was a significant increase in the number of local radio stations that began to operate in Jamaica and increasingly featured dancehall music. In addition, music videos became a popular method of promoting music.

Harding claimed that the process of recording and mixing music on a computer was initially not taken seriously by the local recording establishment, who viewed it as a trend or novelty. Established Jamaican music professionals were largely sceptical about the application of computer recording despite the significant impact that these systems were having in North America and Europe. Harding felt that this attitude was, in part, the product of ignorance regarding the principles of digital recording – a reluctance to change or modify existing recording practices – but perhaps most significantly, it was the product of a general lack of computer literacy in Jamaica at that time. Underlying this is the fact that Jamaican music practitioners saw no need to follow changes in technology simply on the grounds that they were popular elsewhere.

Harding's development as an MRP is informative because he describes a competitive and commercial music industry operating in Jamaica during the 1990s in which audio engineering played a central role. This is evident not only in the process of sound creation and performance-mixing, but also in the need to adapt the sound of dancehall music to a wider range of media, including radio and television. In addition, Harding explains that effective audio-engineering skills were essential for a successful MRP because there was an increasing demand for music productions to establish a personalized sonic signature, especially in an environment where everyone had access to the same drum machines, samplers and synthesizers.

Harding describes a Jamaican music industry where the focus 'was not about spreading knowledge but about establishing control over a specific set of sounds', and if those sounds proved successful, everyone then came to you in order to gain access to them. In this sense, audio-engineering practice became a principal skill that the MRP was required to master in order to become established in the dancehall music community. Harding felt that, at the time of his entrance into the Jamaican music industry, the lack of peer support, high cost of renting studios and hiring musicians made music production a high-risk enterprise. The new technologies not only offered him an alternative pathway into music production, with greater sustainability, but his success was, in part, dependent on his ability to harness this new technology and adapt local sounds and musical values into an expanding range of media that was moving beyond the sound system.

The Significance of Local Radio

During the 1990s there was a growing need for successful records in Jamaica to not only be effective when played on a sound system, but also on domestic radio. A dynamic growth in the number of local radio stations changed the way in which dancehall music was promoted and, according to Harding, this new focus on radio provided him with what might be considered a competitive advantage over other producers. It allowed him to utilize his formal training and experience as a disc jockey and focus on producing a 'radio-friendly' sound, for which the

Pro Tools system proved to be an important asset. The ability to save and retrieve, and update mixes at will, made it easy to work on multiple songs or multiple versions of songs, and move back and forth as creativity, need or 'vibe' dictated. In my interview with James Peart in August 2010 he commented on a sense of liberation that Pro Tools provides to the user and explained that when working on a song, 'the vibe just takes me to lay a track on a next song and with Pro Tools I can do that, and when I'm finished, go straight back to working on the first song'. Peart describes how the Pro Tools system allowed him to work on multiple music projects in a seamless spontaneous manner, which not only contributed to his productivity but also changed the way in which he made production decisions.

Dramatic and subtle changes could now be made to a song production and then saved as a new version of the song in the session file. In the event of a critical mistake, the file could be discarded and the original reopened but the system also allowed the user to 'undo' a series of actions, similar to the undo function found in a word processor. This allowed the operator to make unlimited attempts to perfect technical and creative processes before saving them as part of the session file. In this sense, computer-based recording offered a music production environment that was forgiving of the inexperienced audio engineer and music programmer in a way that was impossible with analogue or modular digital recording systems. The Pro Tools system therefore provided Harding with an effective method of perfecting his audio-engineering and music-production skills, while offering him a distinct competitive edge over his rivals. The system provided him with the opportunity to produce finely honed mixes, customized to the demands of different media formats.

Harding also realized that there was a need to tailor the sound of his recordings to a form that would be considered appropriate in the music markets of North America and Europe, representing his ultimate commercial goal. He describes a significant investment of his time and resources, experimenting with different types of equipment, samples, synthesized sounds and mixing strategies in order to establish mixes that could project well on the various types of media that reproduced his music products.

Harding describes how his first hit record in Jamaica was noted as having a 'clean, radio-friendly sound', and the assumption of many was that this was a characteristic of the Pro Tools system. However, Harding confirms that this was not the case, claiming that the real difference in the sound of his music was derived from the way in which Pro Tools allowed him to manipulate and craft sound as a data file and explore a variety of interpretations. Harding claims that his early success was described as the 'digital computer sound' with which he became associated and represents the first accurate use of these terms to describe a local sound recording. Ultimately his association with this sound and the commercial success he enjoyed helped him to become one of the, 'in demand guys'.

I asked Harding for an example of one of his productions that encapsulated the above discussion and he referred to the song 'Who Am I' (VP Records, 1998) by the dancehall artist Beenie Man. This song was a significant hit in Jamaica but also experienced commercial success in the North America and UK markets. The song was released on Harding's 'Playground Riddim' (1997), receiving substantial amounts of radio play locally and abroad, but it was also a hit on Jamaican sound systems. According to Harding, the UK-based radio disc jockey David Rodigan felt that Harding's sound was so distinct that he located Harding's telephone number and called to commend him on the quality of his radio mixes.

It is significant that Harding identifies human agency, in the form of audio-engineering practice, as a critical factor, which he employed to solve a range of issues concerning sound, its replication and consumption on different types of media. By developing a thorough understanding of the Pro Tools recording system, Harding was able to refine the sound of his music productions so that they achieved significance in a wide range of locations, thereby increasing his potential for commercial and creative success.

Harding emphasized the growing importance of radio-friendly mixes in the production of JPM and a growing trend for promoting dancehall music through this medium. According to Harding, many dancehall producers were familiar with mixing for the sound system and, although local radio stations would accept and play their music, this was not the case in North America. As the manager of Sean Paul, Harding describes the type of response he has encountered when talking to radio-station personnel and record-company executives in the USA. He claims:

> When I have to bring the records to them, you know the radio station guys are saying, and even the labels, 'We can't play this! We love the song, but the mix is horrible!', and a radio station is not afraid to tell a label they think it's horrible. 'I like the song, I like the artist but I can't play this beside a Britney Spears or Justin Timberlake or whoever, sonically it's just going to make my radio station sound really crappy.'

Harding's testimony highlights issues that are significant for the international success of JPM by identifying differences in the values of music production and consumption between North American and Jamaica. He notes the difficulty associated with creating music that maintained local relevance, particularly for dancehall music, but was also able to find acceptance with North American radio programmers. He also notes a change in the consumption of music in Jamaica, during the 1990s, where dancehall music found growing acceptance on local radio despite the difficulties associated with obtaining airplay in North America. The important point that Harding makes is the vital role that sound plays in the commercial success of a sound recording and how traditional musical performance was increasingly being replaced by the need for a sound recording to register a sonic impact on the listener.

It seems likely that Harding's formal training and experience as a disc jockey in Canada, in addition to his decision to engineer his own sound recordings with Pro Tools, had sensitized him to the vital importance of sound. Working from a perspective that understood North American and Jamaican sensibilities, Harding was able to try and bridge the gap that separated these two sonic value systems and produce music that was successful in both local and foreign record markets. Harding, in effect, employed his audio-engineering and music-production skills to harness the potential of computer-recording formats, and tailor them to the riddim production method, in doing so dramatically changing the way in which dancehall music was made.

It is notable that the sound with which Harding became associated was not described as the 'Harding sound' but as the 'computer sound', suggesting a perception that is focused on the technology rather than those who direct its usage.[34] In addition, it should be noted that the name 'Playground Riddim' was not derived from a song that was featured on the riddim, but was chosen by Harding who decided to identify his riddims as independent and autonomous creative works. It is not clear whether Harding was the first to start this practice of providing the riddim with an independent name, but it emphasizes the central importance that riddims had assumed in JPM and the ability of the riddim creator to assert authorship of the riddim as an autonomous work, a practice that is now common. The subsequent success that Harding enjoyed, both locally and overseas was cause for many to re-evaluate their approach to music production in Jamaica, evident in the growth of computer recording systems during the late 1990s and beyond.

Finding Musicality in Dancehall Music

As discussed in Chapter 5, dancehall music is criticized in Jamaica for a range of perceived social, moral and musical failings, often evidenced by its unconventional approach towards the pitching of vocals and use of diatonic harmony. To the establishment, the emergence of the non-specialist MRP was seen as a further decline in musical values representing not only a rejection of established recording models but also established musical concepts and production values in favour of what might be described as an, 'intuitive approach', to making records. To provide a sense of the shape and form that this perceived 'musical decline' assumed it is appropriate to highlight some of the changes that became evident. They include the use of major-key harmonic progressions to underpin minor-key vocal melodies or vice versa. In addition, some vocal melodies were performed in unrelated keys to the riddim over which they were recorded and poorly pitched vocal performances often seemed to make it onto the finished record. It also became common in Jamaica for international hit songs, written with multiple chords and distinct multiple section arrangements, to be performed by dancehall singers, who maintained the original melody over a repetitive two-chord harmony structure causing what many perceived as abrasive discordance.

---

[34] As mentioned earlier, this terminology was used in a derogatory way by some music professionals, although based on Harding's testimony the terms were also employed to describe a difference that was perceived in his music.

An example of this can be found in the Tracey Chapman song 'Fast Car' (Elektra, 1988), which was originally performed in the key of A major, employing the chords D major, A major, F♯ minor and E major, arranged as two independent progressions to form a multiple part song. The song was adapted locally by Wayne Wonder (1989), but performed in the key of D major, with the same melody but performed over the 'Taxi Riddim', based on a repetitive D major to A major, chord progression.

While the reggae establishment objected to, and ridiculed, this unconventional use of melody and harmony, assumed to be the product of musical illiterates, it was, however, welcomed by Jamaican music consumers. They embraced this new, and often-discordant sound and as a result, many music producers, irrespective of their background and training, were encouraged to accept and at times employ this unconventional use of melody and harmony in their work. While this area of JPM production remains largely unexplored, it is also contentious where established and new notions of what constitutes 'good popular music' clash.

What we see during the 1990s is the establishing of new harmonic boundaries based on the riddim-production method, where multiple songs were performed over one riddim, using performance-mixing as a music-arranging tool. It is also important to point out that whatever deficiencies were perceived in the unconventional use of harmony and melody, rhythmic content was often complex, with a strong, groove-based sensibility incorporating engineered rhythms and dynamic sound textures. While it is clear that some of the new recording practitioners had limited musical understanding, in terms of music theory or performance, I contend that this does not mean that their use or misuse of harmony, melody and rhythm was unmusical. So little research has been performed in this area that it is difficult within the confines of this study to say more than that this represents an area in desperate need of further investigation.

It would be fair to say that dancehall music's use of rhythmic structures is less contentious than its use of harmony and that this in part might be the product of its primary function as dance music. I was particularly interested in discussing how Jeremy Harding, as a producer whose values are anchored in urban and dancehall music featuring the drum machine, approached the concept of rhythm and sound.

During my discussions with Harding It became apparent that he was in the process of preparing to record live drums, which were to be edited and sampled for use in his personal drum library. I therefore offered my services as an engineering assistant, adjusting and changing microphones in the recording studio based on Harding's instruction from the control room. Participating in the recording process was instructive because Harding's selection of microphones, preamps, processing and instructions for microphone placement offered a sense of his values as a recording practitioner. Harding came across as an audio engineer/musician/ producer with a highly developed sense of hearing evident in his direction to the drummer and the sounds he created. The attributes that Harding demonstrated were far removed from the image of the stereotypical dancehall producer and it became apparent that he had a precise and detailed image of the sounds and musical textures that he set out to capture and edit into samples .

During the course of these sessions I had noticed that there were a number of different drum machines available in the studio and asked Harding: 'Why do you have so many drum machines, is it because they each offer a different range of sounds?' Harding explained that the drum machines were not kept for their sounds but because 'different machines, programmed with the same beat and drum sound produce grooves that feel different'. Harding claimed this had an important impact on the sound of the riddims he produced and therefore different machines were used to create different rhythmic templates in his music. He also suggested that this perception of drum grooves and the interaction of drum machines was common in the production of urban music, which included rap and hip-hop.

Although initially sceptical of this claim and the highly nuanced perception of rhythm that it implied, Harding's comments are substantiated by the manufacturer of the Logic 9 sequencer software (Apple Inc.). The July 2009 release of the Logic software included an option for programmers to emulate the rhythmic feel and groove of different drum machines, including the models employed by Harding. It therefore seems apparent that Harding is not the only musician/programmer who is sensitive to the rhythmic nuances produced by drum machines, and it is reasonable to deduce that the sensitivity to the rhythmic grooves that he describes is shared by a range of popular music creators that the Logic software caters to.

Harding's comments are reason for pause and consideration, because he describes a use of technology that includes a highly developed sense of sound, timing and groove. While this was applied to the rhythmic characteristic of the drum machine it also represents a perception that could be applied to live performance and was reflected during the live drum recording sessions in which I participated. In effect, Harding implies that some dancehall music has a complex underlying structure, highly sensitized to rhythmic feel and groove, which is far from simple and is in much need of further study. Harding's testimony highlights a fascinating use of sequenced sounds with a focus on rhythmic nuances that may exist in earlier forms of JPM, but are yet to be documented.

The significance of Harding's comments are that they demonstrate the existence and utilization of 'global perspectives' as noted by Greene (Greene and Thomas, 2005, p, 2), in which some Jamaican music practitioners continued to explore, adapt and selectively apply technology to meet specific local demands. The variations in the characteristic timing and groove of drum machines, as highlighted by Harding, and the way in which they influence the performance of live instruments, using the RPM, adds a new dimension to Charles Keil's discussion of participatory discrepancies. The information provided by Harding suggests that this concept might be expanded to include the increasingly complex, mathematically derived rhythmic templates that are employed in partially programmed music such as dancehall music.

Although Keil's observations are made in the context of non-programmed music, Harding brings attention to a style of live musical performance, typically employed in dancehall music, which is derived from, and influenced by, machines that have the potential to imitate the way in which humans create rhythmic grooves.[35] Harding stresses a facet of drum machines, implied by informants in earlier chapters, claiming they have a significant impact on the way in which musicians interpret musical ideas and, ultimately, the sound of the finished riddim in dancehall music. Harding's selection and adaptation of this technology suggests the existence of an underlying range of local musical values that are significant, but yet to be fully explored.

A Difference in North American and Jamaican Sensibilities

Jeremy Harding represented a valuable informant for my research because he had operated at the highest levels of commercial success in both Jamaica and North America, as well as having an intimate understanding of the relationship between creativity and technology in the process of music production. I asked Harding if he could identify specific differences in the attitudes of Jamaican and North American audio engineers and the sounds that they tended to create. He responded: 'The Jamaican sound is produced for the street corner and foreign sound is produced for the radio.'[36]

Harding explained that producing music for traditional forms of music consumption in Jamaica provided both challenges and opportunities for the audio engineer. He identifies a sense of freedom on the part of Jamaican audio engineers who, traditionally, were not constrained by the strict sonic confinement associated with creating radio-friendly mixes.[37] He acknowledged that during much of the 1990s, the dancehall still represented the main arena in which local records had to be accepted in order to attain commercial success, although the use of radio was becoming more prominent. Records were increasingly being promoted on local radio and through music videos, but they still had to meet the sonic standards set by the sound system. Speaking from his perspective as a MRP, Harding adds:

---

[35] See Keil and Feld's discussions in *Music Grooves* (2005, p. 96), but I also note that whereas Keil and Feld discuss complete musical performances, Harding refers to a performance of a musical fragment made from a two- or four-bar rhythmic template in which the musical groove has to be established.

[36] Harding explained that by 'the street corner', he meant the sound systems and other forms of music consumption found in the music reproduction systems of automobiles, record shops and domestic music systems. In Jamaica, these music-reproduction systems usually accommodate an emphasis on low frequencies.

[37] The term 'sonic confinement' is used here in association with 'radio-friendly', because music heard via this medium is typically heard through a small speaker such as those that were commonly found on portable transistor radios, and mixing for this format represents a specific set of challenges for the audio engineer, especially in the production of dance music in which low frequency and rhythmic projection are important.

> When I've worked with guys outside of Jamaica, I think the engineers seem to behave a lot more technical in how they're doing things, they watch the meters a lot, they're very concerned with one or two dBs of difference here and there. They have specific sort of guidelines, like I always use this compressor on the bass, I always use this type of equalization on the vocals ... they're very detailed and structured in how they work.

In comparison, when working with Jamaican engineers:

> I've seen guys work more of a vibe, I've seen sessions where the whole board is in the red ... It doesn't matter if it's in the red, if they're hearing it and it sounds good, they're going to go for it, ya know, I've seen that approach a lot more.

Harding states that, in his experience, foreign engineers practise a formalized recording methodology that is based on the creation of accepted and approved sound vocabularies using tried and tested methods, largely aimed at creating radio-friendly sounds. By comparison, Jamaican audio engineers are intuitive and spontaneous, creating music suitable for reproduction on sound systems, rhythmically driven, with small dynamic ranges and emphasized low frequency, designed to encourage dancing.

The technical and sonic capabilities of the sound system allow it to accommodate a variety of production standards, as seen in Chapter 1, where local mento, North American popular music and exclusive recordings could all be employed during an evening's entertainment. The critical point to make here is that sound systems depended on music that had a great vibe or feel and when this was considered 'right' everything else became secondary. This lies at the core of local values and explains how some outsiders interpret JPM as being poorly produced.

It is also significant that the technical operators of the sound system had access to a range of sound altering devices that were liberally applied to compensate for any perceived inadequacies in a sound recording. We therefore see a trend in the use of spontaneity and manipulation of sound in the production and reproduction of JPM that represents a consistent theme that can be traced to some of the earliest Jamaican commercial sound recordings.

I asked Harding if he could provide any examples to demonstrate the way in which Jamaican audio engineers might spontaneously alter or influence the sound of a record, marking the difference in attitudes between Jamaican and North American audio engineers. Harding offered the example of a song recorded and produced by Don Bennett for the artist Sean Paul, entitled 'Give It Up To Me' (Atlantic, 2005).

Harding explains that Bennett is an example of the most recent generation of MRP working in dancehall music. Bennett largely employs the riddim-production method and typically builds reusable riddims recorded in his home studio and using Pro Tools. However, the stature of Sean Paul as an internationally signed recording artist demanded that Bennett create a hybrid riddim (discussed in Chapter 7) for this particular song.[38] At the time, Harding was acting as the manager for Sean Paul and with his background in music production maintained an overview of the new music being produced for Paul's upcoming album. Harding explained that the instrument tracks for Bennett's production were recorded at Circle House Recording Studio, in Miami, USA and the vocals were recorded at Bennett's home studio in Kingston, Jamaica.[39] Bennett, like Harding, is a music practitioner who performs all aspects of the music-production process and Bennett created the first mixes of the completed song at his home recording studio in Jamaica.

The mix was presented to Harding, who approved it and passed it onto the Atlantic Records label chairman, Craig Kallman. Despite Kallman's approval of the song and its musical arrangement, he did not like Bennett's mix and informed Harding that he intended to have the song remixed by a prominent US mixing engineer. However, each time a new mix was completed and returned to Harding and Bennett, they were of the opinion that, an element was missing from the sound. After several attempts to complete the mix, Harding suggested to Kallman that he and Bennett should be present at the next attempt to mix the song, in the interest of making the final rendition acceptable to both Jamaican and North American sensibilities.

For the final mix, Kallman employed the services of audio engineer Dave Pesado, and booked Larrabee Studio North in Los Angeles for the mixing session.[40] The mix was performed on a Solid State Logic 9000 series mixing console, and the label assigned a US producer, Ron Fair, to oversee the session. The music producer Jack Joseph Puig was also present as an observer during the session.[41] Harding states that as the mix was proceeding, both he and Bennett felt that there was something missing from the sound and they informed Pesado of their concern. Ron Fair suggested that Harding and Bennett make whatever adjustments on the mixing board that they thought were appropriate in an attempt to find consensus regarding the sound. Harding explains:

> We were tweaking on the board [mixing console] and so my friend Don says, [to Dave Pesado] 'where is the hi- hat reverb send?', they show him and he puts reverb on the hi-hat, everybody stops and says 'you're putting reverb on the

[38] Sean Paul's record company, Atlantic, did not want Bennett to retain ownership of the riddim and record multiple artists over it; however, they did require that the riddims used for Sean Paul achieved an authentic, local dancehall music sound.

[39] Circle House Recording Studio is owned and operated by the Jamaican group Inner Circle. It is considered one of the leading recording studios in Florida but, importantly, is familiar with the specialist needs of Jamaican music clients.

[40] Pasado is known as a mixing engineer and has worked for The Black Eyed Peas, Justin Timberlake, Elton John, Jamiroquai, and Christina Aguilera. Pasado also mixed the soundtracks of popular films such as *White Men Can't Jump*, *Hurricane*, *Nutty Professor II: The Klumps* and *Men of Honor*.

[41] Fair has produced music for Christina Aguilera, Prima J, Vanessa Carlton, The Black Eyed Peas, Girlicious, The Pussycat Dolls and Keyshia Cole.

hi-hat?' and he's like, 'yeah', and they're like 'wow! reverb on the hi-hat', and they're making notes, [Harding later clarifies that these were mental notes] reverb on the hi-hat and looking at the settings, like, how much reverb and what's the delay time on the reverb and my friend Don is looking at me like, 'what's the big deal?' I'm like, Dude, obviously they don't put reverb on hi-hats, but to them this is the secret reggae sound now, they're trying to learn, putting reverb on the hi-hat, and I'm looking at them, like, you guys have the Grammy's … we're just some kids in Jamaica with our Pro Tools rigs … they were shocked.

This recollection by Harding highlights his and Bennett's approach towards an audio engineering process that is not constrained by set formulas, established sound treatments or mixing strategies. The apparent shock of these very successful and highly acclaimed US producers and audio engineer, described by Harding, is the product of a basic popular-music recording practice in which reverb is rarely placed on hi-hats. By the time of the Larabee North mixing session, none of the song mixes up to that point had included, nor is there any suggestion that the US engineers ever considered including, reverb on the hi-hat. Bennett's suggestion to make this unorthodox addition, although met with surprise, eventually received unanimous approval and was included on the final mix and eventually released on the album entitled *The Trinity* (Atlantic Records, 2005).

The above anecdote provides a sense of how North American and Jamaican music practitioners differ in their approach to the production of music and is worthy of deeper consideration. From Harding's perspective, the US-based participants of the above mixing session seemed to assume that Jamaican audio engineers employed a similar approach to recording as their US counterparts. Fair, Pesado and Puig made the assumption that placing reverb on the hi-hat was one of the formulated sound signatures that contributed towards 'the Jamaican sound', but that was not the case. Harding confirmed that Bennett was simply reacting to the mix in a manner that was not constrained by preconceptions or established recording conventions, or the use of formulated sounds. Putting reverb on the hi-hat was not a common practice for Bennett or indeed found in Jamaica, but intuitively, this is what he felt the song needed.

The decision by Kallman, as the chairman of Atlantic Records, to remix a song is not unusual. However, in spite of his misgivings concerning Bennett's original mix, Kallman still seemed determined, by Harding's account, to obtain both Harding and Bennett's approval of the final mix. In doing so, Kallman seemed to recognize an importance located in the sonic sensibility of Harding and Bennett, despite the vast range of expertise available to him through the Atlantic Records organization.

Harding's account of this mixing session documents an important sonic contribution that Bennett, in particular, made to the final mix of 'Give It Up To Me'. That contribution was anchored in an evaluation process that was unconstrained by the models and protocols that Bennett's US counterparts adhered to and was performed with a perspective that included audio engineering values. In this sense,

Bennett was functioning as a representative of the Jamaican MRP, offering a range of sonic sensibilities, based on local values and audio engineering practices that allowed him to identify the need to place reverb on the hi-hat.

This also demonstrates that a record company such as Atlantic Records recognized the value of Bennett and Harding and attempted to corral their intuitive approach towards music production. Dave Pesado and Ron Fair were primarily employed by Atlantic to temper and mould Bennett's creation into a format that was considered appropriate for American radio consumption, echoing Harding's earlier comments. This represents a difference in sonic perceptions that were negotiated through audio-engineered sound required to retain a sensibility that was linked to Jamaica's sound system culture, but presented in a form that could be readily digested by North American media. It is also instructive that despite Atlantic appointing a renowned audio engineer to conduct the new mix, Ron Fair, as a producer, was also appointed to oversee the session: this highlights another significant difference between the Jamaican and North American approach towards music production.

Harding is a notable figure in the Jamaican music industry because he represents one of the first non-specialized MRPs to achieve significant local and international success with dancehall music. This was achieved without him working through the ranks of the music industry as either audio engineer or musician. Harding's path to becoming a MRP was therefore a product of the new programmable instruments and the new digital recording formats, together with his own determination to practise and hone his creative and technical skills to the point where he could compete commercially with the local and then international recording establishment.

In addition, Harding's work is notable because the audio engineering and musical approaches that he selected were intended to function with a computer-recording format, which was adapted to the framework and values of the RPM. As such, Harding managed to maintain the aesthetic of a recording practice that was based on vibe, utilizing spontaneity and an intuitive approach towards music-production. However, he was also able to take advantage of the new facilities that computer recording offered, and present Jamaican music in ways that were palatable to a diverse audience and range of media outlets.

Harding's testimony in this chapter demonstrates once again how creativity is brought to audio engineering processes and applied through a framework of local values in the production of music that becomes distinctly Jamaican. This is the same fundamental process that is also evident in the creation of emphasized bass by Graeme Goodall, and the drum programming and creation of drum sounds by Cleveland Browne.

From my perspective, the testimony of Harding is critical in the discussion of how the audio engineer has influenced the development of JPM and how the role of recording participants has changed. Harding demonstrates how local sensibilities can be applied through programmed music, but particularly programmed drumbeats, combined with engineered sounds. This is in direct contradiction to commentators such as Bradley, who claim:

> Once 'Under Mi Sleng Teng' had introduced a sound and a structure that wasn't traditionally Jamaican – that is, Jamaican as perceived by largely uncomprehending black Americans – and computerization allowed usage of the same samples as hip-hop, US airwaves friendly 'reggae' tunes stopped being a contradiction in terms. (2000, p. 519)

What Bradley fails to realize is that the sampled sounds used in the production of dancehall music are no more 'Traditionally Jamaican' than the Fender bass and Hammond organ that was used in the production of reggae. In addition, the comprehension of foreign audiences regarding the 'Jamaicaness' of musical products has little to do with musical structures and is much more about the stereotypes that the marketing arm of music corporations promote. With this comment in mind, a re-evaluation of dancehall music is perhaps appropriate, but in the context of recognizing that JPM music is not limited to any one set of structures, image, rules or interpretations. Sound, rhythm, melody and harmony can all be subject to a distinctly Jamaican interpretation that naturally evolves and changes over time. This is evident in a range of transitions that include emphasized bass, the creation of drum sounds, the RPM, engineered rhythms and reverb on the hi-hat. These are examples of how recording participants negotiate and adapt technology to meet a range of local demands, which ultimately provide the unique sonic characteristics of JPM.

Chapter 9
A Jamaican Recording Studio Ethnography

Through the normal course of my work as a practising musician, I had the opportunity of conducting an ethnographic study of a recording session as participant/observer. To the best of my knowledge, this represents the first example of this type of study to be conducted in Jamaica and although limited by the work I am offered, it is representative of recording practice in Jamaican, in 2008. The intention is to provide the reader with an inside view of the recording practitioner's world. This world is populated by human beings as well as technology and in this context it was crucial to be able to document interactions between participants as well as the interactions between participants and recording technologies.

While many of the discussed changes that took place in the production of JPM have been described in terms of recording models and recording strategies, I acknowledge that these represent only flexible frameworks that vary widely in the details of their implementation and practice. The very nature of JPM, based on spontaneity and vibe, is often in conflict with the predetermined parameters that these recording structures suggest. Therefore, this chapter also tries to capture a sense of how spontaneity is induced into, and influences, the recording process, becoming a catalyst for exploration and creativity.

Selecting an Appropriate Recording Session

A principal objective of this ethnography was to access a real world recording setting in Jamaica where the process of data collection had minimal impact on the actions of participants. I therefore conducted the study covertly, but at the close of the sessions informed the recording participants of my actions and objectives, requesting their permission to formally document my observations. In addition to providing permission, the participants also agreed to participate in follow-up interviews where the events of the recording sessions would be discussed in detail. Furthermore, as a mark of respect and acknowledgement, both participants were provided with a copy of the chapter and invited to comment on any issue or make correction, which would have been incorporated in the text, but both felt the content was an accurate description of events.

In regard to the collection of data during the sessions, I made it a point of attending sessions early so that I could take notes and pictures of the recording studio environment before the other participants arrived. Notes were discreetly made on a note pad before and during the recording sessions, which were expanded and documented within a 24-hour period. I was also able to gain access to the guide mixes that resulted from each session and therefore substantiate much of the musical detail found in the notes.[1] These guide mixes also proved invaluable when compared to the finished sound recording, which was commercially released on compact disc, and allowed an assessment to be made of the post-session work that each sound recording received.

The decision to use a guitar session as the basis for the study was based on a range of live and studio work that I encounter as a music professional. I found that working as a guitarist on a recording session presented me with the best opportunity for collecting the widest and most detailed range of data in which my influence as both participant and researcher was minimized. Although I was keen to collect data, I remained cognizant of the fact that I was being paid as a professional musician to perform a task, which remained my first priority. Although some of my music industry colleagues were aware of my involvement with the study of JPM, and how my experiences as a musician made up part of that research, they were unaware of specific details regarding the topic of my study or the fact that I was keeping a record of some work experiences.

The criteria for selecting the subject recording session was based on the following preferences:

- The location of a setting where the recording studio represented a purpose-built, professional recording facility. A professional recording studio functions and operates on the basis of its ability to satisfy the demands of those individuals who rent it, and the subsequent success of their music products. I reasoned that a professional recording facility therefore offers a relatively neutral setting to observe the work of recording participants.[2]
- The audio engineer employed for the session, should be a career audio engineer as opposed to a career musician who also engineered music projects or was acting as a MRP.
- The project being recorded should have some acoustic instruments that required the audio engineer(s) to use microphones for their sound capture. This offered an opportunity to compare how basic recording techniques had evolved since the 1950s. If the session consisted of only pre-recorded samples or synthesizers, the potential for comparative analysis of engineering techniques would be reduced.
- The recording project, if possible, should represent the work of a single audio engineer to avoid the difficult task of trying to differentiate who was responsible for various aspects of the recording. During the follow-up

---

[1] A guide mix is a rough mix of the music compiled at the end of the recording session that, in the case of the studied session, was made to be presented to the artist and executive producer. I asked the audio engineer if he could furnish me with a copy of these, which he agreed to do.

[2] This excludes home studios, which typically serve the demands of their owner without consideration for what the ambient music market demands in terms of a recording facility.

interview stage of the study It was preferable to have one audio engineer who could speak with authority regarding all aspects of the resulting engineered sound and its creative components

- The study should be of a recording session where the resulting music could be described as popular music, intended for commercial release by a record company as opposed to other types of music production intended for use in advertising or film.

Other possible guitar recording sessions that I was employed for during the selection period for the study included work for Beres Hammond, Maxi Priest and Richie Stevens. However, even with these well-established artists, the recording process took place in a mixture of recording environments and circumstances that were not considered ideal. It is worth noting that out of the three artists mentioned above, only Richie Stevens was present to provide creative input during the recording process. In the case of Maxi Priest the audio engineer Michael McDonald assumed the role of creative director but the sound recording was sent to me as an email attachment and was recorded by me in my own studio. In the case of Beres Hammond, a number of guitar tracks were recorded for creative producers Clive Hunt, Michael Fletcher and audio engineer Errol Brown who also provided creative direction.

Although I had no control over the work that I was offered, or the choice of recording studio, I felt it was important to locate a session that was representative of local popular music production, employing an established professional recording facility with professional participants and that my involvement in the recording should be limited to playing guitar. While the following description is representative of recording practice in Jamaica it can only be considered a small example of the diverse range of recording activities that make up Kingston's recording studio life.

The Rationale for a Recording Studio Ethnography

The sessions chosen as the subject matter for this chapter were commissioned by an artist/producer (A/P) who is considered successful in the local and international recording industry. His musical career began with a reggae group, but in recent years he has established himself as both a music producer and a solo artist, and he has been the recipient of several Grammy awards from the Recording Industry Association of America. The recording sessions were therefore commissioned by someone who might be considered part of a small group of Jamaican entertainers, positioned at the pinnacle of their profession, enjoying international success and recognition with representation through international music publishers, distributors and record companies.

The name of the A/P will not be disclosed for the purpose of this study, primarily because he was not present at the recording sessions. In addition, I had no direct contact with the A/P and my business arrangements were finalized through his personal assistant and Glen Browne (who provided creative direction during the course of the sessions). It was felt that maintaining the A/P's anonymity protected the best interests of all parties concerned, while having minimal impact on the ethnographic material presented here.

The Audio Engineer Appointed to the Recording Session

The recording sessions were conducted at the Tuff Gong Recording Studio (Hope Road), over four dates between 1 February 2008 and 5 February 2008, each lasting between four and five hours.[3] The sessions were part of project to record an acoustic album of which the A/P was the recording artist and credited as the producer.[4] The audio engineer employed by the A/P for the recording sessions was Gregory Morris, who in 2008 represented the youngest generation of audio engineers currently working in Jamaica. Born in 1982, in St Thomas, Jamaica, Morris began working for the Tuff Gong organization in 2003. Morris had enrolled in a computer-programming course at the University of Technology, when he was offered an audio-engineering apprenticeship at Tuff Gong's Bell Road studio (formally Federal Recording Studio). Morris explained that he developed a deep interest in music while still in school, through an association with a small local sound system in St Thomas. Working with the sound system helped to focus his attention on the sonic quality of records and how some had distinct features such as, 'driving bottom end' or 'clarity', while others sounded 'dull' or 'muddy'. Morris recalls wondering why these records sounded so different, and this stimulated his interest in the process of recording music.

Morris explained that as an apprentice audio engineer, he was required to provide general assistance to the senior audio engineers with tasks that ranged from setting up microphones to clearing up after sessions and running errands. According to Morris, he did not receive any formal training at the Bell Road studio, but learnt his craft by watching the senior audio engineers conduct recording and mixing sessions.[5] Morris claims that the management of the Bell Road studio

---

[3] The Hope Road location is where the original Tuff Gong Recording Studio, built by Bob Marley, is located. It is now commonly referred to as 'The Museum', because it houses the Bob Marley museum, a local tourist attraction. It should not to be confused with the Tuff Gong Recording Studio, formally known as Federal Recording Studio, built by Ken Khouri on Bell Road. For clarity, I will refer to these two locations as the Hope Road and Bell Road studios respectively.

[4] The term 'unplugged' is commonly used to describe a project in which musicians and artists who mostly employ electronic instruments perform or record acoustic arrangements of their music.

[5] Morris explained that his training included no formal study of audio engineering in regard to electrical or acoustic theory. His learning process was not enhanced by the use of

encouraged their senior engineers to mentor the trainee engineers, but Morris felt that some engineers were reluctant to share information. He felt that these engineers used this as a tactic to protect their own position in the hierarchy of the Tuff Gong organization and with recording clients.

Morris claims that Shane Brown and his father, Errol Brown, two senior Tuff Gong engineers were notably different, developing a good working relationship with him and acting as his mentors.[6] They were not only willing to share information openly, but encouraged his enquiry and entry into the world of recording. Morris also claimed that the Internet proved to be an important tool for accessing information from recording forums, equipment manufacturers and recording studio websites. From these various sources, Morris was able to form a more detailed understanding of studio-related technologies and how the wider music industry functioned.

Morris describes the circumstances that led to his first recording session as an audio engineer. He was assisting on a session with Shane Brown in 2004, working with what he describes as a 'difficult client'. The studio had been booked for a mixing session and Brown had started the preparation work for that process but the client then decided that he wanted to record additional instrumental parts onto the song. Brown reluctantly asked Morris to set up a microphone in preparation to record these new tracks while he brought the microphone input up on the mixing console. This was assigned to a track on the 24-track tape recorder and Brown set the appropriate recording levels.[7] Brown then asked Morris to take over the session and left without returning. Morris was left alone to continue recording the additional tracks and conclude the session. He states that, from that point forward, he was allowed to work, initially with new and 'less important' studio clients as a junior Tuff Gong audio engineer.

At the time of my interview with Morris, he had established himself as one of the senior resident audio engineers at the Bell Road studio, but is regularly employed by several well-established Jamaican artists for both local and overseas work, including live performances and recording sessions. This association implies that Morris's work is held in high regard by a number of artists whose commercial success ensures that they have a wide selection of audio engineers to choose from. Morris therefore represents a new generation of successful Jamaican audio engineers, working with the top layer of JPM artists. That success is substantiated

---

books or other formal teaching aids, but was 100% hands-on training that depended on the qualified engineers at Tuff Gong sharing their knowledge.

[6] Shane Brown would be now classified as an MRP emerging from his role as an audio engineer. Brown is now considered a successful artist manager and music producer.

[7] Note that this session took place in approximately 2004–05 and that Tuff Gong as a leading Jamaican commercial studio was still using an analogue 24-track tape recorder.

by a number of local and international music-industry awards for recordings in which his work has played a significant role.[8]

The Hope Road Studio

I was contacted by telephone on 28 January 2008 by Glen Browne and asked to play guitar on an undisclosed number of songs that were part of an album project.[9] Browne is a well-known Rastafarian bass player, bandleader, arranger and music producer who is well respected in the Kingston musical fraternity.[10] He has a long-standing association with a number of established Jamaican artists that include Jimmy Cliff, Ziggy Marley, Luciano, Monty Alexander and, most recently, Taurus Riley.[11]

My professional relationship with Browne goes back to the mid-1980s. Since that time we have worked together on live and recording projects as independently employed musicians, but have also employed each other in a wide range of music-related work. I would therefore describe my relationship with Browne as long standing and professional, with a good personal rapport.

During the initial telephone call, Browne explained that he was acting as an agent for the A/P who had requested that I lay some acoustic guitar overdubs on a selection of previously recorded backing tracks, and we arranged to start work at 8 pm on Friday 1 February 2008.[12] The session was scheduled to take place at the Hope Road studio.

The Hope Road studio was constructed on premises originally owned by Island Records, and purchased by Bob Marley during the 1970s, in a prime residential area of Kingston. The main building on the property would locally be described as a large 'colonial style' home, constructed with what appears to be a block and steel ground floor and a wooden frame first floor. The property stands in a large

---

[8] Although Morris has not received any awards directly for his engineering work, he has either acted as the main recording engineer or shared these duties on international award winning album projects for artists such as Damien and Stephen Marley.

[9] Glen Browne is the brother of Cleveland Browne, interviewed in preceding chapters.

[10] Glen and Cleveland Browne are part of a well-known musical family in Jamaica. Other members of the family who work in Kingston's musical community include Danny and Dalton Browne (brothers), and Richard and Robert Browne (Glen's sons).

[11] These Jamaican artists cover a wide musical spectrum from traditional 'roots reggae' associated with artists such as Jimmy Cliff to jazz with Monty Alexander who regularly features Jamaican folk music in his performances. Ziggy Marley, Luciano and Taurus Riley represent current Jamaican popular artists but all the examples share a strong melodic and harmonic component in their music, unlike contemporary Jamaican dancehall music, which tends to have a stronger rhythmic feature.

[12] The arranged time for the recording session was primarily the result of Morris's, Browne's and my other commitments, and the availability of the studio, bearing in mind that most of the larger Kingston studios work on a 24-hour, seven day a week basis.

lot of land, now contained by high walls and fences with a number of outbuildings that have been constructed since Marley's ownership. The buildings include the housing of the Bob Marley museum, a recording studio, a restaurant, a rehearsal room, a beauty salon, domestic dwellings, and offices. Guided tours of the property are offered to tourists and include the recording studio, which is located on the ground floor of the main house, provided it is not being used.

Although this is the original location where Bob Marley recorded some of his music, the studio underwent a major renovation in the 1990s and has now been reconfigured, updated and completely re-equipped. A Solid State Logic 4000 G series, 40-channel mixing console was installed in the studio with new racks of outboard equipment and monitors.[13] Most recently, the studio had acquired a Pro Tools High Definition recording system, which represented the recording industry's most popular digital recording format in 2008.[14]

During the 1990s, the Marley family purchased the site where the Federal Recording Studio was located, in an industrial area of Kingston, and relocated the commercial operations of the Hope Road studio to that location, renaming the Federal studio Tuff Gong. The Hope Road studio was refurbished at around this time and is now treated as a personal facility for the extended Marley family, their close friends and associates.[15] During the period of my employment for the sessions under discussion, members of the Marley family and their friends appeared to use the Hope Road premises to work, socialize and play a regular game of football in the compound car park.

My personal experience as a recording professional suggests that there are marked differences between the studio protocols of Jamaica and those of Europe and North America. I have observed that commercial European and American recording studios treat the recording rooms as a sanctuary that is largely isolated from outsiders and potential interruptions, especially once a recording session begins. The atmosphere of many Jamaican recording studios, however, might be described as 'relaxed' and 'informal'. The recording spaces are often accessible to people who may not be directly associated with the recording process or the recording participants. It is therefore not unusual to have outsiders present at a recording session who play no role in the recording process. The distractions and interruptions that they may cause are largely tolerated and accepted as part of the studio landscape and what might be considered local studio culture. Although the

---

[13] Monitors, in the context of a recording studio, refer to the loudspeakers used to critically evaluate the musical material being recorded.

[14] Pro Tools is the name of a software/ hard ware based computer-recording system made by Digidesign that is commonly acknowledged as being the recording industry's standard format for multi-track-based popular-music recording.

[15] Bob Marley had three children with Rita Marley, but adopted two children belonging to Rita from a previous relationship. In addition, he had eight children with separate women. Several of these children are active in various roles in the music industry and work formally with the Tuff Gong organization.

Hope Road studio should be considered a private recording facility, it appears to subscribe to this informal policy for conducting recording sessions.

The multi-functional role of the Hope Road complex ensured that there were always a substantial number of people on the premises and many had free access to the inner sanctuary of the recording-studio spaces. For example, members of the supporting musical groups, associated with members of the Marley family, were attending rehearsals at the complex at the same time as the guitar sessions under discussion. Some of the group members would periodically pass through the studio and 'hail-up' the recording participants.[16] On two occasions, these individuals sat in on the session, without invitation, observed what was taking place and offered comments of encouragement with no discernable discomfort on the part of Browne or Morris.

On other occasions, there were distractions during the recording sessions caused by activities taking place in the main studio recording room that faced the control room. I was later informed by Morris that some members of the Marley family and their associates were using the main studio room to listen to music. Although the sounds of these activities were isolated from the control room, the participants were visible through the sound-proof glass that separated the two rooms and this sometimes created a surreal effect as we recorded music at one tempo and rhythmic feel, but could see people moving, out of sync, through the studio glass, reacting to music set at a completely different tempo. This could be distracting, especially during the performance of rhythmic guitar parts, but was tolerated.

In addition, there were interruptions as these individuals came and went, to and from the studio. The outer door leading to the inner studio rooms was often slammed and both Morris and Browne, on several occasions, had to stop the recording session and remind those concerned that a recording was in progress, at one point locking the outer studio door to reduce the number of interruptions. Although both Morris and Browne voiced frustration, no other action was taken.

Another point of distraction was focused on the entrance door to the control room, which had a small glass window covered by a curtain on the inside of the door. People passing the control room would open the door and stick their head in to see who was working and on several occasions this actually interrupted recording. It was therefore necessary for Morris to pin back the curtain that covered the glass, so that passers-by could see that a recording was in progress. This proved to be a successful strategy but resulted in a steady stream of curious faces that appeared at the window.

Other distractions were experienced during one of the day-time sessions as a result of a Bob Marley museum tour. The tour included the main building, which houses the recording studio, and although the tour did not include the studio because it was being used, recording had to be temporarily stopped because the

---

[16] 'Hail up' is a local term best translated as an informal verbal or body language greeting or acknowledgment.

footsteps of tourists could be heard on the stairs outside the studio control room, and in the rooms above the control room. At this time Morris simply suggested that we wait for the tour to be completed before continuing to record.

Morris informed me that the level of activity at the Hope Road studio was above normal as a result of preparations for the annual Bob Marley birthday celebrations, due to take place on 6 February. To the outsider, the informal attitude and state of technical preparedness that became evident during the guitar sessions might seem to be the product of an unprofessional or uninformed attitude towards the recording process. However, my professional experience suggests that this approach is simply grounded in a value system that is not consistent with those found in North America and Europe.

JPM is undoubtedly influenced by a wide range of cultural, social, economic and technical forces that have resulted in a recording strategy that can be described as 'relaxed'. However, it should be noted that this 'relaxed' atmosphere represents part of an approach toward recording that aims to establish a creative and inspirational setting. Many Jamaican recording participants refer to this atmosphere as 'vibe', which was noted in previous chapters. When the vibe is right then all other considerations become secondary.

Despite the interruptions evident during the guitar sessions, I would describe the atmosphere at the Hope Road studio as friendly, relaxed and informal, with no tangible sense that the interruptions were having an impact on the quality or creativity of the recording process. It should be noted, however, that this apparent tolerance might have been encouraged by the fact that the A/P had no evident restrictions on recording budget or allotted studio time, and this is not typical of every recording session in Jamaica. In addition, the majority of interruptions were in some way connected directly to activities associated with the extended Marley family. I sensed that there was some frustration on the part of Morris and Browne, but they seemed reluctant to try and change what appeared to be a normal mode of operation at the Hope Road studio.

Preparation for Recording

There were no written scores for the session or provision of preparatory materials such as demo recordings or backing tracks. In the telephone conversations with Browne, prior to the recording session, there was no description of the project or type of material to be recorded other than the request to play acoustic guitar on a recording involving the A/P. In my experience this is not unusual and is typical of the way in which many recording sessions are arranged and prepared for in Jamaica.

Without a definitive description of the type of material being recorded, I selected a Lopez Martin classical guitar, built in the late 1960s with what I describe as an aged mellow tone that has proved suitable for recording popular music, and a 1964 Gibson B25 steel-string acoustic guitar. The B25 was chosen because it is a small-bodied instrument and does not produce the low-frequency content typically associated with a jumbo or dreadnought-sized instrument. This is significant because the Hope Road studio has two relatively small recording rooms that, in my opinion, demand close microphone placement if an optimal acoustic guitar sound is to be achieved.[17] This type of microphone placement captures less of the room sound, but tends to emphasize the low-frequency content of the instrument due to the microphone's proximity effect.[18] In addition, the emphasis of low-frequency sound in JPM meant that audio engineers often equalized instruments in the process of shelving different sounds into an allotted sonic space, as discussed in previous chapters.

The use of smaller bodied instruments removed the need for drastic equalization and, in my opinion, this improved the recorded sound of the guitar. The selection of instruments was therefore based on the absence of information regarding the material to be recorded, the choice of recording studio, the recording artist and my understanding of local recording processes. Although Browne was not familiar with the actual songs to be worked on, it was assumed that they would be multiple-instrument, popular-music productions with a dominant rhythm section.

Browne met me at the studio and introduced me to Gregory Morris, who I was meeting and working with for the first time. I commented to Browne that 'we're both underdressed for the occasion', in casual trousers and T-shirts, because Morris was wearing dress trousers, shirt and jacket. We shook hands, talked a little and I joked that he was the best-dressed audio engineer that I'd ever seen in Jamaica. Morris laughed and explained that he was coming from a formal function related to the Bob Marley birthday celebrations.

I asked Morris which of the two recording rooms he wanted me to record in so that I could put the acoustic guitars in that room and let them acclimatize to the room's air conditioning before tuning them.[19] Morris then explained that I would have to record in the control room because the cabling that connects the isolated recording rooms to the control room had 'gone bad'. It was suggested that rats might have 'eaten out' the cables.[20] I voiced a concern to Morris that this method might introduce unwanted noise onto the guitar tracks and suggested

---

[17] As described in earlier chapters, small recording rooms tend to create audible standing waves that become increasingly noticeable, as the microphone is moved away from the instrument, influencing the sonic characteristic of the instrument in the low and low mid frequency ranges.

[18] Some directional polar patterns on microphones tend to emphasize low frequency when placed close to the sound source and this phenomenon is known as the 'proximity effect'. By choosing an instrument with a lighter low-frequency range, the proximity effect would tend to be less noticeable.

[19] The air conditioning is a central system designed for use in professional recording studios that operates without any discernable noise.

[20] Recording studios are normally connected by a network of cables that run in recessed ducts set into the walls, floor or ceiling of the physical structure. They are typically designed to allow easy access for maintenance and upgrading.

running a temporary microphone and headphone cable through the cable duct for the session. Morris explained that he was not sure where the duct was located, and he believed that the wooden flooring in the control room had been installed over the duct by mistake, making it inaccessible. Morris added that Chow, the maintenance engineer for the Hope Road and Bell Road studios, was so busy at the Bell Road studio, that he rarely had time to attend to maintenance problems at the Hope Road studio, which was not used on a regular basis.

Morris asked, 'do the guitars have an output jack?' referring to built-in pick-ups that would avoid the need for using a microphone, but Browne interjected that: 'I want a real acoustic guitar sound not the sound of a pick-up'. In a recording-studio setting, the term 'real' is an ambiguous and often misleading description of sound that can be interpreted in a number of ways.[21] As the session unfolded it became evident that Browne wanted the recorded guitar sound to have the characteristics of what might be described as the instrument's 'natural acoustic sound'. A passive or active pickup is designed to capture the string vibration, but is unable to capture the full acoustic characteristics of the instrument or the room in which it is recorded.[22] We were therefore limited to recording in the control room, using a professional condenser microphone, which is very sensitive and would be placed as close to the instrument as possible with the intention of keeping the ambient noise of the recording room to a minimum level.[23]

As the performer I viewed the technical quality of the recorded guitar sound to be the responsibility of the audio engineer or individual who was acting as the producer. I had been informed prior to the session that the A/P would act in this capacity, but in his absence Morris and Browne seemed to assume the responsibilities of that role. I was unaware of any discussion regarding the possible negative consequences of recording in the control room and Morris appeared to make the unilateral decision to continue the session, stating that he felt that the resulting guitar tracks would be fine. No further discussion took place regarding the recorded quality of the guitar, in this and the subsequent sessions.

In the subsequent interview with Morris, post recording session, the choice of recording studio, recording method and the sound of the guitar were discussed

---

[21] In my experience as a professional recording musician, the term 'real' is often associated with an existing recorded example of an instrument rather than the sound of the actual instrument. The term suggests a 'natural sound', but often that is not what the user of the term requires. If unsure, I typically ask the individual for a recorded reference. In the case of Browne, through my experience working with him I assumed that he meant a natural acoustic sound.

[22] A passive or active pick-up system depends on the direct mechanical movement of the guitar string to function. Passive devices produce a relatively weak signal with limited tonal variations. An active device is typically powered by a battery that allows amplification and equalization of the signal before it leaves the instrument.

[23] The 'noise floor', in this instance, refers to the level of ambient room sound in relation to the captured level of the instrument.

in detail. Morris was asked if he was initially concerned about the recording quality of the guitar tracks and using a close micing method, in the control room. He said:

> I worried for like the first day, but after you left [meaning Browne and me] I was soloing[24] the tracks, it was pretty clean, I mean in a situation like that, after listening to the tracks I just had to be aware of like, people, going up the stairs and stuff like that

The testimony of Morris demonstrates an awareness of the potential problems and concern for the recording quality of the recorded guitar, but, despite these concerns, he felt it was worth trying at least one recording session to see what musical results could be achieved. Without any prior knowledge of the type of instrument to be recorded and Browne's insistence on using a microphone, Morris, in his capacity as a Tuff Gong audio engineer, could have reasonably requested that the session be postponed and rescheduled at the Bell Road (old Federal) studio because of these technical difficulties. He would have been supported in his rationale to make that decision by the fact that the existing backing tracks were all recorded at the Bell Road studio.[25] However, Morris decided to try recording in this unconventional way, demonstrating self-confidence in his own engineering skills, a willingness to experiment, and a readiness to make production decisions without consulting either the A/P or Browne as the A/P's creative representative. The A/P, of course, would ultimately bear the financial costs of the recording, including the fees charged by Browne and myself.

Morris would later inform Browne and me that the Hope Road studio was typically being used for laying guide tracks with a microphone, or final tracks that did not require the use of a microphone, like the output of a synthesizer or drum machine.[26] He informed me that the Neumann U87 microphone and stool, set up in the control room, had been left there from previous recording sessions.[27] This, in conjunction with the fact that both recording rooms were being used for activities not connected with work taking place in the control room, suggested that the technical problems evident at the Hope Road studio had been apparent for some time.

Figure 9.1 shows the rear of the studio control room and the location where the guitar tracks were recorded. The Akai MPC drum machine, Guinness bottles,

---

[24] 'Soloing' is the term used by audio engineers to describe the process of isolating an individual instrument on the mixing board so that it can be auditioned and clinically analysed for any problems concerning the sound quality or performance.

[25] All of the other backing tracks were recorded by Morris and were created by live instruments with no synthesizers or drum machines.

[26] The term 'guide track' refers to the recording of a musical idea where the intention is to modify, improve or perfect the performance later, and it is therefore a temporary track.

[27] The Neumann U87 might be described as an industry-standard microphone that can be used to capture a wide variety of source material.

Figure 9.1   The microphone and stool positioned at the rear of the control room.
From the author's archive, February 2008

Rizla cigarette papers and small quantity of ganja (marijuana) were left from the previous recording session. It is appropriate to note that although the use of ganja fits the perceived stereotype of Jamaican musicians, the reality is different. Michael Veal states: 'While it would be difficult to find a Jamaican musician of the roots era who was avowedly anti-ganja, some Jamaican musicians nevertheless felt that the prominence of this theme led to a distorted view of reggae in the world at large' (2007, p.17).

Although not the focus of this study, it is appropriate to point out that a substantial number of musicians from the roots era, including dedicated Rastafarians such as Glen Browne, are not ganja smokers.[28] From my personal experience, as a professional musician, I would suggest that it might be difficult to find a reggae, jazz, rock or pop musician anywhere who is avowedly anti-ganja, or, for that matter, many other legal and illegal substances. In my experience I have not found Jamaican musicians to be more prone to the use of illegal drugs than their foreign counterparts. My personal observation is that Jamaican musicians are generally minimal users of both legal and illegal substances, contrary to the

---

[28] I describe Browne as a 'dedicated Rastafarian', meaning that this represents his religion and way of life, which differentiates him from individuals who style their personal image on Rastafarian themes such as dreadlock hairstyles and smoking ganja.

popular stereotype, which is often the product of a record company's marketing department and/or the local perception that many foreigners respond positively to this image.

The Process of Recording

As the performer, and being intimately familiar with audio-engineering practices, (unknown to Morris) I was initially sceptical about the prospect of recording acoustic guitar with a large diaphragm condenser microphone in the control room. In addition to the increase in ambient noise that would unavoidably be recorded with the guitar, close micing techniques place a unique set of demands on the performer. The normal extra-musical sounds associated with a guitar performance, such as fingerboard squeaks, right-hand damping, which can cause a low frequency thump as the side of the palm hits the strings, the breathing of the performer and general noises induced by the performer's normal physical contact with the instrument, can become exaggerated and over emphasized. Close micing therefore creates additional constraints and demands on the performer. Without being familiar with the technical demands of the music or the type of performance required for the recording, I was therefore concerned that a satisfactory guitar sound might not be attainable if recording was limited to the use of close micing and employing a U87 microphone.

Morris saw these technical limitations as an opportunity to explore an unconventional recording method and took the unilateral decision to proceed with the session, despite the apparent technical risks and resulting costs. My experience as a music professional working in Jamaica has taught me to put aside any personal misgivings that I acknowledge as being, in part, the product of a European experience, and I therefore follow an approach that might best be described as 'going with the flow'.

In my subsequent interviews with Morris and Browne, we all agreed that certain advantages and disadvantages became evident by locating the performer in the control room. For example, communication between myself, Morris and Browne became more intimate and nuanced compared to performing in an isolated recording room, where communication is limited to performance instructions issued over the talkback system. Being in the same room as Morris and Browne provided me with a direct sense of what they were trying to achieve with my performance. These observations support a claim made earlier by Robbie Lyn in which he describes how moving from the recording room to the studio control-room changed the process of recording. Morris later confirmed that his primary recording experience was based on recording musicians working from the control room without the use of microphones. He explained that despite the difficulties associated with recording with a microphone in the control room, he felt that, 'Nothing beats a try like a fail', suggesting that he is prepared to explore and experiment with new or untried recording methods.

At the time of the recording session, I had serious doubts concerning the wisdom of Morris's recording strategy. Browne and I represented two seasoned music professionals, yet Morris, who was approximately half our respective ages, demonstrated self-confidence by assuming responsibility for proceeding with the session. However, compromises during the recording were made, for example:

- As the performer, I required a headphone instrument balance that assisted me in the performance of the required guitar track. This might have called for certain instruments to be accentuated, for example to help with time keeping. These instrument balances were typically inconsistent with the preferred balance that Browne and Morris would have employed for monitoring the recording. Unfortunately, the mixing console was set up to provide only one headphone mix.[29]
- The inability of Morris and Browne to monitor the tracks being recorded accurately meant that after each track was completed, it had to be carefully checked on the control room monitors for consistency in performance and technical standards, changing the control room mix so that the guitar could be prominently heard.[30]

It should be noted that the ability to record with a microphone in a small control room, such as that of the Hope Road studio, is in part facilitated by the introduction of computer recording, which tends to be quieter than a mechanical multi-track tape machine.[31] However, the audio quality of the recorded guitar tracks was undoubtedly compromised by the increase in the ambient noise coming from inside and outside of the control room. Despite these limitations, both Morris and Browne readily adopted this method of working and I must assume that whatever doubts they had concerning the quality of the recording were superseded by the musical results being achieved.

The recording methodology used to record the acoustic guitar on these sessions is not untypical of amateur or home-recording studios, often situated in one room around a computer-based, digital audio workstation. After the initial session, three additional sessions were scheduled at the Hope Road studio. During that time, a

---

[29] There is an important relationship between a musical performance and monitored balance of instruments. For example, the recording of a rhythmic part demands that the main timing references like snare drum, bass drum and hi-hat be more prominent in the instrument balance, or if an aggressive performance is required then the level of the instrument being recorded needs to be subdued in the monitor balance so that the performer can play with the appropriate attack.

[30] The producer's mix is often balanced quite differently to the headphone mix for the performer. The producer may require that the instrument being recorded is prominent in the mix in order to identify performance issues; the performer may require the opposite in order to maintain accurate time keeping.

[31] Some analogue recording studios place their tape machines in isolated rooms, but the Hope Road studio had the tape machine positioned in the control room.

total of 14 finished guitar tracks were recorded and approved by the A/P using the above recording method.

In a sense this represents a flexible and intuitive approach to the recording process by Morris and Browne, who were directly commissioned by the A/P and would ultimately take responsibility for the creative and technical result of the sessions. A very different recording environment would have resulted if the technical deficiencies of the Hope Road Studio had led to the sessions being moved to another location. During my interviews with both of these participants there was a strong sense that, for them, music-making was about a personal expression that was not overshadowed by concerns regarding studio protocols, technical perfection or following established production methodologies. This aesthetic was reinforced as the sessions progressed and later verbalized in the interviews.

Morris added that his decision to continue recording in this fashion was supported by the approval of the A/P, who although not present during the recording sessions, did audition and approve the guitar recordings. Morris explained that after Browne and I left the studio, he then checked, compiled and edited the new acoustic guitar tracks. He selected the tracks that, in his view, best represented the musical ideas recorded during the session, but also tracks that complimented the existing recording. He then produced a guide mix of the new instrumentation that was copied onto a compact disc and left at the studio for the A/P to collect the following day. The responsibility of selecting, editing, mixing and presenting recorded material to the A/P were production tasks that Morris assumed. The A/P's comments on the creative direction of the guitar tracks were translated to Browne and myself through Morris as his intermediary at the start of the following session. These comments were always positive and represented an approval to continue with the same recording process.

The Concept of Production

During the course of the guitar sessions it was not clear who was acting as the creative producer for the album project, although both Morris and Browne seemed to make production decisions during the guitar sessions. For example, Browne not only acted as the musical arranger for the guitar session, but also made important decisions regarding the creative direction of the guitar tracks. Morris, in his capacity as audio engineer, also made important decisions concerning the recording method, sound and the balance of instruments that were presented to the A/P for approval.

During my interview with Morris, he was asked about the production of the existing backing tracks that he had recorded at the Bell Road studio. Morris stated that during the recording of these tracks, the A/P was required to be in the recording room with the other musicians and left Morris alone in the control room to decide on how individual instruments would be sonically represented in the recording. However, when listening back to the recordings, the A/P would comment on the recorded sound and say: 'That guitar sound is too bright', or 'Make the bass drum a little deeper', or 'Give me a little more presence'. Morris was therefore entrusted to establish the general sonic character and quality of instruments by assuming responsibility for instrument placement, microphone selection and placement, and the application of equalization and control of the instrument dynamics. According to Morris, the A/P contributed to fine-tuning the sounds that he took responsibility for creating.

The question, therefore, becomes: What part of the production did the A/P take direct responsibility for? Based on my experience during the guitar sessions and the account provided by Morris, it would be fair to say that some elements of the creative production for this album were entrusted to Morris, Browne and possibly other, unknown recording participants, but final approval was provided by the A/P. From the perspective of the guitar sessions, the A/P seemed to act in the capacity of an executive producer with Morris, Browne and myself all verbally contracted as his employees.

With this in mind, I asked Morris if he had noticed a difference between working as an audio engineer in Jamaica and the USA. He claimed that the difference was very noticeable and stated:

> Working abroad, especially for someone apart from, like the [A/P]; one, I do a lot less talking in a session. Sometimes it's like I'm the invisible person in the room, so the producer will be there, he'll control the talk back and everything, you're just the bridge between these guys and the equipment. It's like I'll be in there for one hour working and unless I have a technical question there is like, nothing said.

Morris was then asked, how does that experience compare to a Jamaican setting?

> In Jamaica it's different, there's always something, like some producers in Jamaica they're quick to ask your opinion, which I don't mind, but some may lean on the engineer too much.

Morris was asked: Can you give an example of how producers 'lean' on the engineer?

> You'll find guys that come in and they're like, 'Alright, vocals day' you know, the singer comes, and they'll be there [viz the producers] smoking a spliff or cigarette or something 'Yeah man engineer, you deal wid it man!' and they'll be there outside and you're like, what the hell.

Morris claims that he has experienced sessions in which he has been left alone by the so called 'producer' to record and produce the vocal performance, representing the part of a music product that is often considered to be a critical element. He adds that this can cause a level of friction between the producer and engineer, especially when faults are later detected in the vocal production. Morris explained that the producer sometimes tries to hold the engineer responsible for what Morris considers a lack of production supervision. To illustrate this point, he gave the following example regarding the above vocal track:

> Somebody else will walk in, [to the control room] like a well-trained musician and he'll like, 'Oh that little part is off', [the pitch of the voice] and the producer will go 'Engineer you never hear dat!' and sometimes you're like, what the, [implies expletive] you weren't even in the studio [referring to the producer].[32]

Morris claims that the Jamaican recording studio environment often places production demands on the engineer without production credits, whereas in the USA his involvement in the recording process was limited to what he considered strictly technical audio engineering tasks, following the direction of the producer. Working in the USA, Morris was required to play the role of a technical facilitator at the discretion of the producer with minimal involvement in the creative production of the music being recorded.

Morris recognized that Jamaican audio engineers are often required to perform production roles, but accepts this as part of the working conditions and studio culture that is prevalent in Jamaica. From his perspective the Jamaican audio engineer is often undervalued and marginalized, evidenced by the fact that he often does not get formal credit for his work, including his audio engineering role. He cites VP Records, in particular, as a record label that routinely fails to credit audio engineers on its compact disc liner notes. When he has taken this issue up with 'producers', they claim that full credits were submitted to the record label but that, 'there was too much words and they [the record company] decided to cut'. However, Morris also acknowledged that there was a possibility that his name was not included on the list submitted to the record company.

Creating and Selecting Guitar Tracks

The existing musical arrangements for the songs on which I was to add guitar tracks were based on a Nyabinghi style of drumming and percussion.[33] The arrangements, therefore, had a strong association with Rastafarians and some elements of Jamaican folk music. The instrumentation that I heard during the recording sessions included an electric bass guitar, two acoustic guitars, conga drums, hand-held percussion instruments, wind instruments, and vocals. Browne explained that he had been instructed by the A/P to enhance or replace the existing acoustic guitars because they were 'making the arrangements sound too Latin'.

---

[32] The example that Morris used was from an actual session, but he preferred not to identify the individuals involved.

[33] 'Nyabinghi' is an African derived word used to describe a specific type of Jamaican percussion-dominated music.

Browne interpreted this to mean that the A/P wanted the new guitars to provide a musical interpretation that was identifiably 'Jamaican'.

In the follow-up interview with Browne, on 8 March 2008, I asked if he had been formally commissioned by the A/P to act as the producer and/or arranger for the acoustic guitar sessions. Browne stated that:

> He [the A/P] called me and said, 'You remember that guitarist you used on Ziggy's album? [referring to an earlier session for a Ziggy Marley album that I had played on] Im der bout?' [is he available?] Browne said, 'I'll have to check', and [the A/P] responded, 'I wan you call him for me, but I wan you deal wid it' [I want you to take care of it].

Browne interpreted this as a request by the A/P, for him to produce and arrange the guitar tracks on his behalf. I asked Browne if this meant that he would receive production points and be credited for his work on the resulting album and he answered, 'I'm not sure.'

At the start of the first recording session, both Browne and Morris were unsure if the A/P planned to attend the session or even which songs were being considered for new guitar parts. Morris called the A/P's personal assistant into the control room and he was asked if he had this information. The personal assistant was also unsure and left to get instructions from the A/P, returning after about 10 minutes with a list of songs to be worked on. During that time I quizzed Morris about the studio equipment and changes that had been recently made to the studio. The last time I had worked at the Hope Road studio it had been equipped with a 24-track analogue tape machine, now replaced by the Pro Tools system. Morris explained that the Hope Road studio was under-utilized and at times, suffered from a lack of maintenance. For example, the Solid State Logic 40-channel mixing board had a number of channels that were not fully functional. Morris explained that there was also a limited choice of working microphones and outboard equipment kept at the Hope Road location. The session finally started at about 9 pm and Morris brought up the first song selection, which will be referred to as 'Song One'.

Browne, who was given the responsibility for directing the guitar parts, was, like me, hearing the songs for the first time. I positioned myself on the stool in the control room, initially with the Gibson B25 steel-string guitar, and Morris positioned the microphone within 4 inches of the guitar strings, facing the lower section of the sound hole. According to Browne, in his subsequent interview, the A/P had not asked him to listen to the songs prior to the guitar session, and the A/P was therefore depending on our collective ability to create the guitar parts and arrangements spontaneously during the course of the session. However, Morris was familiar with the material and had been responsible for recording the backing tracks and the guide mixes that we would be working with.[34]

---

[34] The term 'guide mix' represents the creative direction of the song, but is based on recorded instrumentation that might still be incomplete or subsequently changed.

Morris initially played the mixes with the existing guitar parts and my first impression was that they had been performed competently with a variety of predominantly arpeggio and strumming techniques, using standard chord voicings. If any criticism were to be made, it would have been that the existing guitar tracks might be described as 'predictable' and very 'Latin' sounding. As the song was being played, I used the steel-string acoustic to establish the key, existing chord movement and voicings that had been used for the existing guitar parts and then considered what non-standard tuning options, if any, were available to me. The song was in the key of B♭ minor and employed a repetitive chord sequence of E♭ minor to B♭ minor with some small variations. I assumed that the choice of key was based on the voice and, in order to enable the use of open strings on the guitar, I initially tried tuning the guitar one semi-tone below concert pitch, so that from low to high, the guitar was now tuned E♭, A♭, D♭, G♭, B♭, E♭. This allowed me to play in the key of B minor, and therefore incorporate open strings into the chord voicings and utilize open positions, providing a wider choice of voicings and representing a stronger register for the instrument, although tonally a little darker as a result of the detuning. Morris then muted the original guitar parts and I tried some textural arpeggio ideas with non-standard chord voicings that allowed the inclusion of open-pedalled strings.

Browne listened to the part I was playing, but suggested I try a more rhythmic strummed figure that he communicated by initially singing and moving his hands as if playing a guitar but then picked up my nylon-string guitar to demonstrate the idea. Some additional experimentation was conducted with the chord inversions and execution of the rhythmic figure, paying particular attention to the way in which it anticipated the beat in addition to the length and emphasis of notes. I then tried playing the part on the nylon-string guitar in standard tuning at concert pitch, and Browne and Morris both concurred that they preferred the sound quality of that instrument for this particular part.

The track was then recorded and checked for consistency in performance and sound. Although we were recording in Pro Tools, which offers the advantage of being able to cut and paste recorded parts, Morris informed us that the song was recorded without any form of timing reference such as a metronome track and, because of slight timing variations in the backing track, each new guitar track had to be recorded in its entirety, as if working with analogue tape.[35] This is an important point to note and reflects earlier discussions regarding the selection of recording techniques that are based on local creative need. Morris informed me that the option of recording to a metronome track, to facilitate cut and paste editing, was rejected by the A/P (Example 9.1).

---

[35] A timing reference is usually the first track recorded, to which all-additional tracks are played. This not only achieves consistent time keeping, but also allows sections within a song to be interchanged with cut and paste editing.

Example 9.1 Notation of first guitar part

Browne stated that he was using the musical reference of a Jamaican mento band and the new guitar track was referred to as the 'mento guitar' figure.[36] He then asked me to over dub the equivalent of what he interpreted as the mento 'banjo part' for which he also suggested a specific rhythmic figure. Although these two parts would typically be heard together in a mento setting, Browne, Morris and I concurred that it would be best to use them alternately to help define different sections of the song, identified by the vocal parts. Because of the inability to use the cut and paste facility in Pro Tools, Browne had to decide in which sections of the song the banjo inspired figure would be used and how the interplay between the two new guitar parts would be established.

Browne made this decision spontaneously and said, 'run the track and I'll show you where to play'. On the initial run through, Morris started recording even though recording levels and the headphone balance were still being adjusted. After the first take, Browne asked me to 'run the track again', but instructed me to vary the rhythmic figure with improvised rhythmic elements during these sections. As the guitar part was being recorded Browne indicated the location of these sections by using hand movements. He would imitate playing a guitar to signify the performance of the banjo figure and throw his hands away from his body to indicate that he wanted me to vary the figure (Example 9.2).

Example 9.2 Notation of second guitar part. Strummed up, down, up on each phrase

Browne's physical directions were impromptu and provided by him in the preceding two bars that led into each (banjo) section. Browne was therefore directing a spontaneous arrangement for the guitar parts, based intuitively on where he felt the second guitar part should perform. Morris was also required to follow the arrangement and mute the first guitar part when the second guitar part entered. Morris then edited the first guitar part so that both parts could be checked for consistency in performance and transitions.

When the new guitar parts were completed and the old ones removed, the feel of the song changed dramatically and Browne then suggested that we try some melody parts in the intro and outro of the song.[37]

---

[36] See the discussion of mento in Chapter 1.

[37] The term 'intro' is an abbreviation for the introduction of the song and 'outro' is a common term used in popular music that refers to the final section of the song, often based

For these parts Browne asked me to improvise some melodic ideas as the song, with the new rhythmic guitar parts, was played back on the studio monitors. After running through the complete song twice, Browne said that I had played an idea in one of the choruses that he particularly liked. I was not sure of the actual part Browne referred to, but Morris had been recording the improvised guitar ideas, even though they would be unusable due to leakage on the guitar track from the control-room monitors. Morris was therefore able to locate quickly the specific melody in question. We listened back to the part and Browne suggested that I simplify the melody and modify the rhythm slightly.

Once the melody had been agreed on I suggested adding a harmony part played as a two-part, double-stopped voicing. I then worked out appropriate fingering and positions for the part while rehearsing it, and suggested performing the part in a different fingerboard position where portamento could be used to help provide shape and emphasis for the musical phrase. Morris and Browne concurred that they preferred this interpretation and I changed back to headphone monitoring in preparation for recording. During this process Morris had anticipated the resetting of the recording level and headphone balance in preparation to record (Example 9.3).

Example 9.3   Notation of third guitar part, intro/outro phrase

While the new guitar parts were being worked out, Morris said very little, but followed closely the predominantly musical dialogue taking place between Browne and myself, and made the appropriate adjustments and edits to the guitar tracks without any need for instruction. Morris was therefore able to significantly enhance and contribute to the creative flow of the session by ensuring that the appropriate section of the backing track was always cued and ready for rehearsing or listening, and recording levels were set in preparation for recording. There was no noticeable break in the creative flow of ideas to reset the recording levels and headphone balance, although on several occasions I stopped recording to request that Morris change some aspect of the headphone balance in order to facilitate the performance of a particular part.

Morris was rarely instructed when to record, when to retake or when to edit a guitar part. He was at liberty to ask for musical parts to be retaken if he felt there was a technical or musical issue, which he did, without approval or question from Browne, and in this sense played a role that was certainly equal to Browne and significantly more than that of a technical facilitator. The decisions taken in regard to the technical and musical quality of the guitar tracks reflected a joint effort in which Morris had at least an equal share. However, Morris had unilateral control

---

on a repetitive vamp and intended to be faded out by the engineer during mixing.

over which tracks or parts of tracks would be retained, compiled or discarded and included in the new guitar mixes that were later presented to the A/P. That said, those decisions were based on a consensus of opinion that included the views of Browne and myself. Morris's involvement in these production aspects of the recording allowed Browne to concentrate on the musical content of the guitar performance and the communication of his creative ideas that were both verbal and physical.

The above melodic part might best be described as a syncopated semi-quaver pattern that was performed with a slight shuffle feel that is difficult to accurately notate.[38] My performance of the guitar part included a rhythmic interpretation, but Browne required a particular rhythmic emphasis within the phrase, which, in terms of the timing, pushed and pulled back on certain notes. When Browne described his rhythmic interpretation of the phrase, he said that it made him envisage 'one a dem big batty [big bottomed] market women carrying basket on her head and walking with a sway of her hips'.

Initially I had some difficulty capturing the exact rhythmic detail that Browne described and, after several attempts at recording the part, he tried to better communicate this rhythmic interpretation by placing one hand on his hip and mimicking a market-woman's walk, in time and syncopation to the music. From my perspective as the performer, I would describe the required change in rhythmic emphasis as being very nuanced but one where the physical movement provided by Browne did help to establish the points of emphasis, especially where notes were required to be pushed or held back, within the context of the overall rhythmic figure. However, there was still a certain amount of uncertainty in my performance that Browne obviously sensed and so every time that this section in the song came up, during recording, he performed his 'market woman walk' across the studio control room as a performance aid. The sight of this heavily bearded and dreadlocked Rasta impersonating a market-woman became a point of amusement for Morris and myself, and we occasionally made eye contact and smiled while Browne was performing his walk.

In addition to these guitar parts, Browne asked me to improvise a track where the nylon-string guitar was used to provide fills and unstructured melodic content to help establish another texture within the song. This track was predominantly made in a single take, but there were several occasions where Browne required me to punch in a replacement or improved performance of a section of the guitar part. At the time of recording this track was considered a 'throwaway track', in other words provided a guitar texture that could be used, if needed, during the mixing of the song and provide an option for filling any perceived gaps in the musical arrangement that emerged from the final mix.

An interesting point to note is that for the guide mix of 'Song One', made by Morris after Browne and I had left the studio, Morris had decided to use the above

---

[38] 'Shuffle feel' is used to describe a rhythmic structure that lies somewhere between the extremes of straight and triplet note values.

melodic guitar part only in the intro section of the song and discard it from the outro. In addition, he included in the mix a single melodic guitar figure taken from the original guitar recordings that Browne and I were unaware of. Furthermore, for the final mix of the song, released on the album, the melodic guitar part had been removed completely but the spontaneous, improvised throwaway guitar track had been included in almost its entirety.[39] As a 'throwaway' track, there were several sections of my performance that were poorly executed but were not erased because of the intended usage of the track. During mixing, someone made a decision to include this spontaneous performance despite the fact that it contained what I would describes as, mistakes.[40]

It is also important to note that, during the guitar sessions, more tracks were recorded than were actually needed for each song. These additional tracks included alternative musical interpretations or independent musical ideas suggested by Glen Browne or me. After each recording session was completed, Morris remained at the studio and edited, selected and mixed the new guitar tracks, which in his sole opinion best suited the needs of the song, and then presented them to the A/P. At the completion of the four sessions, Morris indicated that 25 guitar tracks had been completed in total, but only 14 tracks comprising complete and composite tracks would be used on the actual recordings and my invoice to the A/P's personal assistant reflected that number.[41]

A digital recording system such as Pro Tools has the potential of providing unlimited tracks, unlike analogue recording, which was limited to the 24 tracks available on a multi-track 2-inch tape. Whereas musicians typically charged the client for the final number of tracks committed to tape, with Pro Tools, the musician is required to trust that the producer will only use tracks in the final recording that have been paid for. For the sessions described here, Morris assumed the responsibility of deciding which guitar tracks were to be included in the final sound recordings.

Post-recording Interviews

During my post-recording interview with Browne, I asked him whether delving back into the folk traditions of Jamaica was a production or arrangement strategy that he regularly used, or whether this was a specific technique for this particular project. He answered:

---

[39] Note that the audio examples are taken from the original guide mixes that were presented to the A/P and are not representative of the final mixes that would be commercially released.

[40] When questioning Morris regarding the outcome of this particular mix he stated that the final mix, performed by him, had been lost prior to mastering by the A/P's personal assistant and for this particular song a new final mix was performed by an unknown audio engineer.

[41] A composite track is the representation of a several performances that have been edited into what the editor considers to be the best single performance.

No this is something that kinda comes naturally to me, we heard the songs, we heard the guitar parts, [the original guitar parts] so right there now, the first thing I do which a lot of people don't know, when I'm going into a session, I go inside [pointing to his chest] and I ask supreme creativity to take over, do justice to this piece of work and cause us to work together as one. So what I start to do now is listen, I listen to the riddim [the musical backing track] and trust that divine self to tell me now; hear it de [hear it there], and listen and see how it take place, and always, when I do this, especially when we dealing with that kind of music, [traditional or Nyabinghi music dominated by percussion] and in this situation, having heard what was there before and why him [the A/P] don't want this [the original guitar tracks] so obviously he wants to come closer home [make the sound more identifiably Jamaican] but those people apparently didn't know [referring to the existing guitarists], and I'm hearing the parts, when I hear the parts I start to dance and it sweet me and I tell you, and then we get into trouble. [Browne laughs] When you're working with a musician who knows his instrument and is always trying to understand where this is going, because it is a surprise for the both of us you know, because when the two of us hear it we say, shit! Hear dat![42]

Browne claims that he looks for spiritual inspiration to help him hear the new musical parts needed for a song. He recognizes the correct guitar part in his musical imagination because it stimulates a physical rhythmic movement that might be interpreted as a form of dance, and when it 'sweets me', meaning makes him feel good, he then tells me, as the performer, and my task becomes the musical interpretation of his description of the part including, but not restricted to, language, sound and movement. Browne's comment that, 'It is a surprise for the both of us', refers to the fact that the eventual performance is largely spontaneous and becomes a combination of what Browne hears and the way in which I interpret his direction. In this sense the guitar tracks represent a combination of our creative efforts. Browne expanded on this theme by saying that, in his experience, session musicians only want to play what comes to them naturally and this often results in a repetition of their established musical vocabulary. As a producer/arranger, he likes to work with musicians who are willing to stretch themselves and try to accommodate the ideas that he hears. In doing so, the resulting performance is often a surprise to both parties.

Browne's creative direction on the guitar sessions was therefore based on a primary need to create music that inspired a physical response from the listener. This seems to be a theme that is common in Jamaican popular music with a long

---

[42] Browne uses the term 'riddim' to describe the backing-music track, even though the music, to the best of my knowledge, was not intended for use with multiple songs. His use of the term is not incorrect but an example of the flexible way in which terminology is employed and has to be assessed in the context of a sentence. It should be noted that Browne's use of the term 'riddim', in this context, means backing-track.

tradition. During my interview with Errol Brown in January 2008, he described Duke Reid producing music in the 1960s by tapping out the rhythm of the bass line on the bass player Jackie Jackson's knee in an attempt to make the song as 'danceable' as possible. I can also add that, in my experience, when working on music backing tracks in the recording studio, I have heard musicians on several occasions describing something being missing from the musical arrangement or mix by commenting that, 'The riddim haffe dance', meaning that (The backing track needs to make you want to move rhythmically). These studio sessions remind us that JPM has a critical connection to physical movement and dance, which represents a common thread connecting both popular and traditional forms of music in Jamaica.

In the limited context of this ethnographic study, Glen Browne's and my contributions are relatively easy to assess, because the currency of our creativity and musical craft is easily located in the harmony, melody, rhythm and performance that can be scored and defined within the context of a musical tradition. The influence of Gregory Morris is more difficult to define, yet is clearly evident in the sounds that he captures, selects, edits and balances as an interpretation of the various elements that make up this sound recording. Even more difficult to define is the attitude that Morris brought to the recording session. His decision to continue recording at the Hope Road studio and the atmosphere that he helped to create were important elements that contributed towards the sound of the recording. From my perspective as a performer, Morris had a significant impact on the flow of creativity that occurred during the recording sessions. Evidence of this can be found in the way in which Morris allowed Browne and myself to work seamlessly through the various musical challenges that were presented during the sessions. He achieved this by not only assuming full responsibility for the technical circumstances of the session but by generally anticipating, removing or avoiding many of the impediments to the musical flow that the process of recording can, and often does, introduce. However, it remains difficult to quantify this contribution.

In an attempt to try and better understand Morris' perspective, objectives and motivation, I discussed specific aspects of the guitar sessions with him and tried to discover his interpretation of the experiences we had shared and witnessed during the process of recording. I asked him if he found it strange or unusual that Glen Browne had communicated a rhythmic detail to me during the sessions using a rhythmic walk. He responded 'No' and went on to explain that from his audio-engineering perspective: 'If you can't dance to it [the music being recorded] at that moment, well, you're probably having second thoughts about it.' Morris is referring to a focal point in the audio-engineering process where a musical performance is interpreted by altering the audio frequencies, contained in a sound. This process is used to emphasize or subdue what are perceived as rhythmic pulses, interpreted through physical movement.

This represents one of the key elements found in local values that are employed to inspire movement, which Browne described as: 'Listening from the waist down', as opposed to Americans and Europeans who listen from the waist up. From Morris's perspective, Browne was contributing towards that process, but using the tools of musical creativity and performance as opposed to sound. This suggests that although the mechanisms are different, Morris shares a common value and musical focus with Browne that critically evaluates the elements of their respective disciplines with the intent of employing them to inspire a particular physical response in the listener. The Jamaican experience seems to suggest that spontaneity, groove and vibe are more efficient conduits for channelling this aesthetic, rather than the pursuit of perfect technical recordings, formulaic recording processes or working within any strict harmonic or melodic structure.

Whereas the musical phrases, lines and figures suggested by Browne contain clear evidence of the above process, they also readily absorb Morris's creative contribution in the form of sound creation and musical balance, helping to inspire a particular musical attitude and rhythmic emphasis that the new musical ideas assume. But what evidence is there to support the idea that Morris was doing anything beyond his technical role of an audio engineer, which is, after all, the task of capturing sound?

It should be noted that this particular album project was unusual in the sense that it was predominantly acoustic with no sampled or synthesized instrument parts. This meant that sound creation was the product of the audio engineer employing microphones and their positioning as primary sound-creation tools. Morris confirmed that he acted as the audio engineer for these sessions despite the majority of his professional recording experience being with the capture and production of electronic instruments that now dominate the vast majority of JPM. Therefore, from a purely technical audio-engineering standpoint, was Morris the best-qualified audio engineer suitable for this kind of acoustic recording project? Is it possible that he was selected for this project by the A/P on the basis of skills that went beyond, and perhaps were considered more important than, technical ability, meaning his sensibility toward spontaneity, groove and vibe?

With this in mind I asked Morris if the A/P had provided him with any specific guidance or instructions in regard to the type of sounds or musical balance that he wanted to create in the initial group recording sessions. If so, were any sound references supplied to Morris as a sonic guide, to which he answered 'No'. From Morris's perspective, he interpreted this lack of direction and sound references as approval by the A/P for him to create a sound palette of his own choosing, based on his own production values and sensibilities. However, the A/P did make suggestions and therefore undoubtedly contributed to the production process, but the creation and choice of sounds was largely left up to Morris. It would be fair to say that this responsibility not only demands a certain level of self-confidence and creativity, but also exceeds the strict technical duties of the audio engineer. The process of 'sound creation' is important in regard to the defining and positioning of a piece of commercial popular music, and in this sense Morris's contribution to the final recording appears to be significant.

The production sounds created by Morris, evident during the guitar sessions but also in the guide and final mixes, were marked by an emphasis on the low-frequency content of certain recorded instruments, such as the electric bass and bandu (a handmade bass drum).[43] They might be described as unnatural in terms of the instrument balance that one would expect from an acoustic ensemble. This undoubtedly gave the production, a sound that was consistent with the mainstream of electronic JPM and not typically what one might expect from an acoustic 'unplugged' recording.

Musicians such as myself were employed to create and perform musical parts, but this was done in response to the sounds created by Morris in the fold back, headphone mix or on the studio monitors, and also in the context of the easy-going vibe that he brought to the recording session. Therefore, it would be fair to say that Morris's choice and selection of sounds not only influenced the final listening experience, but the musical parts created by the rhythm section and overdub musicians.

I asked Morris, 'why do you push the bass and drums so hard and emphasize their low frequency content?' He replied: 'I guess probably, like, from the days of the sound system, ya know, standing in your ear, that drum and bass.' Morris explains that 'standing in your ear' means the drum and bass stand out as dominant features of the music. In this sense, Morris is evidently continuing a tradition noted by Graeme Goodall in earlier chapters, pursuing the sound of emphasized bass. This is notable because in 2008 the sound system can no longer be considered the primary driver of JPM and this particular recording project was intended for the international market, implying that there has been a more general acceptance of emphasized bass, and/or an association with JPM.[44]

I then asked Morris if emphasized bass had a direct connection to making people want to move or dance, and he responded with an emphatic 'Yes!' I asked Morris if he used a particular process or technique to decide what pulses of the rhythm to emphasize. This is a pertinent question because the process of 'toning' instruments using equalization allows the engineer to focus on a narrow band of frequencies and accentuate them. Notes or elements contained in the musical or percussive sounds that are centred on that frequency band are, in effect, pushed forward in the sound field and become pronounced. Morris stated: 'I like to, like, feel it, like, ya know, especially if I'm doing like, dancehall stuff, ya have to put yourself in the middle of the club, to get that kind of vibe.' Morris seems to be suggesting that his creation of sound, in the form of emphasized bass, is realized through his technical manipulation of the equipment, but it is based on a personal value system that is both physically and intuitively derived. He not only retains a vivid sense of what the dancehall sounds and feels like but he claimed that he sometimes arranged to play finished mixes in a club or on a sound system to confirm that he had achieved this aesthetic.

---

[43] See Kenneth Bilby's discussion of Kumina and other Jamaican folk influences on JPM in *Caribbean Currents*, 1995, p. 162.

[44] An interesting note is that although Morris had never heard of Graeme Goodall, he is connected to him through the training he received from Errol Brown, who had apprenticed under Byron Smith, who had been trained by Goodall at Federal, the same studio (renamed Tuff Gong) where Morris now worked.

Morris was not aware of who Graeme Goodall was, yet 50 years later he describes the continuation of an audio-engineering process that Goodall had initiated in the early 1960s. It is appropriate to note that during my discussion with Morris he made no attempt to relate his manipulation of sound to any pre-set engineering practice, such as the choice of microphone, placement, microphone-preamp, equalization or use of a limiter. This is not to say that Morris lacked knowledge or recognized the importance of these devices, but it was my sense that his value system, in regard to sound, was connected to emotive, sociocultural values rather than established technical processes.

From my perspective, as the performer on the guitar sessions, Morris seemed highly tuned to a spontaneous recording approach. Without direction, he not only captured the performances, but also the rehearsing and the working out of ideas, which ensured that no idea was lost and proved to be invaluable as the session progressed. I contend that although Morris's creative and artistic input cannot be easily quantified, closer examination of the recording process, in the context of the creative objective, implies that he played an essential creative, as well as technical, role.

In *Capturing Sound*, Mark Katz refers to producers and audio engineers as 'recordists' and claims that they 'fall outside (or perhaps in between) the traditional triad of composer, performer and listener. They might be thought of as sound shapers, artists in their own right who collaborate with performers and composers' (2004, p. 44). Therefore, Katz recognizes that many compositions and musical performances only become feasible through the interface of engineered sound. During the guitar sessions, Morris clearly and effectively demonstrated that process in action.

Based on my interview with Morris, I had the impression that his professional relationship with the A/P was one where he was employed not only for his technical engineering skills but also for the sounds, values and musical sensibilities that he brought to the recording process. These attributes materialize when Morris is allowed a certain amount of freedom during recording, but I was interested to discover if the A/P recognized this creative contribution. I asked Morris what process the A/P used, if any, to evaluate his unsupervised work in the studio and if there are occasions when the A/P disapproved of creative decisions he sometimes made. Morris claimed that his close work with the A/P gave him a good understanding of his likes and dislikes, but there were times when the A/P disapproved of the decisions he made:

> Sometimes it's like a weird situation, where I would go ahead and do something that he [the A/P] didn't really like, he would try and drill me on [question him] 'Why did you?' Ya know, and he would try to find out, 'So how come you let him do that, why?' I would try to explain and he was like, 'OK', and then he would say 'So why didn't you let him try this?' [laughs]

Morris was describing a situation where he was directing a musical performance in the absence of the A/P, who on hearing the results showed disapproval. This seems to imply that while the A/P recognizes Morris's ability to perform creative tasks, he accepts that, occasionally, Morris's work will not meet with his approval. On these occasions he tries to discover what transpired and suggest alternative approaches that might have been considered. This suggests a recording methodology where Morris might be described as the A/P's surrogate producer, for at least some production duties.

By the end of the guitar sessions and post-recording interviews, it was evident that both Morris and Browne enjoyed a high level of trust placed in them by the A/P, demonstrated in the creative freedom that they both enjoyed during the guitar sessions. It is not possible for me to comment on what the creative expectations of the A/P might have been, but the fact that he allowed four recording sessions to proceed without his presence suggests that he was content with this working arrangement and the creative results it produced.

It became evident in the interviews and by listening to the sounds created during these sessions that the relationship between sound and physical movement was very significant and sat at the core of the creative process for both Browne and Morris. I use the term 'physical movement' here because what Browne and Morris describe seems to be more than the creation of music that is simply intended for people to dance to. It is as if the motivation for bodily movement has acquired an importance in JPM but this does not necessarily have to result, literally, in dance. Although beyond the scope of this study, the testimony of Browne and Morris suggests the existence of a physical connection between the listener and music, achieved through low-frequency sound waves as they pass through the body, acting as a vehicle for a wide range of subtle rhythmic elements.

The absence of a formal creative producer during the guitar sessions reiterates a theme that has been repeated throughout this book, going back to the work of Donald Hendry and Graeme Goodall. It is the absence of the producer that, in part, requires the audio engineer and musician to pursue practices that go far beyond the realm of technician or performer. There is a temptation to try and evaluate these production practices based on standards and values established elsewhere. However, this would fail to recognize that the international status and success of JPM might well be the product of these practices. My intention is not to pass judgement on these issues, nor debate the underlying moral, ethical and creative questions that they raise, but simply to try and evoke a better understanding of the way in which JPM has and continues to develop.

What becomes clear in this chapter, and indeed throughout this book, is that the Jamaican audio engineer and musician demonstrate a level of authority, and routinely make production and creative decisions during the recording process in Jamaica. This chapter demonstrates that, despite changes in technology, the audio engineer and musician continue to provide critical elements in a spontaneous recording process built on feel, groove and vibe with the goal of producing music that inspires a particular kind of physical movement in the listener. As such, the audio engineer represents the unsung hero of JPM, the lynchpin around which many of its unique characteristics have developed, who has, and continues to exert a constant and ongoing influence on the development of JPM.

Conclusion

While this book has focused on the development of JPM through the work of audio engineers and musicians, it raises a number of questions regarding the post-1950 popular music canon. Few would disagree that recording processes and music production systems have had a significant influence on this important body of music. However, the details of what music professionals refer to as 'music production', meaning the process of turning a musical idea into a recorded product, remains largely untapped. The information offered in this study, although limited to JPM, emerges from a focus on some of these 'music production' practices, particularly those involved with sound creation, the technology on which it depends and the human agency that often provides its direction. Although the introduction and ongoing integration of digital technology has caused seismic shifts in all spheres connected to the music industry, it remains important for us to understand where and how the sounds of popular music evolved.

From my perspective, the role of the audio engineer represents an area that is not only under-studied but is also under-appreciated. In the case of JPM, the audio engineer's influence is relatively easy to detect given the fact that many Jamaican 'producers' limit their activities to executive duties. Despite this, there is still a disproportionate division of credit for the achievement of successful sound recordings, in favour of the musician, with nominal consideration for the audio engineer's role. This book therefore underlines the need for a more detailed assessment of how technical processes influence music creation, performance and capture. In the context of JPM, the findings of this study suggest that musical performance and sound creation often function in a symbiotic relationship, but this phenomenon is in no way limited to Jamaican recording studios.

Although Geoff Emerick is widely recognized for his audio engineering contribution to The Beatles' seminal album, *Sgt Pepper's Lonely Hearts Club Band* (Parlophone, 1967), I contend that the full extent of his creative contribution is yet to be fully assessed. In reading the various accounts of The Beatles' recording sessions there is consensus regarding Emerick's important technical and creative contribution to this album in particular.[1] However, Emerick's achievement in sound creation becomes absorbed by more tangible areas of music production and is often credited to the musician, arranger and/or producer. Other seminal sound recordings of the 1960s also suggest that the audio engineer played a critical role in the development and shaping of popular music. Is it coincidence that Phil Spector's 'wall of sound' and the Beach Boys seminal album *Pet Sounds* (Capitol, 1966)

---

[1] See Martin and Hornsby (1979); Lewishohn (1988); Emerick and Massey (2006).

were recorded at Gold Star studios under the guidance of Larry Levine as audio engineer? Could Spector or Brian Wilson have created the new sounds associated with their music in any similarly equipped studio at that time with any audio technician? I suspect not, and it seems clear that Levine and Emerick, played a crucial role in the seismic shifts that occurred in the sound of popular music during this period. Assessing and acknowledging the creativity and ingenuity of these audio engineers does nothing to diminish the contribution of other recording participants. This study therefore suggests that the rigorous appraisal of sound recordings should include a detailed assessment of sound creation, which can complement but also be complemented by other forms of musical analysis.

This study of JPM has demonstrated how sound creation and manipulation, like a musical performance, can be intensely creative, and can also influence and change the creative approach of musicians in a range of often subtle but measurable ways. Sound, like melody and harmony, is often easy to replicate but difficult to conceptualize and originate in a popular music recording session. However, this is not to say that every audio engineer is able to expand the sonic horizon of popular music. In fact, in Chapter 8, Jeremy Harding notes the existence of a formulated approach towards audio engineering in North America in 2008, which responds to the needs of radio stations and conforms to an established sonic standard. The role of the audio engineer therefore can respond to a wide range of needs that require both technical and creative skill; functioning in a freeform or formulated structure, providing purely technical services or the inspiration and vibe of a spontaneous recording environment.

This study set out to investigate the influence of recording procedures on the development of JPM and it uncovers a clear trend where audio engineers represent a position of authority, intrinsically involved with the creation, direction and production of JPM as a spontaneous recorded product. This is evident in the very first sound recordings made by Donald Hendry at the start of the 1950s, and continues in the work of Gregory Morris in 2008. Jamaican audio engineers therefore emerge from this study as multi-faceted recording practitioners who wield a significant level of authority in Jamaican recording studios, evident in unique sonic developments such as the emergence of emphasized bass in the 1960s and performance mixing during the 1980s. Their work might be described as the lubrication of a dynamic musical engine, but while every 'horsepower' of that engine's performance is influenced by the efficiency and characteristic of the lubricant, it remains largely hidden. Wallis and Malm appropriately defined JPM as a 'Studio product' (1984, p.169) and, as such, JPM offers a particularly effective site for the study of audio engineering practice and an example of the ways in which the audio engineer can influence the development of popular music.

Another goal of this book was to challenge the notion that music production standards in Jamaica were somehow inferior to those practised elsewhere, as if there is a single pre-eminent recorded sound that all recording participants in the world subscribe to. The contents of this book attest to the fact that recording in Jamaica is often intended to meet the demands of a local aesthetic, with limited consideration for values being employed elsewhere. I have argued that recording studios represent complex tools, designed, built and operated for the purpose of creating and capturing sounds that are considered appropriate for specific music products, within a culture. A deeper understanding of popular music has to therefore grapple with how and why specific tools are chosen and the way in which they are adapted and applied to meet commercial, cultural and creative needs.

In my assessment, our understanding of the development of JPM has been significantly hindered by a prejudice toward dancehall music, led by an establishment that has pursued the misrepresentation of music technology in the production of post-1980s JPM. It is not clear to me why these voices and their assertions have not been more vigorously challenged by the academy, given the erroneous basis of some claims. I contend that this narrative and its application of pre-1980s recording values, as the benchmark for Jamaican creativity, are not only inappropriate but detrimental to the study of JPM. It is therefore hoped that this book's discussion of production practices used in post-1980s JPM will help to counter this negative and largely unfair perception that dancehall music seems to have acquired. While certainly not without fault, criticism of dancehall music, in my view, should be based on rigorous and analytical debate of actual production practices and the unique way in which creativity emerges in this music.

While considering the recording studio culture of Jamaica, a number of underlying themes have emerged during the writing of this book, which are worthy of final mention. My discussion regarding the Rediffusion radio service, represents an important element of the unique form of musical exposure that Kingstonians enjoyed at the turn of the 1960s. It provides an explanation for how Kingston's largely impoverished society gained access to foreign-recorded music during this period. My findings suggest that Kingston's music consumers, of all classes, emerged during this period with a familiarity for a wide selection of recorded music and production sounds. I saw a need to include this information, not only as a component that undoubtedly influenced producers of locally recorded music, but as information that might help to explain the popularity in Jamaica of North American country music that seems to have had a significant local impact and is yet to be explored.

During this critical period of the late 1950s and early 1960s, Kingstonians enjoyed a rich and unique soundscape, dominated during the day by the Rediffusion system and at night by the low-frequency rumble of multiple sound systems playing American popular music as well as a growing and eagerly anticipated range of local music products. It is therefore hoped that the findings of this study will not only have an impact on JPM scholarship but also highlight a potential seam of information that lies in the study of recorded products and the way in which they are consumed in Jamaica.

The need for this study is, in fact, long overdue because the generation of audio engineers who dramatically changed popular music during the 1950s, 1960s and 1970s are disappearing at a dramatic rate. Sadly, during the course of my research for this book, Coxsone Dodd, Jim Taylor, Lynn Tait, Joe Gibbs, Byron Smith and Errol Thompson all died. This study therefore not only establishes that the audio engineer had a significant influence on the development of JPM, but that there is an urgent need to gather the oral histories of these important contributors and document their work before it is entirely lost.

Appendix A
Recording Models

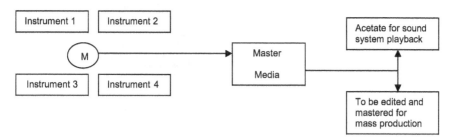

Figure A.1   The single-microphone/single-track recording model (1948–58)

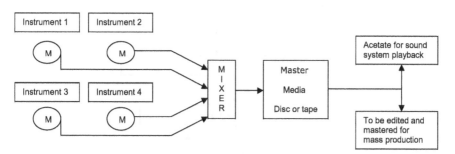

Figure A.2   The multi-microphone/single-track recording model (1958–63)

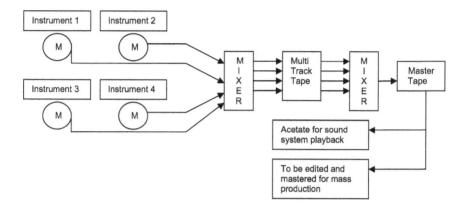

Figure A.3   The multi-microphone/multi-track recording model (1963–82)

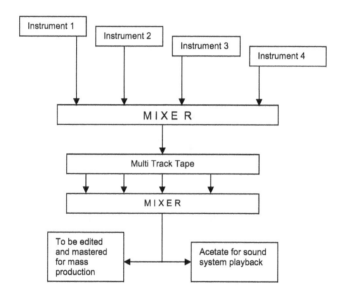

Figure A.4   The serial (one instrument at a time) multi-track recording model (1982–92)

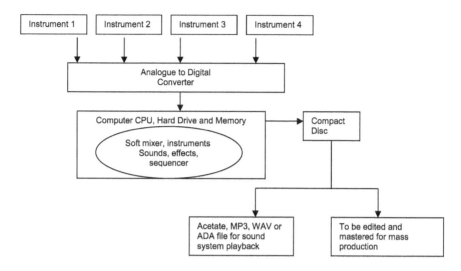

Figure A.5   The computer-based recording model (1992–present)

Appendix B
Interviewee List

The following table represents a list of the primary informants, their respective area of work and dates on which interviews were initiated. In many cases multiple interviews were conducted.

Name		Role	Month	Year
Arkwright	Frank	Mastering engineer	June	2006
Ashbourne	Peter	Multi-role producer	July	2008
Brown	Errol	Audio engineer	January	2008
Browne	Cleveland	Producer/Audio engineer	July	2008
Browne	Glen	Arranger/musician	March	2008
Coote	Paul	Music collector	April	2007
Couch	Peter	Producer/musician	February	2008
Coxsone	Dodd	Producer/Audio Engineer	February/March	2002
Cummings	Melvis	Broadcast engineer	June	2009
Davy	Noel	Musician	January	2006
Dunbar	Sly	Musician/Producer	November	2009
Fletcher	Michael	Musician	January	2006
Goodall	Graeme	Audio engineer	July	2006
Harding	Jeremy	Producer/Audio engineer	January	2008
Harriot	Derrick	Singer/Producer	September	2009
Hendry	Donald	Audio engineer	June	2007
Hussey	Dermott	Broadcaster	July	2006
Khouri	Paul	Producer/Audio engineer	June	2002
Khouri	Richard	producer/Audio engineer	June	2010
Lee	Bunny	Producer	June	2006
Loddington	Jake	Broadcast engineer	April	2010
Lyn	Robbie	Musician	January	2006
McDonald	Michael	Audio engineer	June	2008
Mathews	Walter	Broadcast engineer	May	2006

Name		Role	Month	Year
Morris	Gregory	Audio engineer	March	2008
Peart	James	Musician/Audio engineer	December	2005
Perkins	Lascels	Singer	June	2006
Seaga	Edward	Producer	February	2008
Scorpio	Jack	Producer/Audio engineer	May	2006
Sindrey	Dennis	Musician	July	2006
Stewart	Steven	Audio Engineer/Musician	April	2001
Teape	Robert	Broadcast engineer	June	2006
Whitter	Glen	Audio engineer	June	2006

Appendix C
Glossary of Music-related Terms

The glossary has been compiled from answers given during the interviews and questionnaire. It also includes terms that came up during interviews. In this event, verification of the term was obtained from at least two other sources before being included.

Bang
Piano-specific term used to describe the single chord, off-beat figure typically associated with reggae and rock steady.

Bubble
A semi-quaver rhythmic figure performed on the organ, associated with Reggae but also found in later styles of JPM.

Check (also 'Chop')
Guitar-specific term used to describe the single chord, off-beat figure typically associated with ska, rock-steady. reggae and dancehall music.

Check-a
Guitar-specific term used to describe the double quaver rhythmic figure typically associated with reggae and rock-steady.

Come again (also 'Flash it Back' and 'Lick it Back')

A performance directive given to a selector or band by a performer requesting that they return to the start of a piece of music.

Conscious
A style of music and lyrics with a positive, very often Rastafarian perspective.

Dance Hall
A specific type of venue associated with the sound system. Usually the venue was open air and in the 1950s might have been called a lawn.

Dancehall
A style of music that developed during the 1980s and became known for its uses of drum machine and dominance of deejay vocalists. Dancehall music was more rhythmically diverse and used faster tempos than reggae. It very often employed

gimmicky musical trends and styles of lyrics that were frequently censored by the media using sensationalist lyrics that took, what some perceived as, radical positions on sexuality and gangsterism.

Dub
1. A type of audio engineered music created from pre-existing recordings.
2. Can be uses as a direction during a live performance indicating that only drum and bass should play.
3. Used to indicate the process of recording or copying musical material.

Fast Food
Slang term used by musicians to describe music that is not musically challenging but provides income.

Feel
Described by most informants as an emotion that comes out of music but also represents a term used in conjunction with other descriptive words to provide performance instruction. The term is often applied to indicate the need for small subtle changes in the nuance of a performance, for example 'Play it with a sticky feel'.

Groove
The term was generally thought to represent the rhythmic interaction and sense that instruments provided the listener with. Most informants associated the term with a strong repetitive pulse that was hypnotic and steady. This produced a physical reaction from the listener, which was described as making you want to move but not necessarily dance.

Haul 'n' Pull Up
This is a term used by deejays to instruct the individual operating the turntables of a sound system to stop the music abruptly and restart the song or follow additional instructions from the deejay.
The term is also used to direct a group of musicians during a live performance, who also prepare to restart the song or follow additional instruction from the deejay.

Herbal Pounding
Describes the style of reggae music associated with Rastafarian philosophy and includes the smoking of ganja.

Kotch
This term is an example of Jamaican English that means 'resting place'. The term implies an improvised seat where an individual may rest. In terms of the performance of JPM the term represents a place in a repetitive rhythmic

structure that acts as a point of punctuation, typically in the form of a rest in the musical phrase.

Mix

1. The balancing and sonic treatment of instruments in a multi-track recording .
2. The term can be used in a live performance to indicate that the group plays pre-determined rhythmic structures (engineered rhythms), typically in unison, and octaves with all instruments playing the same rhythmic figure. Direction to 'mix' is typically given by the performer or the musical director of the group.

Monkey

A double semi-quaver rhythmic figure. Performed most commonly on the organ but can be performed on electronic percussion. The name is derived from its apparent imitation of the sound made by a monkey.

Nice-up

To make something attractive and feel good or inspirational.

One Drop

Denotes a drum beat most commonly associated with reggae but also used with preceding and later styles of JPM. It is recognized by the use of the side stick that plays with the kick drum on the third beat in the bar.

Rattle

A term used to describe a snare drum flourish used particularly in folk-influenced dancehall music.

Describes a fast succession of decorative notes played on the guitar, typically while it duplicates the bass line at a higher octave.

Reasoning, or To Reason

To discuss, debate or problem solve.

Riddim

Jamaican/English for the term 'rhythm'.

A music backing track used as the base on which multiple songs are performed.

A live performance term typically used in dancehall music to direct the drummer and bass player to stop playing.

Rockers

There are various definitions but this is most commonly associated with a militant style of reggae being produced during the early 1980s and typified by the work of Sly Dunbar and Robbie Shakespeare, incorporating the steppes drum beat.

Roots
1. A general term used to describe music from the rock-steady and reggae era.
2. Used to describe a value system and sensibility associated with Rastafarians.

Shuffle
A term used to describe a rhythmic interpretation of quavers played in the form of triplets. But it is typically performed somewhere between these two rhythmic values.

Steppes
Denotes a drumbeat based on four crotchet kick drum pulses in the bar.

Top
A performance directive given to a selector or band by a performer requesting that they return to the start of a piece of music.

Version
1. Is used, as in Standard English, to describe a rendition of a piece of music that has been adapted in some way. i.e. Eric Clapton's version of 'I Shot The Sheriff'.
2. An abbreviation for Version B-side, meaning the instrumental mix of an A side of a record.

Version B-side
The instrumental mix of the A-side of a record. Version B-sides were often used as a vehicle for the audio engineer to introduce new sonic textures to the sound recording. These were used by sound-system selector to provide interest for its patrons or to be used as a generic backing track over which the live performance of singers or deejays could be featured.

Wheel
A performance term that directs a selector or live band to stop the current piece of music being played abruptly.

Wheel and Come-again
A performance directive combining the term 'wheel' and the term 'come-again'. It directs the selector or live band to stop abruptly and restart the current song from the start.

Select Bibliography

Alleyne Dillion. 1999. *Taxation and Equity in Jamaica 1985–1992: Who Bear's the Burden?* (The Press, UWI, Kingston, Jamaica).

Amos, S.W. (ed.). 1977. *Radio, TV & Audio Technical Reference Book* (Butterworth, London).

Attali, Jacques. 1999. *Noise: The Political Economy of Music*, (University of Minnesota, USA).

Bainbridge, David. 1992. *Intellectual Property*, 4th edition (Pearson Education Ltd, Harlow, UK).

Ballou, Glen. M. (ed.). 1991. *Handbook for Sound Engineers* (Butterworth-Heinemann, Newton, USA).

Barz, Gregory and Cooley, Timothy (eds). 2008. *Shadows In The Field: New Perspectives for Fieldwork in Ethnomusicology* (Oxford University Press, New York).

Bayley, Amanda. (ed.). 2010. *Recorded Music: Performance, Culture and Technology* (Cambridge University Press, UK).

Beebe, Roger. Fulbrook, Denise and Saunders, Ben (eds). 2002. *Rock Over The Edge: Transformations in Popular Music Culture* (Duke University Press, USA).

Bennett Andy. 2001. *Cultures of Popular Music: Issues In Culture and Media Studies* (Open University Press, Buckingham, UK).

Best, Curwen. 2004. *Culture @ The Cutting Edge: Tracking Caribbean Popular Music* (University of The West Indies, Kingston, Jamaica).

Bilby, Kenneth. 1995. 'Jamaica', in Manuel, *Caribbean Currents: Caribbean Music From Rumba to Reggae* (Temple University Press, USA).

Borwick, John (ed.). 1994. *Sound Recording Practice* (Oxford University Press, New York).

Brackett, David. 2000. *Interpreting Popular Music* (California University Press, USA).

Bradley, Lloyd. 2000. *This is Reggae Music: The story of Jamaican Music* (Grove Press, New York).

—. 2002. *Reggae: The Story of Jamaican Music* (BBC, London).

Brady, Erika. 1999. *A Spiral Way: How The Phonograph Changed Ethnography* (University Press of Mississippi, USA).

Braithwaite, Edward Kamau. 1971. *Folk Culture of the Slaves in Jamaica.*(New Beacon, London).

Braun, Hans-Joachim. 2002. *Music and Technology in the Twentieth Century* (Johns Hopkins University Press, USA).

Brown, Roger and Griese, Martin. 2000. *Electronic Dance Music Programming Secrets* (Pearson Education Limited, London).

Byron, Reginald (ed). 1995. *Music, Culture, & Experience: Selected Papers of John Blacking* (University of Chicago Press, USA).

Cable, Michael. 1977. *The Pop Industry Inside Out* (W.H. Allen, London).

Carter, L. Kenneth. 1997. *Why Workers Won't Work: The Worker In a Developing Economy, A Case Study of Jamaica* (Macmillan, Oxford, UK).

Cassidy, F.G. and Le Page R. B (ed). 2002. *Dictionary of Jamaican English 2ndEdition* (University of The West Indies Press, Kingston, Jamaica).

Chanan, Michael. 1995. *Repeated Takes: A Short History of Recording and Its Effects On Music* (Verso, London).

Chevannes, Barry. 1995. *Rastafari: Roots and Ideology* (Syracuse University Press, USA).

Cogan, Jim and Clark, William. 2003. *Temples of Sound: Inside The Great Recording Studios* (Chronicle, San Francisco).

Cooper, Carolyn. 1993. *Noises in the Blood* (Duke University Press, USA).

—. 2004. *Sound Clash: Jamaican Dancehall Culture At Large* (Palgrave-McMillan, New York).

Cox, Christopher and Warner, Daniel (eds). 2006. *Audio Culture: Reasonings In Modern Music* (Continuum, New York).

Cunningham, Mark. 1996. *Good Vibrations* (Sanctuary, London).

Dawe, Kevin (ed.). 2004, *Island Musics* (Berg, Oxford, UK).

De Koningh, Michael and Cane-Honeysett, Laurence. 2003. *Young Gifted and Black: The Story of Trojan Records* (Sanctuary, London).

Emerick, Geoff and Massey, Howard. 2006. *Here, There and Everywhere: My Life Recording the Music of The Beatles* (Gotham, New York).

Eisenberg, Evan. 1987. *Recording Angel: Explorations in Phonography* (McGraw-Hill, New York).

Everest, F. Alton. 1991. 'Fundamentals of Sound', in Ballou, *Handbook for Sound Engineers* (Butterworth-Heinemann, Newton, USA).

Feld, Steven. 1982. *Sound and Sentiment: Birds Weeping, Poetics and Song in Kaluli Expression* (University of Pennsylvania Press, USA).

Fikentscher, Kai. 2003. '"There's not a problem I can't fix, 'cause I can do it in the mix": On the Performative Technology of 12-Inch Vinyl', in Lysloff and Gay, *Music And Technoculture* (Wesleyan University Press, USA).

Fletcher. 1996. 'A reader's guide to Vintage Gear'. *Mix: Professional Audio and Music Production*, Volume 20, Number 11 (Cardinal Business Media Inc.).

Foehr, Stephen. 2000. *Jamaican Warriors: Reggae Roots & Culture* (Sanctuary, London).

Francis-Jackson, Chester.1995.*The Official Dancehall Dictionary: A Guide to Jamaican Dialect and Dancehall Slang* (LMH Publishing, Kingston, Jamaica).

Frith, Simon. 1981. *Sound Effects* (Pantheon, New York).

—. 1988. *Music For Pleasure* (Routledge, New York).

— (ed.). 1988. *Facing The Music* (Pantheon, New York).

—. 1996. *Performing Rites: On the value of Popular Music* (Harvard University Press, USA).

Frith, Simon and Goodwin, Andrew (eds). 1990. *On Record: Rock, Pop and The Written Word* (Routledge, London).

Geertz, Clifford. 1973. *The Interpretation of Cultures* (Basic Books, New York).

Giddings, Philip. 1990. *Audio Systems Design and Installation* (Focal Press, Burlington, USA).

Gillett, Charlie. 1996. *The Sound of The City: The Rise and Fall of Rock and Roll* (Souvenir Press, New York).

Gilroy, Paul. 1987. *There Ain't No Black in the Union Jack: The Cultural Politics of Race and Nation* (University of Chicago Press, USA).

Gracyk, Theodore. 1996. *Rhythm And Noise: An Aesthetic Of Rock* (Duke University Press, USA).

Greene, Paul and Porcello, Thomas (eds). 2005. *Wired for Sound: Engineering and Technologies in Sonic Cultures* (Wesleyan University Press, USA).

Guilbault, Joselyne. 1993. *Zouk: World Music In The West Indies* (University of Chicago Press, London).

Gunst, Laurie. 1995. *Born Fi Dead: A Journey Through The Jamaican Posse Underworld* (Payback Press, Edinburgh, UK).

Hagerman, Brent. 2011. 'You Can't Go To Zion with a Carnal Mind: Slackness and Culture in the Music of Yellowman' (PhD dissertation, Wilfrid Laurier University).

Harford, Tim. 2006. *The Undercover Economist: Exposing Why The Rich Are Rich, The Poor Are Poor – And Why You Can Never Buy A Decent Used Car!* (OUP, New York).

Hebdige, Dick. 1987a. *Cut 'N' Mix* (Routledge, London).

—. 1987b. *Subculture: The Meaning of Style* (Routledge, London).

Henry, Balford. 2003. 'Ken Khouri: Pioneer of Jamaican recording industry', *Sunday Gleaner*, 28 September.

Hesmondhalgh, David. 2002. *The Cultural Industries* (Sage, London).

Hesmondhalgh, David and Negus, Keith (eds). 2002. *Popular Music Studies* (Bloomsbury, New York).

Hope, Donna. P. 2006. *Inna Di Danchall: Popular Culture and the Politics of Identity in Jamaica* (UWI Press, Kingston, Jamaica).

—. 2010. *ManVibes: Masculinities in Jamaican Dancehall* (Ian Randall Publishers, Kingston, Jamaica).

Howard, Dennis. 2010. 'Political Patronage and Gun Violence in the Dancehall', *Jamaica Journal*, Volume 32, Number 3 (Institute of Jamaica).

Jackson, Blair. 2001. 'Roy Halee', *Mix: Professional Audio and Music Production* (Cardinal Business Media Inc.).

Jahn, Brian and Weber, Tom. 1998. *Reggae Island: Jamaican Music in the Digital Age* (Da Capo, New York).

Jensen, Joli. 1998. *Nashville Sound: Authenticity, Commercialism and Country Music* (Vanderbilt University Press, USA).

Johnson, Howard and Pines, Jim. 1982. *Reggae: Deep Roots Music* (Proteus, London).

Jones, Steve. 1992. *Rock Formation: Music, Technology, and Mass Communication* (Sage, London).

Katz, David. 2003. *Solid Foundation: An Oral History of Reggae* (Bloomsbury, London).

Katz, Mark. 2004. *Capturing Sound: How Technology Has Changed Music* (University of California Press, USA).

Keil, Charles and Feld, Steven. 2005. *Music Grooves* (Fenestra, Tucson, USA).

Kozul-Wright, Zelka and Lloyd, Stanbury. 1998. 'Becoming a Globally Competitive Player: The case of the Music Industry in Jamaica' (Discussion Paper No 138, UNCTAD).

Larkin, Colin (ed). 1994. *The Guinness Book of Who's Who of Reggae* (Guinness Publishing, London).

Levi, Darrell E. 1989. *Michael Manley: The Making of a Leader* (Heinemann Publishers (Caribbean) Limited).

Levine, Lawrence. 1977. *Black Culture and Black Consciousness* (Oxford University Press, New York).

Lewin, Olive. 2000. *Rock It Come Over: The Folk Music of Jamaica* (UWI Press, Kingston, Jamaica).

Lewisohn, Mark. 1988. *The Beatles Recording Sessions: The Official Abbey Road Studio Session Notes 1962–1970* (Harmony Books, New York).

Linn, Karen. 1994. *That Half-Barbaric Twang: The Banjo in American Popular Culture* (University of Illinois Press, USA).

Lull, James (ed.). 1992. *Popular Music and Communication* (Sage, Newbury Park, USA).

Lysloff, Rene and Gay, Leslie. 2003. *Music And Technoculture* (Wesleyan University Press, USA).

Mac Queen, Colin and Albanese, Steve. 2002. *Pro Tools Power: Practical Tips and Concepts for the Efficient us of Pro Tools* (Muska and Lipman, Cincinnati, USA).

McClary, Susan and Walser, Robert. 1990. 'Start Making Sense: Musicology Wrestles with Rock', in Frith and Goodwin, *On Record: Rock, Pop and The Written Word* (Routledge, London).

McMillan, John. 2005. 'Trench Town Rock: The Creation of Jamaica's Music Industry' (Case study, Graduate School of Business, Stanford University, 2005).

Maingot, P. Anthony. 1994. *The United States and The Caribbean* (Macmillan, London).

Manley, Michael. 1990. *Politics of Change: A Jamaican Testament* (Howard University Press, Washington).

Manuel, Peter. 1993. *Cassette Culture: Popular Music and Technology in North India* (University of Chicago Press, USA).

— (ed). 1995. *Caribbean Currents: Caribbean Music from Rumba to Reggae* (Temple University Press, USA).

—. 2009. *Creolizing Contradance in the Caribbean* (Temple University Press, USA).

Manuel, Peter and Marshall, Wayne. 2006. 'The Riddim Method: Aesthetics, Practice and Ownership in Jamaican Dancehall', *Popular Music* Volume 25, Number 3 (Cambridge University Press, UK).

Martin, George and Hornsby, Jeremy. 1979. *All you Need Is Ears: The Inside Personal Story Of The Genius Who Created The Beatles* (St Martin's Press Inc., New York).

Meintjes, Louise. 2003. *Sound of Africa: Making Music Zulu in a South African Studio* (Duke University Press, USA).

Millard, Andre. 1995. *America On Record: A History Of Recorded Sound* (Cambridge University Press, New York).

Miller, Chernoff, John. 1979. *African Rhythm and African Sensibility: Aesthetics and Social Action in African Musical Idioms* (Chicago University Press, London).

Moorefield, Virgil. 2010. *The Producer As Composer: Shaping The Sounds Of Popular Music* (Massachusetts Institute Of Technology Press, Cambridge, USA).

Morton, L. David. Jr. 2004. *Sound Recording: The Life Story of a Technology* (Johns Hopkins University Press, USA).

Moser, C.A. and Kalton, G. 1971. *Survey Methods in Social Investigation* (Dartmouth Publishing Company Ltd, Aldershot, UK).

Myers, Helen (ed). 1993. *Ethnomusicology: Historical and Regional Studies* (Macmillan, London).

Neely, Daniel. 2007. 'Calling All Singers, Musicians and Speechmakers: Mento Aesthetics and Jamaica's Early Recording Industry', *Caribbean Quarterly* Volume 53, Number 4).

—. 2008. '"Mento, Jamaica's Original Music": Development, Tourism and the National Frame' (dissertation, New York University).

Negus, Keith. 1996. *Popular Music In Theory: An Introduction* (Wesleyan University Press, USA).

Nettl, Bruno and Bohlman, Philip, V. (eds). 1991. *Comparative Musicology and Anthropology of Music* (University of Chicago Press, USA).

Neuenfeldt, Karl. 2005. 'Nigel Pegrum, "Didjeridu-Friendly Sections", and What Constitutes an Indigenous CD: An Australian Case Study of Producing "World Music" Recordings', in Greene and Porcello, *Wired For Sound: Engineering and Technologies in Sonic Cultures* (Wesleyan University Press, USA).

New Grove Dictionary. 2001. *New Grove Dictionary of Music and Musicians,* ed. Stanley Sadie and John Tyrrell, 2nd edition (Macmillan, Basingstoke).

Nisbett, Alec. 1962. *The Technique of The Sound Studio: Radio & Recording* (Focal Press, London).

—. 2000. *The Sound Studio,* 6th edition (Focal Press, London)

O'Brien-Chang, Kevin and Chen, Wayne. 1998. *Reggae Routes: The Story of Jamaican Music* (Ian Randle Publishing, Kingston, Jamaica).

Padel, Ruth. 2000. *I'm A Man: Sex, Gods and Rock 'n' Roll* (Faber, London)

Panton, David. 1993. *Jamaica's Michael Manley: The Great Transformation (1972–92)* (Kingston Publishers, Kingston, Jamaica).

Plattner, Stuart (ed). 1989. *Economic Anthropology* (Stanford University Press, USA).

Powera, Norbert. 2003. *Microphone Practice: Tips and Tricks for Stage and Studio* (PPV Medien, Bergkirchen, Gemany).

Powney, Janet and Watts, Mike. 1987. *Interviewing in educational Research,* Routledge, London).

Prendergast, Mark. 2003. *The Ambient Century: From Mahler to Moby – The Evolution of Sound in the Electronic Age* (Bloomsbury, London).

Ramnarine, Tina K. 'Music In the Diasporic Imagination and the Performance of Culture (Dis)placement in Trinidad', in Dawe, *Island Musics* (Berg, Oxford, UK).

Rice, Timothy. 2008. 'Toward a Mediation of Field Methods and Field Experience in Ethnomusicology', in Barz and Cooley, *Shadows in the Field* (Oxford University Press, New York).

Rivera, Raquel Z. Marshall, Wayne and Pacini Nernandez, Deborah (eds). 2009. *Reggaeton* (Duke University Press, USA).

Robson, Colin. 1993. *Real World Research: A Resource for Social Scientists and Practitioner-Researchers* (Blackwell Publishers Ltd, Oxford, UK).

Rose, Tricia. 1994. *Black Noise: Rap Music and Black Culture in Contemporary America* (Wesleyan University Press, USA).

Salewicz, Chris and Boot, Adrian. 2001. *Reggae Explosion: The Story of Jamaican Music* (Harry N. Abrams, New York).

Saville-Troike, Muriel. 2002. *The Ethnography of Communication: An Introduction* (Wiley-Blackwell, Massachusetts, USA).

Schafer, Murray R. 1977. *Our Sonic Environment and The Soundscape: The Tuning of The World* (Destiny, Rochester, USA).

Schuler, Monica. 1980. *Alas Alas Kongo: A Social History of Indentured African Immigration into Jamaica, 1841–1865* (Johns Hopkins University Press, USA).

Schultz, Barbara. 2009. 'A Flexible Production Home in Kingston', *Mix: Professional Audio and Music Production,* 1 February, at: http://mixonline. com/studios/profiles/on-cover-hard-records/ (accessed November 2010).

Schusky, Ernest L. and Culbert, Patrick T. 1987. *Introducing Culture* (Prentice-Hall Inc., Englewood Cliffs, USA).

Scott, Derek. 2010. *Musical Style and Social Meaning* (Ashgate, Farnham, UK).

Seaga, Edward. 1969. 'Revival Cults in Jamaica', *Jamaica Journal* Volume 3, Number 2, June (Institute of Jamaica).

—. 2009. *Edward Seaga: My Life and Leadership Volume 1: Clash of Ideologies 1930 –1980* (Macmillan, Oxford, UK).

—. 2010. *Edward Seaga: My Life and Leadership Volume II: Hard Road To Travel 1980–2008* (Macmillan, Oxford, UK).

Sherlock, Philip and Bennett, Hazel. 1998. *The Story of the Jamaican People* (Ian Randle Publishing, Kingston, Jamaica).

Sneider, Frieidrich and Klinglmair, Robert. 2004 'Shadow Economies Around The World: What Do We Know' (Discussion Paper No 1043, IZA, Bonn Germany).

Southall, Brian, Vince, Peter and Rouse, Allan. 1997. *The Recording Studios, That Became a Legend: Abbey Road* (Omnibus Press, London).

Stanley-Niaah, Sonjah. 2006. 'Kingston's Dancehall Spaces', *Jamaica Journal*, Volume 29, Number 3 (Institute Of Jamaica).

—. 2010. *Dancehall: From Slaveship to Ghetto (African and Diasporic Cultural Studies* (University of Ottawa Press, Canada).

Sterne, Jonathan. 2003. *The Audible Past: Cultural Origins of Sound Reproduction* (Duke University Press, USA).

Stolzoff, Norman. 2000. *Wake the Town and Tell the People* (Duke University Press, USA).

Stone, Carl. 1989. *Politics Versus Economics: The 1989 Elections in Jamaica* (Heinemann Publishers Caribbean, Kingston, Jamaica).

Stinati, Dominic. 1995. *An Introduction to Theories of Popular Culture* (Routledge, London).

Taylor, Don. 1994. *Marley and Me* (Kingston Publishers Ltd, Kingston, Jamaica).

Taylor, Timothy. 2001. *Strange Sounds: Music Technology and Culture* (Routledge, London).

Théberge, Paul. 1997. *Any Sound You Can Imagine: Making Music/Consuming Technology* (Wesleyan University Press, USA).

—. 2003 '"Ethnic Sounds": The Economy and Discourse of World Music Sampling', in Lysloff and Gay, *Music And Technoculture* (Wesleyan University Press, USA).

Thomas, Hugh. 1977. *The Slave Trade: The Story of The Atlantic Slave Trade* 1440–1870 (Touchstone, New York).

Throsby, David. 2002. 'The Music Industry in The New Millennium: Global and Local Perspectives' (UNESCO, Paris).

Titon, Jeff, Todd. 1995. *Early Downhome Blues: A Musical and Cultural Analysis* (University of North Carolina Press, USA).

Toop, David. 1995. *Ocean Of Sound: Aether Talk, Ambient Sound And Imaginary Worlds* (Serpent's Tail, London).

Toynbee, Jason. 2000. *Making Popular Music: Musicians, Creativity and Institutions* (Arnold, London).

—. 2007. *Bob Marley* (Polity Press, Cambridge, UK).

Van Maanan, John. 1988. *Tales of The Field: On Writing Ethnography* (The University of Chicago Press, USA).

Veal, Michael. E. 2007. *Dub: Soundscapes & Shattered Songs in Jamaican Reggae* (Wesleyan University Press, USA).

Walker, Klive. 2005. *Dubwise: Reasoning From The Reggae Underground* (Insomniac Press, Toronto, Canada).

Wallis, Roger and Malm, Krister.1984. *Big Sounds From Small Peoples: The Music Industry in Small Countries* (Pendragon Press, Hillsdale, USA).

—. 1990. 'Patterns of Change', in *On Record: Rock, Pop and The Written Word* (Routledge, London).

Warner, Timothy. 2003. *Pop Music Technology and Creativity: Trevor Horn and The Digital Revolution* (Ashgate, Aldershot, UK).

Waterman, Christopher. Alan. 1990. *Juju: A social History and Ethnography of an African Popular Music* (University of Chicago Press, USA).

Waters, M. Anita. 1985. Race, *Class, and Political Symbols: Rastafari and Reggae in Jamaican Politics* (Transaction Publishers, New Jersey, USA).

Whitter, Michael. 2004. 'Music and The Jamaican Economy' (UNCTAD, WIPO).

Wicke, Peter. 1987. *Rock Music: Culture Aesthetics and Sociology* (Cambridge University Press, USA).

Winner, Langdon. 1986. 'Do Artifacts Have Politics?', in *The Whale and The Reactor: A Search for Limits in an Age of High Technology* (University of Chicago Press, USA).

Wong, Deborah. 2003. 'Plugged in at Home: Vietnamese American Technoculture in Orange County', in Lysloff and Gay, *Music And Technoculture* (Wesleyan University Press, USA).

—. 2008. 'Moving: From Performance to Performative Ethnography and Back Again', in Barz and Cooley, *Shadows In The Field: New Perspectives for Fieldwork in Ethnomusicology* (OUP, New York).

Zak, Albin. J. III. 2001. *The Poetics of Rock: Cutting Tracks, Making Records* (University of California Press, USA).

Reports/Manuals

Borwick, J.N. 1956. *Programme Operating Handbook (Sound Broadcasting), Central Programme Operations Department, BBC*. Written and compiled by J.N. Borwick, Instructor, Central Programme Operations Department, BBC.

Statistical Institute of Jamaica. 2003. Population Census 2001, Jamaica Volume 1 County report.

Videography

Fenn, Suzanne and Letts, Don. *Dancehall Queen* (Palm Pictures, 1997).

Henzel, Perry and Rhone, Trevor. *The Harder They Come* (Island Films, 1972).

Jobson, Dickie and Thomas, Michael. *Countryman* (Lions Gate, 1982).

Martin, Darnell. *Cadillac Records* (Sony Pictures, 2008).

Moormann, Mark. *Tom Dowd & The Language of Music* (Palm Pictures, 2003).

Index